Adult Learning: a Reader

Adult Learning: a Reader

edited by

Peter Sutherland
University of Stirling

KOGAN
PAGE

London • Stirling (USA)

First published in 1997
First paperback edition 1998

Kogan Page Limited
120 Pentonville Road
London N1 9JN
UK

Stylus Publishing
22883 Quicksilver Drive
Sterling VA 20166
USA

British Library Cataloguing in Publication Data

A CIP record for this book is available from the British Library.

ISBN 0 7494 2795 7

Designed and typeset by Kate Williams, London
Printed and bound in Great Britain by Clays Ltd, St Ives plc

Contents

CONTENTS

Acknowledgments

Thanks to Clare Andrews, the original editor who commissioned the book at Kogan Page, and to Pat Lomax, who has looked after us since writing commenced.

One of the American contributors spent the summer on the Stirling University campus with the editor. Thanks to Paul Hettich for his helpful discussions and advice about communal sections of the book.

Thanks to the journal *Adult Education Quarterly* for permission to reproduce the article by Jack Mezirow, 'Contemporary paradigms of learning' (*Adult Education Quarterly*, 46(3), 158–73).

Thanks to the ACER for permission to reproduce Figure 2.1 from the book *The Early Years* (1994) and to the *Australian Journal of Education* for permission to publish Figure 2.2.

List of Contributors

Elizabeth Beaty, Principal Lecturer, Teaching and Learning Unit, University of Brighton.

Loraine Blaxter, Research Fellow in the Department of Continuing Education, University of Warwick, Coventry.

Gillian Boulton-Lewis, Professor in the School of Learning and Development of the Faculty of Education at Queensland University of Technology.

Gloria Dall'Alba, Research Fellow at the Karolinska Institute, Sweden.

Barry Dart, Lecturer in the School of Learning and Development of the Faculty of Education at Queensland University of Technology.

Ian Dennis, Head of Department and Prinicipal Lecturer, Department of Psychology, University of Plymouth.

Arlene Franklyn-Stokes, Senior Lecturer, Department of Psychology, University of Plymouth.

James Hartley, Professor of Psychology at the University of Keele.

Paul Hettich, Professor in, and Head of, the Department of Psychology, Barat College, Illinois.

Sherria Hoskins, postgraduate student in the Department of Psychology, University of Plymouth.

Christina Hughes, Lecturer in the Department of Continuing Education, University of Warwick, Coventry.

Ference Marton, Professor and Director of the Department of Education and Educational Research, Gothenburg University.

Jack Mezirow, Emeritus Professor of Teachers College, University of Columbia.

Ian Mowatt, Lecturer in the Department of Language and Media, Glasgow Caledonian University.

Stephen Newstead, President of the British Psychological Society, Professor of Psychology, University of Plymouth.

Glyn Owens, Professor of Psychology, University of Auckland.

Hitendra Pillay, Lecturer in the School of Learning and Development in the School of Education, Queensland University of Technology.

John Richardson, Professor and Head of the Department of Human Sciences, Brunel University, London.

Ronald Schmeck, Professor in the Department of Psychology of the University of Southern Illinois at Carbondale.

Gerda Siann, Professor of Gender Relations, University of Dundee.

Peter Sutherland, Lecturer in Education in the Department of Education, University of Stirling.

Malcolm Tight, Senior Lecturer in the Department of Continuing Education, University of Warwick, Coventry.

Keith Topping, Director of the Centre for Paired Learning, Department of Psychology, University of Dundee.

Mark Trueman, Head of Department and Professor of Psychology, University of Keele.

Introduction

The publication of Ference Marton's ideas in 1976 stimulated, into a new and very fruitful mode, the field of research into the learning of traditional-age students. It has thrived ever since, through the work of Entwistle, Ramsden and others.

The field of research into mature students is a newer one. In the UK at least it was stimulated by an expected shortage of students in the early 1990s. This led to a corresponding branch of academic study, involved largely in the evaluation of the success or otherwise of students entering higher education without conventional qualifications. This book examines the learning of both traditional-age and mature students. There are two dominant focuses. In Section I, *Cognitive processes* and Section II, *Learning and education*, we examine the different aspects of the learning of individual adults. Hence there are chapters on information processing and metacognition as well as on behaviourist and cognitive approaches.

The overall aim is to investigate different aspects of both categories of adult learners: traditional age and mature. The aspects will include both their learning processes and their learning strategies. From the most pertinent relevant points which arise, implications for teaching will be deduced.

In Section III, *Adults interacting in groups*, we continue the initial focus on learning, but now examining small groups rather than individuals. The subsequent focus is on the mature adult, starting from Chapter 10 of Section IV, *The context of education*, and continuing through the whole of Section V, *The particular context of the mature student in higher education*.

The combination of two focuses, traditional-age and mature adult learners, may not be entirely coherent, but mature adult learners represent the current interests of researchers. Thus, distinguished authors such as Ference Marton, Malcolm Tight and John Richardson are better able to address learning in mature adults, than in traditional-age students. Ideally, perhaps, there could have been two separate books. However, I believe that learning in the mature adult is a special case of adult learning, in some ways a case study, and that the latter focus grew out of the earlier one.

It was not possible to include every aspect of adult learning in a book of a little over 200 pages. For instance, it was decided that, important though they are, it was not possible to include: Bandura's perspective (social learning theory); David Boud's work on autonomy; or self-directed learning. However, several subfocuses are included, such as informal learning and work-based learning. The book is therefore concerned with many different aspects of adult learning.

As can be seen from the list of contributors, an intercontinental team has been assembled. This has produced a cross-fertilization of ideas from different countries. However, this does throw up the difficult problem of nomenclature. Different countries have different terms for what are here called 'traditional-age' students and 'mature' students. In this book these are subsumed under the generic term 'adult' learners.

No particular theoretical orientation has been prescribed. Authors were free to use whatever theoretical background they believe helps them to make a worthwhile elucidation of some aspect of the adult learner.

In Section I, Jack Mezirow provides an introduction to the book as a whole by considering the various paradigms of learning that currently exist. This leads into a discussion of a number of varying and stimulating approaches to cognitive processes. Mezirow argues his case in favour of the transformative perspective as opposed to the traditional 'objective' one.

Gillian Boulton-Lewis outlines the information processing model and various ideas on the post-Piagetian postformal operational stages of thinking. These have a great deal of relevance to the pedagogic style of teaching; a relevance discussed in Section VI, *Implications for teaching*.

Barry Dart examines the closely related field of metacognition from a constructivist standpoint and writes of some empirical work that he has done. He argues that the field of metacognition is a particularly relevant one for teachers since there is such a strong element of self-monitoring and learning how to learn. Teachers should be aware of both of these and encourage their students to adopt them.

Section II continues with and expands on this theme of linking adult learning with education. Paul Hettich provides a broad longitudinal perspective. He reviews research done across a degree; studies into how both traditional-age (aged 18–22 years) and mature students change whilst they study for a four-year US degree. He starts with the well-known work of Perry on men students and Belenky *et al.* on women students; then introduces us to some of the more recent US work of King and Kitchener and Baxter Magolda.

Ron Schmeck narrows the focus to the micro-level of tactics, while also examining the correlation of the use of particular tactics with broad personality differences among adult learners. He uses his Inventory of Learning Processes (ILP) scale to categorise adults into a spectrum of ten categories, varying from agentic analytic (work-seeking) to conventional (simply obeying accepted rules). Glyn Owens analyses behaviourist approaches in general; then applies his analysis to adult learners in particular. He argues for a number of positive applications, despite the limitations of applying such a simplistic model to adults. Less simplistic is experiential learning. Peter Sutherland argues the case for a fruitful link between it and constructivism.

Current interest among teachers in providing learning in small groups is the focus of Section III. Ian Mowatt and Gerda Siann provide an overview; which leads into Keith Topping's exposition of peer tutoring within small groups.

The context in which learning is experienced is so important that it is worthy of a section in its own right, Section IV. Workplace learning is one of the exciting new areas for academic study. Hitendra Pillay offers a practical and useful analysis of the strategies that adults use to acquire the necessary knowledge and skills. He argues that workers do not find it easy to learn domain-specific and generic knowledge simultaneously. If his findings are borne out in university and college settings, there will be significant implications for teachers. These are addressed in Section VI.

Malcolm Tight and his colleagues broaden the issue beyond the narrow and artificial confines of pure academic study by considering the work, home and social lives of mature students and how these factors affect their academic learning. Tight's chapter links into Section V, where the focus is on an evaluation of the educational experiences of mature students. One set of authors focuses particularly on mature women. Beaty *et al.* report on the personal experiences of women students aged 30–50 years.

Three sets of authors focus on the mature learner in general (both genders). By means of a review of the literature, John Richardson compares how mature students cope with education, in comparison with traditional-age students. James Hartley complements this literature-based approach by reporting on a small-scale, empirical, comparative study of the performance of mature and traditional entry students at one English university. Steve Newstead *et al.* have a particular interest in the problem of cheating, both in exams and in essays. What is the relative likelihood of traditional age and mature students cheating? This phenomenon has aroused considerable interest in the educational media in Britain and we are pleased to be able to publish some additional data in this book. Newstead *et al.* also have some data on what motivates traditional-age and mature students.

The first two sections focus on various concepts of how adults learn as individuals. In Section III the focus switches to how adults learn in groups. The concepts explored in these first three sections have enormous implications for teaching, explored in Section VI.

In Section IV the context in which this learning takes place is examined. This leads into Section V where the particular context of the mature adult is examined in considerable detail. In some cases this examination of the context indicates directly and in other cases implies indirectly what sort of context universities, colleges and workplaces should provide for both students (particularly mature women students) and workers. The sort of context and the types of teaching that this implies are analysed in Section VI, where Peter Sutherland also provides an overview of the book.

Various themes permeate the book as a whole. The crucial effects of life events on the mature learner is one. Most of the authors who write about the mature learner emphasise this, so many chapters have links with more than one section. Readers are advised to use the index to maximise the usefulness of each topic and to aid the user-friendliness of the book.

Most of the contributions have been specially commissioned, with the exception of Jack Mezirow's opening chapter (which is reprinted with the permission of *Adult Education Quarterly*), and most authors have adopted a psychological approach; including both the approaches to learning tradition of Marton and the experiential learning tradition of Kolb and Knowles. In terms of research methodology, chapters are contributed from both the softer, qualitative approach (such the phenomenological chapter of Marton's team) and the harder, quantitative approach (such as those of Boulton-Lewis and Dart).

Besides the majority of contributions that come from either of these psychological perspectives, there is a minority of contributions from other discipline bases; for example, Mezirow, who adopts a cross-cultural comparative perspective in order to examine the whole scene of adult learning, and the Tight team, who adopt a sociological approach.

Our approaches and methodologies have been eclectic, but whatever approach or methodology chosen, the adult learner (both traditional age and mature) is the focus of interest for all who wrote for or read this book.

SECTION I

COGNITIVE PROCESSES

CHAPTER 1

Cognitive Processes:
Contemporary Paradigms of Learning

Jack Mezirow

What learning means depends upon a set of presuppositions. The theories of learning must be understood in light of these assumptions but also in light of a second set of presuppositions pertaining to the nature and function of learning theory itself. This is a time when such long established concepts as cognition, rationality, language and development are under challenge, and the very concept of reality itself is the subject of spirited debate. In this climate the concept of learning is undergoing significant transformation.

This chapter reviews the current debate over the nature and meaning of learning, which pits a diverse group of social cognitivists against the tradition of Western rationalism. Transformation theory (Mezirow, 1991), a critical theory of adult learning, provides a dialectical synthesis and an alternative with a fresh look at the nature of learning and learning theory. The tenets and assumptions of three paradigmatic contexts are described and compared. The question of the relationship of transformation theory, as a learning theory, to the realities of local culture in which learning is situated is elaborated.

The objectivist paradigm:
the Western rationalistic tradition

John Searle (1993) characterises the Western rationalistic tradition as predicated upon five principles.
1. Reality exists independently of mental and linguistic representations of the world such as beliefs, experiences, statements and theories.
2. At least one of the functions of language is to communicate meanings from speakers to hearers, including meanings that refer to objects and states of affairs in the world that exist independently of language. Truth is a matter of the accuracy of representation. Statements attempt to

describe how things are. These statements are true if things in the world are as the statements about them say they are.

3. Knowledge is objective. It neither depends on nor derives from the subjective attitudes and feelings of a particular investigator. 'The objective truth or falsity of the claims made is totally independent of the motives, the morality or even the gender, the race or the ethnicity of the maker'.

4. Logic and rationality are formal. There are two kinds of reason: the theoretical, which aims at what it is reasonable to believe; and the practical, which aims at what it is reasonable to do. Logic is central to this concept. These procedures, methods, standards and canon only operate in the context of a previously given set of axioms, assumptions, goals and objectives.

5. Intellectual standards are not 'up for grabs'. There are both objectively and intersubjectively valid criteria of intellectual achievement and excellence. Some criteria are 'objective', independent of the sensibilities of the people who apply them: others are intersubjective, appealing to widely shared features of human sensibility.

In this tradition, learning and the cognitive world are sensitive to, correspondent with or reflective of events in the objective world. Learning and the cognitive system are central to the production of behaviour. Behaviour is 'adaptive' to the extent that what is learned is correspondent with reality and behaviour is dictated by what is learned. Language is guided by cognition. We communicate knowledge or understanding if the categories of language reflect, or are somehow systematically linked to, the features of the cognitive system, and this system is accurately reflective of the real world. Language conveys knowledge but does not constitute it; it is the vehicle for expressing the state of the individual's cognition. The most significant learning is that which enables the learner to understand and shape his or her behaviour to better anticipate and control the real world. The educational process is to transmit accurate representations of the real world, ideally established as such by scientific test.

This position has fostered a common interpretation, which holds that judgements about liberty, responsibility and rationality – whose voice will be heard, who should be rewarded, what to teach, what to prohibit – should be made according to objective, value-neutral, universal criteria acknowledged as valid by all informed, objective and rational persons. Similarly, 'some ideas are better than others, some values more enduring, some works of art more universal. Some cultures, through we dare not say it, are more accomplished than others and therefore more worthy of study' (Henry, 1994).

The interpretist paradigm: the cognitive revolution

The challenge to the Western rationalistic tradition, sometimes under the eclectic banner of postmodernism, has come from various sources. One has been the increasing evidence that points to the essential capacities of the individual to organise, select, attend to or otherwise act upon the environmental givens (Semin and Gergen, 1990). Chomsky's (1959) influential critique of Skinner's theory of language development demonstrated that to learn a language it is essential to consider the innate knowledge potential of the learner. This and the work of many others have contributed to what Semin and Gergen hail as 'the cognitive revolution', a growing recognition of the importance of the structures of the mind that an individual brings to his or her encounters with the world, and of the self-perpetuating proclivities of these structures.

Vygotsky argues that cognitive categories are social in origin, as are the forms of thought in which these categories are embedded. Consequently, understanding is inherently a social rather than a biological act; it cannot be cut away from the sociocultural circumstances of the agent. Others contend that private cognitions may be understood as the internalised by-products of publicly shared discourse (Semin and Gergen, 1990).

Richard Bagnall (1994) writes,

> 'the concept of the interpretive nature of all human perception focuses on our inability to separate fully what we perceive to be the case from the frameworks of our understanding, expectation and subconscious figuration that we bring to the perceptual task. Given the irremediably normative nature of these frameworks, we are unable, also, to separate entirely matters of fact from matters of value – the former, indeed, may be seen as reducible to the latter. All belief, then, is seen as being contingent on the perceptual and linguistic frameworks through which it is mediated, and all knowledge is seen as being provisional and relative to the context of its generation.'

Phenomenologists, drawing upon the works of Husserl, Heidegger and Merleau-Ponty, see subject and object as one. Making a distinction between the experiencing agent and the object of experience is misleading. The agent brings his own frame of reference, which is an integral element constituting the experience. To understand others, one must gain access to their lived experience so as to clarify and elucidate the way they interpret it.

A significant methodological alternative to the tradition's empirical–analytical studies of external reality is the development of hermeneutics, the study of the meaning of texts, which has broadened its scope to focus on discourse and the development of interpretive understanding. In sociology, symbolic interactionism and ethnomethodology have evolved into other 'qualitative' research approaches to the study of language and social inter-action.

Another powerful source of criticism of the tradition has been derived from Nietzsche and Heidegger by Derrida and his followers, who attempt to deconstruct it, and Foucault, who has demonstrated how social reality is defined by nature and distribution of domination, power and influence. Their influence, and that of Baudrillard, Lyotard and others, have resulted in a widespread concern over a corrosive commodification of the culture and a profound suspicion of metanarratives, including the concepts of rationality and discourse.

For some, this reasoning leads to a relativistic conviction that truth must be understood in the context of language games, the rules of which are agreed upon by local players. Truth becomes a contingent, exclusive formulation of local culture. Such universal values as freedom, democracy, justice and equal-ity are similarly viewed with deep reservation as artefacts of the Enlighten-ment, with what these critics judge to be the failed project of modernity; phenomena limited in origin and relevance to Western culture.

Social cognitivists see subjectivity, intentionality and learning as functions of forms of life and systems of language; they are elements of a linguistically disclosed world in which the local character of truth, discourse and validity is asserted. This position posits the intrinsically social character of structures of meaning, the historical and cultural variability of categories of thought and principles of action and their interdependence with the changing forms of social and material reproduction.

A case point in the world of international politics was the recent World Conference on Human Rights at which 40 Asian countries approved a state-ment contending that standards of justice and fairness should be tempered by 'regional peculiarities and various historical, cultural and religious back-grounds'. A related abortive attempt by seven countries to redefine human rights as 'Western' provoked a *New York Times* editorial with the headline, 'Ending torture isn't colonialism' (13 June 1993).

For many who challenge the tradition, understanding exists in the lan-guage used to describe or explain the world rather than in the external world itself. Language involves generalisations over specific instances, time and space, which makes 'intersubjectivity' (relating to another person who has a sense of agency like oneself) possible.

To communicate, content is ascribed to a known class; ie it is generalised. Thinking reflects reality in a generalised way. Syntax and semantics provide a generalised structure for language. Dictionary definitions of human traits may similarly be understood as idealised semantic abstractions that determine the use of person terms in everyday communication. In this sense, knowledge and information about persons and the world are embedded in the medium of language. We are essentially beings constituted by, and engaged in, inter-pretive understanding.

Words acquire meaning from their relationship to meaning schemes or 'language games' and to other words through social interchange. Thus language is entirely social in origins, uses and implications. Reality is a social construct. Languages sustain and rationalise relationships and favour some patterns of cultural life over others. Words of emotion sustain family life and the language of intentions enables us to have criminal trials.

To summarise, the cognitive revolution has led to an argument that holds that human beings are always and necessarily local, temporal, partial, embodied and purposive and cannot attain objectivity, neutrality or such universality as that commonly attributed to rationality.

Principles and definitions are empty until interpreted, and every interpretation rests on a chain or network of assumptions and stipulations, which cannot all simultaneously be examined. Criteria and values do not come from nowhere (or from God or the nature of things), but from their proponents' histories and interests. Since the latter must differ, so must the former, fundamentally and irreducibly. Ergo, to invoke objectivity, formal equality and other purportedly nonpartisan, noncontroversial principles is bad faith, an effort to place one's perspective or goal above criticism (Scialabba, 1994).

The critics of the tradition ask, if cognitive structures delimit and distort our understanding or experience, how can learning or education do anything more than reify existing forms of cultural understanding? How can the educators truly inform the culture of a reality that does not correspond with the array of existing understandings? It would appear that education can serve only to reify further existing categories of understanding. Learning, acquiring the common understandings of the culture, perpetuates that culture. Cultural frames of reference constitute the boundaries and formulae with which the learner differentiates, acquires values and integrates experience. Learning is a matter of more fully realising the nature of a culturally defined frame of reference or of acquiring new meaning schemes for the culture.

Transformation theory

Key propositions

1. A learning theory framed as a general, abstract and idealised model, used to explain the generic structure, dimensions and dynamics of the process of learning can be useful to action oriented adult educators. A learning theory should be grounded upon the nature of human communication. Seeking agreement on our interpretations and beliefs is central to human communication and the learning process.
2. Learning is understood as the process of using a prior interpretation to construe a new or revised interpretation of the meaning of one's experience in order to guide future action.

6

3. We make meaning by projecting images and symbolic models – 'meaning schemes' (see 6. below) based upon prior learning – on to our sensory experiences, and imaginatively use analogies to interpret new experiences.

4. Construal of meaning may be intentional, propositional (unintentional, incidental) or presentational (without the use of words – talking to ourselves or others – as when we discern or intuit presence, motion, directionality, kinaesthetic experience and feelings) (Heron, 1988).

5. Sense perceptions are filtered through a frame of reference, which selectively shapes and delimits perception, cognition and feelings by predisposing our intentions, expectations and purposes.

6. A frame of reference has two dimensions. One is a meaning perspective consisting of broad, generalised, orienting predispositions – habits of mind – that act as three sets of codes: (a) sociolinguistic (eg ideologies, social norms, language games); (b) epistemic (eg learning styles, sensory preferences, focus on wholes or parts or on the concrete or abstract); and (c) psychological (eg personality traits or repressed parental prohibitions that continue to dictate ways of feeling and acting in adulthood). The second dimension is the resulting formulation, a meaning scheme, constituted by the cluster of specific beliefs, feelings, attitudes and value judgements that accompany and shape an interpretation. A more fully developed (more functional) frame of reference is one that is more: (a) inclusive; (b) differentiating; (c) permeable (open to other viewpoints); (d) critically reflective; and (e) integrative of experience.

7. A belief is a habit that guides action. Beliefs become crystallised in concepts. Any action guided by a belief is also a test of that belief. When the actions dictated by beliefs (and the interpretations articulating them) fall in practice or become problematic through changing circumstances, our frames of reference may be transformed through critical reflection on their assumptions. We can transform our meaning schemes by becoming critically reflective of the assumptions supporting the content and/or process of problem solving. We may transform our meaning perspective by becoming critically reflective of our premises in defining the problem. Reflectivity involves reasoning and/or intuition. Transformative learning refers to transforming our frame of reference to become more inclusive, differentiating, permeable and integrative of experience. Seeking agreement on our interpretations and beliefs and the possibility and potential of critical reflection are cardinal concepts in the adult learning process.

8. Learning occurs in one of four ways: by elaborating existing meaning schemes; learning new meaning schemes; transforming meaning schemes; and transforming meaning perspectives. Transformations may be epochal or incremental. The most personally significant transformations involve a critique of premises regarding one's self.

9. There are two distinctive domains of learning with different purposes, logics of inquiry and modes of validating beliefs: instrumental learning, learning to control and manipulate the environment or other people (eg task-oriented learning and communicative learning); and learning what others mean when they communicate with you, often involving feelings, intentions, values and moral issues (Habermas, 1984). Most learning involves elements of both domains. Problem solving follows a hypothetical–deductive logic (test a hypothesis, analyse its consequences) in instrumental learning and a metaphorical–abductive logic (make an analogy, let each step dictate the next one) in communicative learning.

10. We establish the validity of our problematic beliefs in instrumental learning by empirically testing to determine the truth that an assertion is as it is purported to be. In communicative learning, we determine the justification of a problematic belief through (a) appealing to tradition, authority or force or (b) rational discourse. Discourse involves an informed, objective, rational and intuitive assessment of reasons, evidence and arguments and leads toward a tentative, consensual, best judgement. Consensus building is an ongoing process and always subject to review by a broader group of participants. The nature of human communication implies the ideal conditions for discourse (and, by implication, for adult education as well).

11. Taking action on reflective insights often involves situational, emotional and informational constraints, which may also require new learning experiences. A transformative learning experience, involving a transformation of meaning structures, requires that the learner makes an informed and reflective decision to act. This decision may result in immediate action, delayed action caused by situational constraints or lack of information on how to act, or a reasoned reaffirmation of an existing pattern of action. Reflective action may be taken to effect changes in the sociolinguistic, epistemic or psychological areas.

12. Development in adulthood is understood as a learning process. Instrumental competence in coping with the external world involves attainment of task-oriented performance skills, which may involve reflective problem solving and sometimes problem posing. Communicative competence, which includes coping with the social world and the world of inner subjectivity, refers to the ability of learners to negotiate their own purposes, values and meanings rather than to simply accept those of others. A learner may acquire communicative competence by becoming more aware and critically reflective of assumptions and more able to freely and fully participate in discourse and to overcome constraints to taking reflection action.

The emancipatory paradigm

The line of development of the emancipatory paradigm that provides a context for transformation theory may be traced from Socrates, who 'in his words and deeds embodies the basic conviction that there is a type of self-reflection that can free us from the tyranny and bondage of false opinion' (Bernstein, 1985) through Marx and Freud to Freire and Habermas. Following Habermas, transformation theory constitutes a dialectical synthesis of the objectivist paradigm of learning and the more recent interpretive paradigm and its concern for socially constructed structures of meaning, the significance of language in creating meaning, the centrality of critique and a sensitivity for cultural diversity. But Habermas and transformation theory go beyond this synthesis to posit an alternative view of rationality and learning and of the nature of theory itself.

The synthesis is accomplished by recognising the validity of two major complementary and interactive domains of learning. One is instrumental learning, learning to control the environment and others, which takes the form of task-oriented problem solving. The other is communicative learning, learning what one means when one communicates with others. This commonly involves values, motives, intentions, feelings, ideals and moral decisions. Knowledge is derived from both instrumental learning and scientific inquiry regarding the independent reality of the world and a set of shared, subjective, often taken-for-granted interpretations; a reality created through the process of communicative learning that is socioculturally constructed through language. Learners need to appropriate a critical stance and language that will enable them to understand the ways in which these different discourses encode different meaning perspectives and schemes.

Habermas transcends both the tradition and the revolution by grounding understanding and learning in the very structure of human communication. We cannot make sense of the concepts of meaning, understanding and interpretation unless we evaluate the validity claims implicit in our speech acts: that what I say is intelligible; that its propositional content is true; that I am justified in saying it; and that I speak sincerely, without intent to deceive. To say that one acts rationally or that a statement is rational is to say that the action or statement can be criticised or defended by the speaker so that they may be justified.

Where instrumental learning limits justification of rational acts or expressions to knowledge of the object world, communicative learning requires that something is rational only if it meets the conditions necessary to effect an understanding with at least one other person. The intrinsic goal of human communication is to bring about a common understanding and mutual trust. Understanding the meaning of an utterance and assessing the validity of a claim are the same. We understand the meaning of a text only to the extent that we recognise why the author felt entitled to put forward certain assertions

9

as true, to recognise certain values and norms as right and to express certain experiences as sincere. It is the orientation of actors to validity claims that makes significant learning processes possible.

Meaning, interpretation and understanding are functions of the rational assessment of the validity claims (justifications) made by those communicating with each other. We have to understand what one counts as good reasons for his or her actions and evaluate these reasons by our own standards of rationality, even if we do not share them. Bernstein (1985) writes, 'we are always in danger of being ethnocentric, but we never escape the horizon of rationality'.

Discourse, understood as that special dialogue devoted to the assessing of reasons, examining evidence and judging arguments in order to achieve a consensual best judgement concerning justifications presented in support of a belief, allows us to test the validity of our beliefs and interpretations. A consensual best judgement holds only until new evidence, arguments or points of view are introduced; consensual validation is an ongoing learning process. In practice, discourse may involve interacting with one individual at a time, including the authors of texts, or with groups of various sizes.

As the interest of reason is in furthering the conditions for its fullest development, non-distorted communication is required and, for this to become possible, we must change the material social conditions required for mutual communication through which we may understand the meaning of our experience.

Thus transformation theory represents a dialectical synthesis of the objectivist learning assumptions of the tradition, by incorporating the study of nomological regularities, and the interpretive learning insights of the cognitive revolution, by incorporating the concept of meaning structures, a sensitivity to the importance of inclusion and interpretation of the meaning of symbolic interaction. But transformation theory goes beyond them to focus on a critically reflective, emancipatory critique grounded in the very structures of intersubjective communicative competence and, through critical reflection, emancipation from communication distorted by cultural constraints on full free participation in discourse.

Searle's first four principles of the Western rationalist tradition pertain to reality construed through instrumental learning. Transformation theory supplements these principles by recognising, through communicative learning, the salience (but not the exclusive role) of language in construal, discourse and reflective action. Searle's fifth principle on rationality and logic and sixth on intellectual standards pertain to both domains of instrumental and communicative learning.

However important the distinction between instrumental and communicative learning, one must not dichotomise these two domains. It is important to emphasise that most learning involves elements of both the instrumental and the communicative. Critical theory highlights the danger of the hegemony of instrumental rationality, which in our society tends to displace communicative rationality, creating a force for objectifying, commodifying and depersonalising.

Problem solving in instrumental learning, as well as in communicative learning, is embedded in a set of assumptions established through a consensus of those involved. Kuhn (1990) has shown how the paradigms that govern scientific enterprise become challenged and how scientific inquiry becomes transformed by critical reflection on dilemmas produced in attempts to make newly discovered data 'fit' established assumptions. Kuhn also notes the validating role of resulting discourse concerning the conditions of inquiry and when findings do not fit the prevailing theory within the scientific community involved. Instrumental problem solving characteristically involves more than cognition alone. Motives, will, intuition, self-concept, interpersonal considerations and emotions are also often important ingredients of task-oriented problem solving in everyday instrumental learning and even in its prototype, scientific inquiry.

On learning theory

Habermas argues that to understand scientific theories formulated within the tradition, we must differentiate empirical–analytical theories from reconstructive theories (like those of Chomsky, Piaget and Kohlberg), which seek to explain universal conditions and rules implicit in linguistic competence, cognitive and moral development and the nature of human communication. Habermas's theory of communicative action (1984, 1987) is one such reconstructive theory.

Transformation theory is also a reconstructive theory. Its focus is adult learning and its primary audience is adult educators. As a reconstructive theory, it seeks to establish a general, abstract and idealised model that explains the generic structure, dimensions and dynamics of the learning process.

Transformation theory does not undertake a definitive cultural critique, but it provides the model constructs, language, categories and dynamics to enable others to understand how adults learn in various cultural settings. These include: the distinctions between instrumental and communicative learning; the four kinds of learning; the nature of meaning schemes and perspectives; characteristics of a better developed frame of reference; forms of construal; memory as a projected imaginative reconstruction of past events; learning through validation of beliefs by appeal to tradition, authority, force or discourse; alternative forms of reflection; critical reflection on problem contexts, processes and premises as the way meaning structures are transformed; epochal and accumulative transformations; the ideal conditions of discourse; and communicative competence. Which of these descriptors are used, the priorities of their use and the way they are used are dictated by a culture, and not by their validity as constructs.

11

To say that one acts rationally or that a statement is rational is to say that the action or statement can be criticised or defended by those involved so that they are able to justify them. Rationality is not, in theory, a culturally partisan privilege, although local cultures may distort the process to make it so.

As I have indicated elsewhere, all contemporary cultures would probably agree that rationality should have the following characteristics: (a) beliefs should contain no logical contradictions; (b) reasons for believing them can be advanced and assessed; (c) concepts will become more intelligible when analysed; and (d) we have criteria with which to know when the belief is justified or not. Most would probably also agree that an interpretation or point of view is likely to be a better one to the degree that it is more inclusive, discriminating, permeable, critically reflective and integrative of experience, although as Tennant (1993) points out, integrative may mean different things in different cultures.

The criticism in the quotation above is misdirected. Transformation theory should be rigorously assessed through a continuing and critically reflective discourse to establish the validity of its constructs, and not its focus or lack of focus on obstructions imposed on the learning process by one or another local cultures. Reconstructive theories are subject to the canons of confirmation and falsification.

The ideal conditions of learning

Transformation theory rescues the belaboured concepts of freedom, justice, democratic participation and equality from attack as parochial political artefacts of the Western Enlightenment. It holds that these values, along with tolerance, education, openness and caring are necessary to the ideal of undistorted communication.

Under optimal conditions, participants in discourse will: (a) have accurate and complete information; (b) be free from coercion and distorting self-deception; (c) be able to weigh evidence and assess arguments as objectively as possible; (d) be open to alternative perspectives; (e) be able to critically reflect upon presuppositions and their consequences; (f) have equal opportunity to participate (including the chance to challenge, question, refute and reflect and to hear others do the same); and (g) be able to accept an informed, objective and rational consensus as a legitimate test of validity (Mezirow, 1991).

These optimal conditions of discourse are also optimal conditions of learning and of education. To the extent that we may think of a common process of learning in contemporary societies, we may also accept (tentatively) a consensus regarding these ideal conditions, which have evolved out of our common experience. These ideals provide the foundation in the nature of adult learning for both a philosophy of education and a political philosophy as well.

The implementation of these ideal conditions within the context of adult education implies a conscious effort by the educator to establish and enforce norms in the learning situation that neutralise or significantly reduce the influence of power and prestige, the win/lose dialogue and the hegemony of instrumental rationality found elsewhere in society. Adult education is predicated upon creating free space for reflection and discourse and a reduction of the power differential between educator and learner. The educator is seen as a collaborative learner, and he or she tries to work herself out of the job of facilitator to become another learner, contributing his or her experience to arrive at a best consensual judgement. Ideally, and this is characteristic of adult education, the relation of educator to learner is one of subject-to-subject, a peer relationship, rather than one of subject-to-object, not uncommon in the education of children.

In adult education, there are well established norms differentiating between education and indoctrination. Thus, with all its cultural limitations, adult education may be understood as a credible response to the postmodernist threat that society's power and influence inevitably corrupt critical discourse and rationality. Adult education is critically reflective of this threat and committed to preventing it from distorting communication and the adult learning process.

References

Bagnall, R G (1994) Continuing education in postmodernity: four semantic tensions, *International Journal of Lifelong Education* 13, July–August, 265–79.

Bernstein, R J (1985) 'Introduction' in *Habermas and Modernity*, R J Bernstein (ed.), The MIT Press, Cambridge, Mass.

Chomsky, N (1959) Review of *Verbal Behaviour* by B F Skinner, *Language* 35, 26–58.

Habermas, J (1984) *The Theory of Communicative Action. Vol. I, Reason and the Rationalisation of Society*, T McCarthy (trans.), Beacon Press, Boston.

Habermas, J (1987) *The Theory of Communicative Action. Vol. II, Lifeworld and System: a Critique of Functionalist Reason*, T McCarthy (trans.), Beacon Press, Boston.

Henry, W A (1994) *In Defense of Elitism*, Doubleday, NY (quoted in the *New York Times Book Review*, 16 October, 30).

Heron, J (1988) 'Validity in co-operative inquiry', in *Human Inquiry in Action: Developments in Paradigm Research*, P Reason (ed.), Sage, London.

Kuhn, T S (1990) *The Structure of Scientific Revolution*, University of Chicago, Chicago.

Mezirow J (1991) *Transformative Dimensions in Adult Learning*, Jossey-Bass, San Francisco, California.

Scialabba G (1994) 'Only words', *The Nation*, 31 January.

Searle J R (1993) 'Rationality and realism, what is at stake?', *Daedalus* 122 (Fall), 55–83.

Semin Gun R I and Gergen K J (1990) *Everyday Understanding*, Sage, London.

Tennant M (1993) 'Perspective transformation and adult development', *Adult Education Quarterly* 44 (Fall), 34–42.

CHAPTER 2

Information Processing, Memory, Age and Adult Learning

Gillian Boulton-Lewis

Learning and information processing

This chapter is concerned with current research and thinking about the human information processing model, the aspects of memory that this includes, cognitive change and development with age and implications for learning in adulthood.

Models of the human information processing system

In this section aspects of the human information processing model including the sensory register, short-term memory, working memory, long-term memory, knowledge and semantic networks are considered. Connections are made between these aspects of memory and the strategies that are used to detect and recognise information, retain it for processing, encoding, transforming and storing in long-term memory (Boulton-Lewis, 1994). The kinds of information, such as declarative, procedural and conditional knowledge, that are believed to comprise the knowledge base are also discussed briefly.

What is learning? It can be described simply as mental activity that includes receiving, storing, retrieving and using knowledge. This process requires interest and often demands effort. It depends heavily on memory processes as described below.

From the mid-1960s models of memory have been proposed in which a distinction has been made between holding information for a short time by repeating it and storing information for long periods by encoding and practising it (Waugh and Norman, 1965). The models have become progressively more detailed and provide a description, modelled partly on computer programs, of the components of human information processing. Of course, the major difference between computers and humans of all ages is that we can choose to a great extent what information we hold in any part of memory whereas computers cannot.

Probably the most influential model of memory has been that of Atkinson and Shiffrin (1968, 1971). The structure that they described included sensory registers, short-term memory, and long-term memory. This was a three-store model in which information was received through the senses, held in short-term memory, where it was processed along with information from long-term memory, and then encoded and stored in long-term memory, which supposedly has an unlimited capacity. This model has been criticised because it did not take into account the level to which an individual person processed the information or the procedures that were used to do that.

More recent structural models of memory and thinking include descriptions of processing and storage components as well as procedures that affect the level of processing of information. A simplified version of such a model is shown in Figure 2.1. Notice that a distinction is made in this figure between short-term memory and working memory.

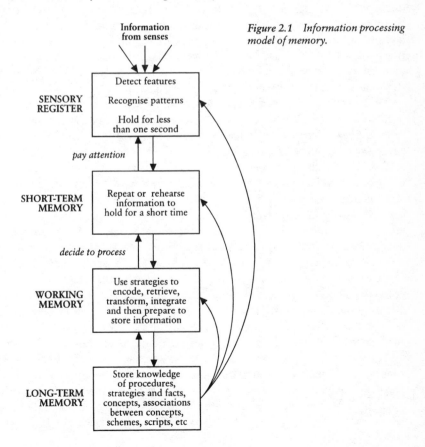

Figure 2.1   Information processing model of memory.

The sensory register

As can be seen from Figure 2.1, the sensory register is where we detect features and recognise patterns of objects or events in our environment. We do this through sight, sound, touch and so on. If we do not pay attention to and process this information then we hold it for less than a second. The sensory register does not change much with age. The ability to perceive information is present soon after birth for most senses. What does change with age is knowledge, based on experience, and that affects what we know about, are interested in, and therefore choose to attend to.

Short-term memory

As the name implies, this is where, in the model but not in any particular part of the brain, we hold information for a short time. It is where you hold, for example, a telephone number while you dial it. You can only hold that information for a few seconds unless you use a strategy to keep it there. That is, you repeat it or, to use the more technical term, you rehearse it. Before information processing explanations of cognitive development were proposed, much of intellectual development was explained in terms of increases in memory capacity and studies were conducted to identify and describe the development of memory span (eg Ebbinghaus, 1885).

Miller (1956) proposed that adults could remember five to nine items of unrelated information. There are more recent theories of how much information adults can remember but Miller's formula is still a good approximate guide to the number of unrelated bits of information that an adult can store and recall for a short time. As memory span tests show (Dempster, 1981) the number of unrelated separate items of information that can be held in short-term memory increase with age to approximately six items of unrelated numbers or words in adolescence. There is no general agreement as to why memory span increases with age. Schneider and Pressley (1989) summarised the present position and concluded that there is no reason to believe that memory span increases are due to some biologically determined growth in capacity, or alternatively due to use of strategies alone, which was another popular hypothesis. They proposed that increases in speed of processing information, due to more efficient carrying out of operations, as suggested by Case *et al.* (1982), might free more space for storage. Siegler (1991, p.75) used the analogy of packing a car boot to explain the workings of short-term memory. The capacity of a car's boot does not change as the owner acquires experience in packing luggage into it. None the less, the amount of luggage that can be packed into the boot does change. Whereas the boot at first might hold three or four suitcases, it might eventually come to hold four or five. With more efficient packing, boot space is freed for additional materials.

Hence the analogy that with a better organised knowledge base and chunking of information, more can be processed more efficiently.

Working memory

In some descriptions of the information processing system short-term and working memory are considered to be the same. Halford (1993) made a strong case for short-term and working memory to be considered as separate parts of the memory structure. Baddeley (1990, 1994) proposed that there is evidence to distinguish short-term store (STS) in memory from long-term store and that there is probably a multi-component working memory system as opposed to STS. This multi-component system would contain a controlling executive system as well as subsidiary systems such as an articulatory or phonological loop. You will see that in Figure 2.1 working memory is described as the part of memory where we combine information from long-term and short-term memory and use strategies such as encoding, retrieval, transforming, and integrating to process information so that it can be stored in, and later retrieved from, long-term memory. When you consciously decide to break your telephone number into parts, or note the pattern of the numbers, you are using working memory.

Long-term memory

Long-term memory contains almost everything that a person knows. This includes procedural and declarative knowledge (Anderson, 1988). Procedural knowledge is knowing how to do things whereas declarative knowledge includes acquisition of facts, concepts, associations between concepts, and schemas and scripts. This last is a set of procedures something like the script for a play and guides our behaviour in familiar situations. For example, people develop scripts to represent such activities as eating in restaurants. You usually do not order dessert before the main course unless you want to puzzle or annoy the waiter or waitress.

As well as storing words as representations of facts and procedures we also store sensory information in the form of events, images, sounds, smells, tastes, movements and so on. Some of these we encode deliberately and some unconsciously enter long-term memory. Basically, it is proposed that the information is organised semantically (according to meaning). The association between concepts in memory is often represented in diagrams in the form of a semantic network, that is a network of meanings. In such a diagram the length of the line joining the concepts is an indication of how close the association is between them. Collins and Loftus (1975), for example, presented a hypothetical example of a semantic network. It was an attempt to provide a diagrammatic representation of the way in which concepts are related in human memory. In the figure the word 'red' is joined by lines of more or less equal length to concepts such as 'orange' and 'fire' on the basis that these ideas would be prompted more or less equally by the word 'red' as a stimulus. On the other hand the line from 'red' to 'fire engine' is longer because 'fire engine' is more likely to cause one to think of other vehicles. I actually think of blood, wounds, first aid and so on when I hear 'red'. Try it yourself and with a few other people. Did you all respond in the same way? As you can see from this activity we all construct an individual knowledge base in long-term memory as a result of existing knowledge and interests from our own unique encounters with our environment.

Long-term memory is believed to be infinite and not to change in capacity with age. What does develop from about five years of age is a range of strategies to encode, store and retrieve information in long-term memory. When we cannot retrieve information from long-term memory it is usually because we have not encoded and stored it effectively, or it has decayed due to lack of use, or there is interference from other memories. Strategies and meta-cognition are not discussed in this chapter because they are considered in other sections of the book.

The effect of development and ageing on aspects of the information processing system

Merriam and Caffarella (1991) asserted that apparent deficits and declines in learning with age are often shown to be functions of non-cognitive factors such as level of education, training and speed of response. Merriam (1993) discussed early research in differences in rate of learning with age. She cited the work of Thorndike *et al.* (1928) who focused on testing people between 14 and 50 years and concluded that between 25 and 45 years adults should learn in much the same way as adults of 20 years. Thorndike *et al.* suggested that the rate of learning declined 1 per cent per year. It is likely that these results were confounded by the fact that the older adults had less formal education. Also, when speed of learning was not important, it was found that adults up to the age of 70 years did as well as younger adults.

Horn and Hofer (1992) described nine broad organisations of cognitive processes, which are summarised as follows.

1. Knowledge derived from acculturation (maintained)
2. Fluency of retrieval of knowledge (maintained)
3. Visualising capabilities (maintained)
4. Auditory capabilities (maintained)
5. Quantitative capabilities (maintained)
6. Reasoning capabilities (vulnerable)
7. Processes of maintaining immediate awareness (vulnerable)

8. Processes in speed of apprehension (vulnerable)
9. Processes for quickly arriving at decisions (vulnerable).

People who are high or low in performance in one of these processes are not necessarily high or low in others. As Charness (1992) suggests, 'age and expertise are individual-difference variables'. The processes themselves relate in different ways to age over the lifespan in individuals in terms of overall cognitive processing. The cognitive processes that decline early in adulthood (1, 2, 3, and 4) are said to be maintained and the processes that decline very slowly from the early twenties, that is reasoning capabilities, processes for maintaining awareness, speed of apprehension and of making a decision (6, 7, 8 and 9) are said to be vulnerable. These processes are also adversely and irreversibly affected by brain damage but usually decline late and little in adulthood. Auditory and visual capabilities actually increase until about 40 years and then decrease gradually. Knowledge, its retrieval, and quantitative capabilities (1, 2 and 5) increase into the sixties before decline is noted. There are individual differences in increase of knowledge with age because some people continue to learn after formal schooling finishes. Individual differences in reasoning abilities (6) do not increase with age but some aspects of reasoning improve with training. Declines in processes of maintaining awareness, and speed of apprehension and decision making (6, 7 and 8) probably result in loss of the ability to comprehend complex relationships. It is suggested that increases in carefulness and persistence with age to some extent compensate for these losses. Decline in vulnerable processes appears also to result from small losses in brain functions related to different lifestyle effects such as consumption of alcohol. The above summary is compatible with Charness's (1992) suggestion, on the basis of Lehman's (1953) data and other research, that peak performances are most likely to occur for people in their thirties; however, it would seem that very competent performance can be maintained into the forties and fifties at least.

Hence it can be concluded that adults generally continue to learn with little change into their forties and that there is a small amount of decline in some aspects of cognitive functioning from then onwards. Most adults, as they age, usually process less information and do it in a slower and less efficient manner. In particular the aspects of cognitive functioning that relate to processing of information in short-term storage and working memory, and hence the preparation and encoding of information for storage in long-term memory, are vulnerable. Knowledge that has already been acquired, the ability to retrieve it, as well as visual and auditory sensory capabilities are maintained, for the most part, into the sixties.

It has been asserted that the research from which the above conclusions are derived consists mainly of studies of information processing abilities outside the domains in which a particular adult has acquired expert knowledge. For example, Rybash et al. (1986) proposed an encapsulation model of adult learning and performance. In essence, in proposing this model, they maintained that fluid capabilities were encapsulated with age and that this explained the simultaneous presence of age-related declines in the components of the information processing system as well as the emergence of postformal styles of thinking and the growth and use of expert, domain-specific knowledge systems. They maintained that psychologists have used ecologically irrelevant tasks to study performance with ageing and that, 'when memory and attention are assessed under domain-specific real-life contexts, there is little evidence for negative developmental change'. They suggested that this can be attributed to the possibility that much adult processing is driven in a top-down fashion, based on knowledge and expertise, rather than in the data-driven bottom-up model assumed in the information processing paradigm. They suggest also that while some components of intelligence, such as fluid mental abilities as described above, decline with age it may very well be that much of adult cognitive performance depends less on these abilities and more on contextual and domain related knowledge. Hence, they suggest that,

> 'Older adults, despite reductions in efficiency and speed of processing with advances in age, may not display comparable reductions in cognitive effectiveness in any of the familiar domains of specialised expertise that they may have developed throughout their lifetime... it appears far too limiting to focus purely on the processes and abilities that define the components of the cognitive system.' (Rybash *et al.*, 1986, p.147)

However, as Charness (1992) states, if there were no changes in cognitive functioning with age one would expect monotonic-increasing functions in performance and research shows this not to be the case. The conclusion that can be drawn from the above is that older adults, compared with younger adults, are less likely to easily develop new knowledge outside their existing domains of expertise. If they do so it is likely to require more time and effort.

Charness (1992) makes similar statements to those above when discussing age and its effect on job performance, asserting that there is little evidence that age *per se* accounts for much of the variance. However, he acknowledges that much of the literature on age and mental performance suggests that age decline is more apparent as tasks become more complex. He makes the arresting statement, on the basis of a range of studies and his own calculations, that,

> 'there is a magic number for this new metric on the importance of initial age differences in performance. Namely, 3 min of practice per year of age difference is all that it takes to eliminate age effects, using the benchmark of the initial performance level of young adults. Put more crudely, by giving up one night of television watching and practising a typical laboratory task, an older adult will perform as well as an unpracticed young adult.' (p.452)

20

Theories of cognitive development and formal and postformal stages of learning in adulthood

Piaget described the development of human thought as occurring in stages until formal operational thinking in adolescence. Since the 1980s a number of theories that can be described as neo-Piagetian have been proposed, most of which attribute the development of cognition and learning to the maturation of and constraints on the capacity to process information (Labouvie-Vief, 1992; Rybash *et al.*, 1986; Demetriou, 1990; Commons and Richards, 1984; Fischer and Farrar, 1988). These are examined below for their description of postformal thought in late adolescence and adulthood. There is also a brief consideration of the SOLO (structure of observed learning outcomes) taxonomy (Biggs and Collis, 1982, 1989; Biggs and Moore, 1993) as it applies to learning in the formal mode in higher education.

Piaget (Inhelder and Piaget, 1958) proposed four stages of cognitive development from birth to adolescence. He described human thinking in terms of developing logical structures. He proposed that the highest level of thinking occurs in adolescents, continues on into adulthood and depends on an abstract system of symbolic logic. He determined stages of thinking in terms of the typical logical operations that a person could be competent in at approximate ages and asserted that all thought for a person in a particular stage would be qualitatively the same. He believed that from about 12 years of age a person usually became capable of formal operational thought. This means that,

> 'the subject becomes capable of reasoning correctly about propositions he does not believe, or at least not yet; that is propositions that he [sic] considers pure hypotheses. He [sic] becomes capable of drawing the necessary conclusions from truths which are merely possible, which constitutes the beginning of hypothetico-deductive or formal thought'.

Piaget did not describe stages of thought beyond the formal operational stage although in his later work he did suggest that normal subjects reach the stage of formal operations 'in different areas according to their aptitudes and their professional specializations' (Piaget, 1972).

Others have since proposed postformal stages and some of their work is discussed briefly below. The view that people develop through discrete stages and that all their responses to cognitive tasks are typical of a particular stage is no longer generally accepted. In particular Piaget's theory did not satisfactorily explain exceptions to the general pattern of development; for example, why a person's apparent level of functioning can differ from one domain to another and why, in some domains, some adults do not ever reach the stage of formal operations. As well as development of cognitive ability, some of the more recent theories of cognitive development also take into account knowledge and experience as factors in cognitive performance.

Rybash *et al.* (1986) presented evidence to support the position that adults can 'think about their accumulated knowledge in a postformal manner' (p.149). They suggested that postformal thinking consists of a number of styles, that this leads adults to conceptualise knowledge as dynamic and active and that they conceptualise reality within an open self-evolving framework, and their knowledge as a relationship between subject and object. Thus, they suggest, knowledge becomes personalised, contextualised and relativistic for adults.

Demetriou (1990) described two theories of cognitive development that deal with development of formal and postformal thought; that of Commons and Richards (1984) and his own (Demetriou and Efklides, 1985). He believes that there are inadequacies in both theories and that there are testable predictions that could result in their integration. According to Commons, Richards and associates there are five stages of development following concrete operations. The first is the stage of abstract operations where a person can represent elements abstractly and perform single operations on them such as permutations and combinations. The next is the stage of formal operations, which is similar to Piaget's stage of that name. The third is that of systematic operations, which is the first of the postformal stages, and allows a person to perform third-order operations and represent a whole network of relations comprising a system. The fourth stage of metasystematic thought allows a person to transform systems and determine relations between systems. The final stage is that of supersystems, which is only postulated at present due to lack of empirical data. Systematic and metasystematic thought were tested using the multisystem problem, one version of which is described by Demetriou as follows.

> 'The task consists of four stories. Each of the stories describes ordered relations and/or equalities between single objects and/or sets of objects (eg relations of the type [A+B+C] > [B+C] > [A+C] > [C] >[0]) [sic]. Thus each story is equivalent to a system comprised of elements and relations. The subject's task is first to decode the relations between the elements of each story and organise them properly... Second the subject must compare each of the stories with the rest.' (p.153)

One story, for example, concerned an Indian man whose tastes in food never varied but whose income did. It described the restaurants and the combinations of dishes that he would choose in order of preference depending on what he could afford. The person reasoning with such stories must construct an exhaustive set of representations that holds across stories and detect any violations. Systematic thinkers attempt to do this but metasystematic thinkers realise that the 'correct' system is one that yields isomorphic transformations across systems (Labouvie-Vief, 1992).

Demetriou and Efklides (1985) proposed detailed levels of postformal thought in six capacity spheres. Three of these are described by Demetriou (1990) as they apply to experimental capacity, relational capacity and the possibility of conceiving reflecting capacity (metacognitive behaviour). For example, on the metacognitive task, which required the subjects to categorise other formal tasks and explain why they were similar, different, or similar and different in some respects, four levels of development were proposed in hierarchical order as follows.

1. Qualitative relations of relations between tasks.
2. Content based reflections and task characteristics but cognitive processes not taken into account.
3. Operations specified, cognitive processes identified but not analysed.
4. Operations analysed, cognitive processes analysed and contrasted. A personal theory of cognitive functioning may exist.

When Demetriou retested these theories he found, *inter alia*, that the developmental sequence proposed by Commons and Richards that culminates in metasystematic thought is closely related to the developmental sequence of metacognitive abilities described by Demetriou and Efklides (1985, p.165) and summarised above. He also found that 'science teachers performed slightly better on the multisystem problem than [humanities] undergraduates, who performed much better than humanities teachers. However undergraduate scores on the metacognitive problem were higher than the other two groups [of teachers]'. He does not explain these results but it could be concluded that discipline area and occupation affect the development of such thought processes.

Fischer (Fischer and Farrar, 1988) also proposed an abstract tier of skill development that included four abstract levels (abstract sets, abstract mappings, abstract systems and systems of abstract systems) that are single principles that can occur between 14 and 26 years of age. He makes it quite clear that one of the most potent factors in organising people's skills is the task; 'a skill is a characteristic of a person-in-context'. When tasks differ, skills differ substantially. The mechanism producing changes in levels of thinking is the emergence of the requisite capacity but this does not necessarily result in changes in skills. The person must take time and effort to use the capacity to develop the skills. In other words Fischer believes that although general capacity is partly a developmental process, acquisition of skills in a task domain requires attention, time and effort at any age.

Biggs and Collis (1982, 1989) proposed, in the SOLO taxonomy, a consistent hierarchical sequence that they call a learning cycle. They distinguished five basic levels in each learning cycle or mode of learning: prestructural; unistructural; multistructural; relational; and extended abstract, which is also the first level in the next cycle. The levels occur and reoccur in the five modes as shown in Figure 2.2. The modes are the representational form for the content of learning. The modes typically appear at the ages indicated on the abscissa in Figure 2.2 and the typical corresponding educational levels are shown on the right-hand side of the Figure. As shown in Figure 2.2, Biggs and Collis suggest that theoretical learning in the formal mode can begin around year 12 and continue to develop through university courses to formal-2 (postformal) knowledge as a result of higher degree study by research. These levels are learning outcomes and hence depend on development as well as learning in a discipline area. The two formal levels are summarised below.

'Formal-1 (from about 16 years of age)... the first of the formal modes makes its appearance when students begin to question how things are and, instead of accepting them, form hypotheses about how they might be. This is theorising proper... Unistructural levels of thinking in the formal mode begin to appear in some students, with respect to their particular specialisations, from around 16 years of age... It certainly does not generalise to all thinking, however, and

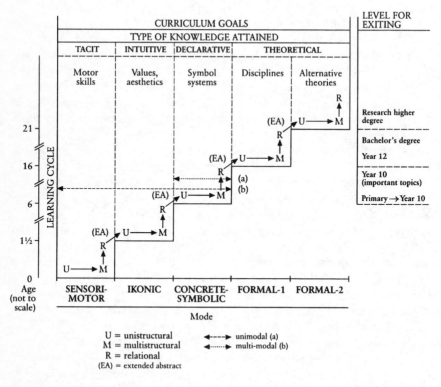

Figure 2.2 *Modes, learning cycle (solo level), curriculum goals and suggested exit levels for schooling (reproduced from Biggs and Collis, 1989).*

24

may not develop in other students at all. Some evidence of formal-1 thought should be essential for admission to university.

Formal-2 [postformal] (from about 20 years)... when one questions the conventional bounds of theory and practice and establishes new ones, one enters [this mode]... [it] may be seen in high level innovations in many fields; it is institutionalised in post graduate study and in basic research.' (Biggs and Collis, 1989, p.157).

Biggs and Collis state that some learning can be cross-modal or multi-modal. A superb dancing or sporting performance, for example, would be multimodal. Some teaching approaches such as problem based learning, to develop the content of professional skills in context, for medical and para-medical degrees, for example, involve multimodal learning. They assert that some adults never progress much beyond the concrete symbolic mode and, if they do, it is often only in selected content areas because of further study as a result of their interest or motivation.

Knowledge, expertise and adult learning

The question of prior knowledge, the advantage that it can provide in adult learning contexts, and the differences between expert and novice behaviour (Glaser and Chi, 1988) are considered in this section.

Rybash *et al.* (1986) proposed that the 'growth and encapsulation of domain-specific knowledge is the most salient feature of adult cognition' (p.147). It is characterised as expert, automatised, intuitive, self-constructed and active. For the purposes of this discussion of age and learning the question of expertise is most important if, as has been asserted by Horn and Hofer (1992), for example, adults who have become experts in a domain can continue to function as experts despite gradual declines in aspects of processing and memory.

Experts are better than novices on many dimensions of performance in particular when speed and accuracy are involved. They usually know what to do and how to do it. Glaser and Chi (1988, p.xv ff.) described the differences between expert and novice behaviour and they are summarised below.

1. *Experts excel in their own domain.*   There is little evidence that expertise in one domain can be transferred to another. For example a driver's expertise is not transferable to expertise in the domain of chess playing.
2. *Experts perceive large meaningful patterns in their domain.*   That is, experts are more likely to perceive meaningful clusters of elements, whereas novices are more likely to perceive the individual elements in their domain. For example chess masters excel in recalling clusters of pieces. This excellence is not necessarily associated with a generally

superior perceptual ability but rather is a reflection of better organisation of the relevant knowledge base.

3. *Experts quickly solve problems in their domain with little error.* Relative to novices, experts execute their skills more quickly and accurately.
   It is postulated that such speed comes from many hours of practice
   which makes the process more automatic and frees memory capacity
   for other processing. It could also be that they have stored a large
   number of condition–action rules.

4. *Experts have superior short- and long-term memory for occurrences in
   their domain.* Experts, as opposed to novices, have higher rates of
   both immediate and delayed recall for events or elements within their
   domain.

5. *Experts represent problems in their domain at a deeper, more principled
   level.* Both experts and novices have knowledge represented by conceptual categories. The experts' categories, however, tend to be 'semantically or principle based', whereas novices' categories are 'syntactically
   or surface-feature oriented'.

6. *Experts spend a great deal of time analysing a problem qualitatively.*
   Experts seek to ponder and understand a problem, whereas novices
   seek immediately to apply formulae in an attempt to solve the problem.
   An illustrative example of such behaviour is given from the work of
   Paige and Simon (1966) where students were asked to solve an algebra
   word problem as follows;

   > 'A board was sawed into two pieces. One piece was two thirds
   > as long as the whole piece and was exceeded in length by the
   > second piece by four feet. How long was the board before it
   > was cut?'

   Some students used equations to arrive at a negative solution whereas
   those who had a mental representation of the problem decided it was
   meaningless because you could not have a negative length.

7. *Experts have superior self-monitoring skills.* Experts are more aware
   of when they make errors, of why they do not comprehend and of when
   they need to check solutions (and of what they do not know). Experts
   also ask more questions.

Tennant and Pogson (1995, p.52) cite the work of Schmidt *et al.* (1990) as
an example of how experience operates to produce medical expertise. They
suggest that clinical competence is content specific, that is it depends on
knowledge relevant to the particular problem, rather than the general reasoning or heuristics proposed by proponents of problem based learning. A four-
stage theory of development of clinical expertise describes the first stage as
dependent on complex learned explanations with little understanding of how
the disease appears in reality. The second stage allows the person to take short
cuts in reasoning without considering all relevant theoretical knowledge. The
third stage depends on 'illness scripts', which are 'a grammar' that provides

rules enabling one to construct mental models of families of diseases. Problem solving is a matter of searching these idiosyncratic scripts. The fourth stage is one where diagnosis is based on similarity between a particular case and some previous patient. This expertise might depend on experience stored in the doctor's memory of a very large number of previous patients.

Charness (1992) suggested that the critical issue, in terms of age and performance, is how the older expert compensates for changes in processing speed and working memory to maintain performance. He gives a good example from research in typing (Salthouse, 1991) of how skilled older operators maintain typing speed by looking further ahead, and therefore give themselves more planning time. He also raises the question as to whether there are tasks where no compensation is adequate and suggests that debates over mandatory retirement ages for airline pilots and others in similar occupations are related to such an issue.

In summary then, expertise depends on learning and experience, is crucial to later adult learning and performance and is the product of time, effort and experience.

Implications for adult learning

In conclusion, aspects of the human information system, which is central to learning and thinking, begin to decline from the early twenties but not significantly until the sixties. However, where older adults have acquired expert knowledge and are not suffering from any disease that would interfere with memory, their performance should be minimally slower but as competent as that of younger adults. Selkoe (1992) cites evidence from two medical studies of the health of a large group of subjects in the USA that indicates that in the 65–74 year age group, 0.4–3 per cent only are likely to suffer from dementia, including Alzheimer's disease. The implications for continued learning in the adult years are that one can expect younger adults to learn new material a little more quickly but that, given time and sufficient motivation, older adults will achieve equivalent learning outcomes. Hence the myth about the difficulty of learning as they get older, which many adults believe, is not well founded and should be dispelled. The positive perspective of the effect of expertise on performance and the need for just a little more effort to learn new material should be promoted with adult learners.

References

Anderson, J R (1988) *Cognitive Psychology and its Implications*, Freeman, New York.
Atkinson, R C and Shiffrin, R M (1968) 'Human memory. A proposed system and its control processes' in *The Psychology of Learning and Motivation*, vol. 2, K W Spence

and J W Spence (eds), Academic Press, New York.

Atkinson, R C and Shiffrin R M (1971) 'The control of short-term memory', *Scientific American*, **225**(2), August, 82–90.

Baddeley, A (1990) *Human Memory: Theory and Practice*, Erlbaum, Hove, UK.

Baddeley, A (1994) *Your Memory: A User's Guide*, Penguin, Harmondsworth.

Biggs, J B and Collis, K F (1982) *Evaluating the Quality of Learning; The SOLO Taxonomy*, Academic Press, New York.

Biggs, J B and Collis, K F (1989) Towards a model of school-based curriculum development and assessment using the SOLO taxonomy, *Australian Journal of Education*, **33**(2), 151–63.

Biggs, J B and Moore, P J (1993) *The Process of Learning*, Prentice-Hall, Sydney, Australia.

Boulton-Lewis, G M (1994) 'Memory, cognition, learning and teaching from three to eight years' in *The Early Years: Development, Learning and Teaching,* G M Boulton-Lewis and D Catherwood (eds), Australian Council for Educational Research, Hawthorn, Victoria. Republished (1995) by Pitman, London.

Case, R, Kurland, D M and Goldberg, J (1982) Operational efficiency and the growth of short-term memory span, *Journal of Experimental Child Psychology*, **33**, 386–404.

Charness, N (1992) 'Age and expertise: Responding to Tallands's challenge' in *Everyday Cognition in Adulthood and Late Life*, L W Poon, D C Rubin and B A Wilson (eds), Cambridge University Press, Cambridge, England.

Collins, A M and Loftus E F (1975) A spreading-activation theory of semantic processing, *Psychological Review*, **6**, 407–28.

Commons, M L and Richards, F A (1984) 'A general model of stage theory' in *Beyond Formal Operations: Vol 1, Late Adolescent and Adult Cognitive Development*, M L Commons, F A Richards and C Armon (eds), Praeger, New York.

Demetriou, A (1990) 'Structural and developmental relations between formal and postformal capacities: towards a comprehensive theory of adolescent and adult cognitive development' in *Adult Development, Vol 2*, M L Commons, C Armon, L Kohlberg, F A Richards, T A Grotzer and J D Sinnott (eds), Praeger, New York.

Demetriou, A and Efklides, A (1985) Structure and sequence of formal and post formal thought: general patterns and individual differences, *Child Development*, **56**, 1062–91.

Dempster, F N (1981) Memory span: Sources of individual and developmental differences, *Psychological Bulletin*, **89**, 63–100.

Ebbinghaus, E A (1885) *Uber das Gedachtnis*, Duncker, Leipzig.

Fischer, K W and Farrar, M J (1988) 'Generalizations about generalization: how a theory of skill development explains both generality and specificity' in *The Neo-Piagetian Theories of Cognitive Development: Toward an Integration*, A. Demetriou (ed.), Elsevier, Amsterdam, Netherlands.

Glaser, R and Chi, M T H (1988) 'Overview' in *The Nature of Expertise,* M T H Chi, R Glaser and M J Farr (eds), xv–xxviii, Lawrence Erlbaum, Hillsdale, New Jersey.

Halford, G S (1993) *Children's Understanding: The Development of Mental Models*, Lawrence Erlbaum, Hillsdale, New Jersey.

Horn, J L and Hofer S M (1992) 'Major abilities and development in the adult period' in *Intellectual Development*, R J Sternberg and C A Berg (eds), Cambridge University Press, Cambridge.

Inhelder, B and Piaget, J (1958) *The Growth of Logical Thinking*, Routledge and Kegan Paul, London.

Labouvie-Vief, G (1992) 'A neo-Piagetian perspective on adult cognitive development' in *Intellectual Development*, R J Sternberg and C A Berg (eds), Cambridge University Press, Cambridge.

Lehman, H C (1953) *Age and Achievement*, Princeton University Press, Princeton, New Jersey.

Merriam, S B (1993) Adult learning: where have we come from? Where are we headed?, *New Directions for Adult and Continuing Education*, 57 (Spring), 5–14.

Merriam, S B and Caffarella, R S (1991) *Learning in Adulthood*, Jossey-Bass, San Francisco, California.

Miller, C A (1956) The magical number seven, plus or minus two: some limits on our capacity for processing information, *Psychological Review*, 63, 81–97.

Paige, J M and Simon, H A (1986) 'Cognition processes in solving algebra word problems' in *Problem Solving*, B Kleinmuntz (ed.), 119–151, John Wiley, New York.

Piaget, J (1972) Intellectual evolution from adolescence to adulthood, *Human Development*, 15, 1–12.

Rybash, J M, Hoyer, W J and Roodin, P A (1986) *Adult Cognition and Ageing*, Pergamon, New York.

Salthouse, T A (1991). *Theoretical Perspectives on Cognitive Ageing*, Lawrence Erlbaum, Hillsdale, New Jersey.

Schmidt, H G, Norman, G R and Boshuizen, H P A (1990) A cognitive perspective on medical expertise: theory and implications, *Academic Medicine*, 65, 611–21.

Schneider, W and Pressley, M (1989) *Memory Development between 2 and 20*, Springer-Verlag, New York.

Selkoe, D J (1992) Aging brain, aging mind, *Scientific American*, September, 97–103.

Siegler R S (1991) *Children's Thinking* (2nd edn), Prentice-Hall, Englewood Cliffs, New Jersey.

Sternberg, R J and Berg, C A (eds) (1992) *Intellectual Development*, Cambridge University Press, Cambridge.

Tennant, M and Pogson, P (1995) *Learning and Change in the Adult Years*, Jossey-Bass, San Francisco, California.

Thorndike, E L, Bregman, E O, Tilton, J W and Woodyard, E (1928) *Adult Learning*, Macmillan, New York.

CHAPTER 3

Adult Learners' Metacognitive Behaviour in Higher Education

Barry Dart

Introduction

This chapter explores metacognition and the use of metacognitive strategies by adult learners in higher education. It draws much of its information from two research studies conducted in a large metropolitan university in Australia. Adult learners are defined as individuals over the age of twenty-five years. This definition is frequently used to identify 'non-traditional' or adult students in higher education (Kasworm, 1990).

In recent years the role of metacognition in learning at the primary and secondary levels of education has been made more explicit, and an increased number of learning activities to facilitate metacognitive thinking have been identified and described. There has been less interest in and emphasis on the use of metacognitive thinking in higher education. However, educators at this level emphasise the importance of metacognition for complex cognitive activities and for self-directedness in learning (Baird *et al.*,1989).

Learning

The familiar, traditional transmission model of teaching, whereby information is transferred from teacher to learners, and in which learners play passive roles, is gradually being replaced by a model based on constructivist learning theory. This emphasises that learners actively construct knowledge for themselves by forming their own representations of the material to be learned, selecting information they perceive to be relevant, and interpreting this on the basis of their present knowledge and needs. In this theory, learners assume more active and interactive roles (Prawat and Floden, 1994).

Thus, in the transmission model of teaching, the teacher is the focus, whereas in the constructivist model of learning the learner is the focus. This is how it should be, for in constructivist learning, the learning drives the teaching, as adjustments need to be made in the teaching role to enable learners to recognise their own relevant ideas and beliefs, evaluate these ideas and beliefs in terms of what is to be learned and how this learning is intended to occur, and decide whether or not to reconstruct these ideas and beliefs. The teacher's role, therefore, includes helping learners to identify their beliefs and working with them to master impediments to understanding. This can be achieved by facilitating student–student and student–teacher interaction: using reflective feedback to enhance the nature of discussions; providing critical feedback related to learners' contributions; and challenging learners' naïve conceptions. Thus, the teacher becomes a facilitator of learning rather than a giver of information.

If learning with understanding, characterised by the making of connections – between aspects of the new material, between new material and prior knowledge, and between informal and formal knowledge – is a desired outcome rather than rote learning and regurgitation of information, then replacement of the transmission model of teaching by constructivist teaching needs to be hastened.

Collaborative learning

Many writers (for example King, 1993) emphasise the importance of social interaction in bringing about changes in understanding. The primacy of collaborative learning is stressed. Peer collaboration is essential to the learning process, as learners construct meaning and understanding through active participation and sharing of knowledge (Resnick, 1987). A change in understanding is more likely to occur through social interactive methods that require learners to explain, elaborate and argue their position to others (Brown, 1988). Constructivist environments should support collaboration among learners and with the teacher, who facilitates social negotiation (Jonassen, 1994).

Negotiation as a process of overcoming obstacles to understanding is seen as a collaborative activity engaged in both by teacher and students (Prawat and Floden, 1994). Collaborative learning groups provide opportunities for learners to examine and refine their understandings. What is important is that 'opposing views become alternatives to be explored rather than competitors to be eliminated' (Roby, 1988, p.173).

These activities necessitate the exercise of reflection and metacognition (Baird, 1991) as well as the acceptance of self-responsibility for learning (Biggs and Moore, 1993). From a constructivist viewpoint, learners must have control over their own learning, as the responsibility for learning and sense-making resides with individual learners. To do this successfully they must possess requisite cognitive and metacognitive knowledge and skills. These together with motivation are seen as the essential components of self-regulation in learning (Zimmerman, 1990), wherein learners purposely seek the attainment of self-selected goals through the appropriate use of strategies designed to optimise their learning. In a similar vein, Biggs (1988) emphasises the importance of metacognition as an essential element in the adoption of a deep approach to learning.

Metacognition

Cognition, or thinking, refers to a learner's capability to attend, acquire, represent and recall information. Thus, it relates to how we perceive, act, think and remember. On the other hand, metacognition or 'thinking about thinking' refers to the knowledge and regulation learners have of their own thinking and learning (Brown, 1978). Therefore, it refers to the ability to reflect upon, understand and control one's learning.

Beyer (1987) provides detailed information about metacognition and its elements and consequently only a brief overview of these elements is given here. Metacognitive knowledge includes one's knowledge about learning (what it is, how it occurs and how one knows when something has been learned), which is implied in one's conception of learning. For example, learning is about developing meaning and understanding, through such activities as reading widely about the topic, discussing one's views with colleagues and attempting to relate the new information to what is already known, and then seeing if one can explain the material in a coherent manner and apply it appropriately.

Metacognitive knowledge incorporates understanding about task characteristics that influence how the learner will approach the learning activity; for example, realising that a critical review essay is more demanding than a descriptive essay, so that different methods of study would be required for each of these learning tasks. It also involves learners recognising their strengths and weaknesses, and assets and liabilities in learning; for example, knowing that they are good at identifying the main ideas from text and organising these into a form that facilitates the integration of these with relevant prior knowledge.

As well, metacognitive knowledge includes information about effective cognitive learning strategies. That is, knowing what they are (declarative knowledge) and how to use them (procedural knowledge); for example, knowing that paraphrasing is one strategy that helps the learner develop connections between new information and relevant prior knowledge. This requires reading for understanding so that main ideas are identified, rewriting of the text in the learner's own words and intentional integration of this with the learner's prior knowledge.

32

Regulation of thinking and learning involves two elements; metacognitive awareness and metacognitive control. Metacognitive awareness results from the learner's conscious self-interrogation in relation to the learning task and activity. For example, what is the purpose of this task? What is this information about? What do I already know about this? What do I need to know? What might I do that will help me in completing this task? How am I going? Does this make sense? How well do I understand it? How does this relate to what I already know? Do I need to try something different? Is there a better way of doing this? By asking questions of themselves relating to cognitive processes and deciding on answers to these, learners can control their approach to, progress through and outcomes of learning.

Metacognitive control involves the key operations of planning, monitoring/directing and evaluating and is related to the degree of awareness developed. Planning involves task analysis, identifying relevant prior knowledge, goal setting, selecting appropriate cognitive strategies (conditional knowledge), anticipating possible obstacles to successful completion of the task and predicting ways of overcoming these. Directing/monitoring includes checking to see that learning is proceeding according to plan and assessing understanding or lack of understanding so that corrective strategies can be used if needed. Evaluating comprises assessment of both the processes used to reach the goal and the product resulting from these processes.

The extent to which adult learners report using metacognitive strategies in their learning in university courses and subjects has been investigated in a number of studies carried out by the author. This research is described and analysed, results are discussed and suggestions are made to improve the use of metacognitive strategies in learning.

Study 1

Dart (1994a) reported research on the adequacy of a goal-mediational model of personal and environmental influences on higher education students' learning strategy use. The sample included 1170 students (293 older than 25 years, of which 182 were female; of the remaining 877, 540 were female) enrolled in courses within ten schools at a large metropolitan university in Australia.

The environmental variables measured were Perceived Lecturers' Goals (PLG) (for encouraging autonomy and self-direction in learning) and Perceived Subject Value (PSV) (in terms of interest and importance for the profession and one's own professional development). The personal variable was Perceived Self-Ability (PSA) (how confident students feel in relation to successful accomplishment of the tasks of the subject and in relation to other students). Motivational variables were students' Mastery Goal Orientation (MGO) (intentions for learning the subject in terms of interest and challenge for learning new material) and Performance Goal Orientation (PGO) (the extent to which students want to be successful through getting high grades). Learning strategies included Elaboration (ELAB) (extent to which students personalise learning material by relating it to their prior knowledge and applying it in order to develop understanding); Metacognition (META) (the degree to which students plan for their learning, monitor their understanding and evaluate this); Collaboration (COLL) (the extent to which students interact with other students to facilitate their learning) and Organisation (ORG) (the frequency with which students plan and structure their study). Descriptions of these variables and the questionnaire used to measure them are given in Dart (1994a). Items for this questionnaire were rated on a five-point Likert scale (5 = strongly agree, 1 = strongly disagree).

In the study reported here using the data of the Dart (1994a) research, confirmatory factor analyses were carried out to determine to what extent the factor structure for the learning influences and strategies is the same for females and males of different age groups. The results of these analyses indicated that the factor structures were invariant, which allowed for meaningful comparisons of subgroup means.

Scores on the learning influences and strategies variables were transformed to a five-point scale because of the differing number of items in the various subscales. A multivariate analysis of variance (MANOVA) of the 1170 subjects' scores on the learning influences/strategies variables with respect to age (25 years and younger vs. older than 25 years) was carried out. This analysis revealed a multivariate age effect (Pillais $= 0.11$; $F = 15.61$; $df = 9$, 1084; $p < 0.001$). Univariate analyses of this effect were significant for: Perceived Lecturers' Goals ($F = 7.5$; $df = 1$, 1092; $p = 0.006$); Perceived Subject Value ($F = 33.3$; $df = 1$, 1092; $p < 0.001$); Mastery Goal Orientation ($F = 38.79$; $df = 1$, 1092; $p < 0.001$); Performance Goal Orientation ($F = 6.05$; $df = 1$, 1092; $p = 0.01$); Elaboration ($F = 81.09$; $df = 1$, 1092; $p < 0.001$); Metacognition ($F = 16.31$; $df = 1$, 1092; $p < 0.001$); and Organisation ($F = 21.65$; $df = 1$, 1092; $p < 0.001$). Table 3.1 indicates the mean scores of each age group for these variables.

Even though differences may be statistically significant, they may have little practical significance. Indices of differences in group behaviour and

Table 3.1 Age differences – significantly different mean scores and effect sizes.

Variable	Young	Old	Effect size
PLG	3.44	3.58	0.18
PSV	3.62	3.92	0.40
MGO	3.74	4.03	0.43
PGO	4.39	4.29	0.16
ELAB	3.31	3.81	0.63
META	3.76	3.96	0.29
ORG	2.70	3.03	0.32

performance are frequently used in meta-analytic studies (Glass, 1976), and they can also be used in individual investigations (Richardson, 1993). One of these indices, the effect size or standardised mean difference (Glass, 1976), is the ratio between mean scores of the two groups compared to the average within-group standard deviation on the variable in question. This index is reported in the results. For purposes of interpretation, Cohen (1969) considers an effect size of 0.20 to be small, a value of 0.50 to be medium, and one of 0.80 to be large.

In all instances except for performance goal orientation, the older age group (>25 years) had higher mean scores than the younger students. However, using Cohen's (1969) suggestions, all of these can be considered small except for Perceived Subject Value, Mastery Goal Orientation and the reported use of Elaboration strategies. As can be seen from Table 3.1 it appears that older students match the profile of the 'good' student to a greater degree than do the younger students.

Correlational analyses between metacognition and the other learning influences/strategies were performed separately for the 'young' and 'old' groups of students. Results of these analyses are reported in Table 3.2. Due to the large sample size, small correlation coefficients were significant with $p < 0.01$. It was decided to only interpret coefficients smaller than 0.30, according to the argument forwarded by Burnett (1991), who maintained that accounting for a minimum of 9 per cent of the covariation was meaningful.

It can be seen from Table 3.2 that for both the young and old students metacognition is more strongly associated with a Mastery Goal Orientation and the use of Elaboration and Organised study strategies. This finding is supported by Dart (1994a) who reported that learners having a Mastery Goal Orientation are inclined to use learning strategies for developing their own meaningful understanding (Elaboration); for planning, directing and evaluating this learning (Metacognition); and for planning their study times (Organisation).

The correlation coefficients for these learning influences and strategies variables were examined using Fisher's (1915) transformation of the cor-

Table 3.2 Pearson correlations between metacognition and other learning influences/strategies for 'young' and 'old' students.

	Young	Old
PLG	0.13*	0.08
PSV	0.17*	0.19*
PSA	0.18*	0.08
MGO	0.30*	0.37*
PGO	0.16*	0.24*
ELAB	0.42*	0.56*
COLL	0.22*	0.20*
ORG	0.30*	0.41*

* $p < 0.01$

relation coefficient to determine whether there were any significant differences between these for the 'young' and 'old' students. No differences were significant.

A further multivariance of analysis (MANOVA) was performed on the learning influences and strategies variables for the 'old' group of students to determine if there were any gender differences. A multivariate gender effect was indicated (Pillais = 0.11; $df = 9, 272$; $F = 3.82$; $p < 0.001$). There were significant univariate differences on: Perceived Lecturers' Goals ($F = 11.35$; $df = 1, 280$; $p = 0.001$); Perceived Subject Value ($F = 4.39$; $df = 1, 280$; $p = 0.04$); Elaboration ($F = 7.04$; $df = 1, 280$; $p = 0.01$); Metacognition ($F = 5.33$; $df = 1, 280$; $p = 0.02$); and Collaboration ($F = 13.49$; $df = 1, 280$; $p < 0.001$). In all instances, female students had higher mean scores than males.

Table 3.3 presents the mean scores for these variables for each gender group as well as the effect sizes. These differences are generally small except for Perceived Lecturers' Goals and Collaboration strategies, which are of a moderate degree. Female students perceived their lecturers to be encouraging self-direction of learning more and they reported collaborating with their peers more in their learning than did male students. This latter finding supports the suggestion by Tarule (1988) that females may have preferences for 'connected' learning strategies, such as collaborative discussion and the sharing of personal experiences. It also provides evidence for Hayes' (1992) finding that females rate higher on support seeking. Overall, the profile of female learners is more positive than males.

Table 3.3 Gender differences for 'old' students – significantly different mean scores and effect sizes.

Variable	Female	Male	Effect size
PLG	3.71	3.38	0.41
PSV	4.00	3.81	0.24
ELAB	3.91	3.65	0.33
META	4.02	3.84	0.28
COLL	3.11	2.87	0.45

Correlation analyses for these older students were performed on metacognition and the other learning influences and strategies to determine if there were any variations according to gender. These results are shown in Table 3.4.

As above, only correlation coefficients greater than 0.30 are interpreted. It can be seen that metacognition is associated with both a Mastery Goal Orientation and a Performance Goal Orientation for the older males as well as Elaboration and Organised study strategies, whereas with females, metacognition is related to a Mastery Goal Orientation and Elaboration and

Table 3.4   Pearson correlations between meta-cognition and other learning influences/strategies for female and male students in 'old' group.

	Female	Male
PLG	−0.02	0.18
PSV	0.11	0.28*
PSA	0.05	0.17
MGO	0.34*	0.42*
PGO	0.21*	0.31*
ELAB	0.64*	0.43*
COLL	0.22*	0.16
ORG	0.46*	0.36*

*$p < 0.01$

Organised study approaches. Again, these were checked to see if any significant differences existed between female and male students. There were no significant differences.

Study 2

In this study, there were 432 students from four faculties of the same university as that in Study 1: Health, 60; Arts, 107; Business, 191; and Education, 74. Students older than 25 numbered 126 and of these 88 were female. Of the remaining 306 students, 221 were female. As well as responding to the same learning influences and strategies questionnaire as in Study 1, students also responded to open-ended questions concerning their beliefs about learning and completed the Study Process Questionnaire (SPQ) (Biggs, 1987). This is a comprehensive measure of study processes. There are six subscales: three measure students' motives for studying (surface, deep, achieving); and three measure the learning strategies adopted by students (surface, deep, achieving). The corresponding subscales for motive and strategy can be combined to produce a score representing, respectively, surface approach, deep approach, achieving approach. Items are rated by respondents on a five-point Likert scale (5 = always or almost always true of me, 1 = never or only rarely true of me).

The open-ended questions concerning students' beliefs about learning were analysed (Taylor, 1994) using the conceptions of learning framework of Marton *et al.* (1993), which indicates at which level within a hierarchy of conceptions a particular response best fits. They found that learning was conceived of in six distinct ways.

1. Increasing one's knowledge
2. Memorising and reproducing
3. Applying
4. Understanding

5. Seeing something in a different way
6. Changing as a person.

In a similar fashion to Van Rossum and Schenk (1984), the first three levels of conceptions were combined to form a 'reproductive' conception of learning and the remaining three levels were combined to form a 'constructive' conception of learning.

A multivariate analysis of variance was carried out on the learning influences and strategies variables and approaches to learning (as measured by the SPQ) for the 'old' group of students to see if there were any gender differences. Results indicated a multivariate gender effect (Pillais $= 0.22$; $df = 12$, 114; $F = 2.73$; $p = 0.003$). Significant univariate differences occurred for: Perceived Lecturers' Goals ($F = 7.92$; $df = 1$, 125; $p = 0.006$); Perceived Self-Ability ($F = 3.96$; $df = 1$, 125; $p = 0.049$); Elaboration ($F = 5.08$; $df = 1$, 125; $p = 0.03$); Collaboration ($F = 6.98$; $df = 1$, 125; $p = 0.009$); surface approach ($F = 4.48$; $df = 1$, 125; $p = 0.04$); and deep approach ($F = 11.50$; $df = 1$, 125; $p = 0.001$). Effect sizes were calculated for each difference. Table 3.5 indicates mean scores and effect sizes for variables on which there are significant differences.

Table 3.5 Gender differences for 'old' students – significantly different mean scores and effect sizes.

Variable	Young	Old	Effect size
PLG	4.07	3.73	0.52
PSA	3.55	3.81	0.40
ELAB	4.10	3.79	0.41
COLL	3.54	3.10	0.50
Surface approach	2.80	3.05	0.40
Deep approach	3.95	3.62	0.62

In all instances except for perceived self-ability and surface approach, females had higher mean scores than males. The finding that males had higher mean scores on Perceived Self-Ability is similar to Hayes' (1992) finding that males appear more confident in classroom situations.

As can be seen from Table 3.6, these differences are of moderate degree and indicate again that female learners are more likely to adopt deep approaches to learning than males, perceive their lecturers as encouraging autonomy and self-direction in learning to a greater degree than males, and engage in more collaborative learning than male learners, even though they are less sure of their ability to succeed than males.

Correlational analyses between metacognition and the learning influences and strategies variables and approaches to learning were carried out for the older students to see if there were gender variations. These results are shown in Table 3.6.

Table 3.6 Pearson correlations between metacognition and other learning influences/strategies; surface, deep and achieving approaches for female and male students in 'old' group metacognition.

	Female	Male
PLG	−0.13	0.31*
PSV	0.01	0.37*
PSA	0.17	0.31*
MGO	0.36**	0.45**
PGO	0.18	0.26
ELAB	0.56**	0.37*
COLL	0.11	0.26
ORG	0.38**	0.48**
Surface approach	−0.20	−0.10
Deep approach	0.49**	0.63**
Achieving approach	0.39**	0.51**

$*p < 0.05, **p < 0.01$

It is evident that similar relationships exist between Metacognition and Mastery Goal Orientation, Elaboration (stronger for females than males), Organised study, and deep and achieving approaches to learning for female and male students. The relationships between Metacognition and deep and achieving approaches to learning provide confirmatory evidence of Biggs' (1988) and Dart's (1994b) findings that teaching intervention aimed at increasing students' use of metacognitive thinking in their learning leads to more frequent application of deep and achieving approaches to learning.

Checking these correlation coefficients with Fisher's (1915) transformation indicated that for Perceived Lecturers' Goals and Perceived Subject Value there were significant differences in these relationships for males and females. This suggests how metacognitive behaviour in males may be influenced through interventions designed to address these environmental variables.

Students' conceptions of learning were correlated with Metacognition. There was a significant relationship for male students ($r = 0.44$, $p < 0.01$) but not for female students ($r = 0.15$). This finding suggests that for male students, teaching and learning environments designed to facilitate the formation of higher level conceptions of learning (Dart, 1994b), that is, 'constructive' conceptions rather than 'reproductive' conceptions, may also influence the use of metacognitive thinking.

Discussion and conclusion

The results of these two studies provide suggestions for the design of teaching and learning environments to facilitate metacognitive thinking and the adoption of deep approaches to learning.

The introduction of intervention programmes that focus on the development of a mastery goal orientation, the use of learning strategies for personalising learning material and connecting it with prior knowledge, as well as for planning and organising study, may lead to more frequent use of metacognitive thinking for both female and male students. Furthermore, if, through their teaching approaches, academic teachers are perceived to be encouraging student control over their learning, independent thinking, and the seeking of meaning and understanding, as well as developing interest in their subject and showing its importance and value for professional development, this may lead to increased metacognitive thinking in male students.

In addition for male students, teaching in ways that enable students to 'get in touch' with their ideas and beliefs relating to the teaching and learning process and that stress that learning involves the development of personal meaning through conceptual development and change is likely to lead to increased use of metacognitive thinking. Earlier work by the author (Dart, 1994b; Dart and Clarke, 1991) provides evidence that this can be achieved.

Twenty-two teacher education students (14 female and eight male; ten of whom were older than 25 years) enrolled in the Post Graduate Diploma of Education (Secondary Teaching) were involved in a specially designed programme in educational psychology (Dart, 1994b). The programme provided opportunities for students to take greater responsibility for their own learning, as well as to learn and apply appropriate cognitive and metacognitive strategies associated with a deep or transformative approach to learning. These experiences included collaborative small-group work involving peer teaching and discussion of their understandings of and responses to questions relating to assigned readings or other material; sharing of writings, concept maps and case studies; and role plays relating to teaching/learning activities such as classroom-management episodes. They were also given experience in developing their own specific questions relating to the material being studied using a constructivist interactive learning strategy that helps them actively process material (King, 1993). Whole class discussion and debate followed small-group work. Assessment included their peer teaching and a learning contract negotiated with the teacher. Peer teaching included self-, peer and teacher assessment, and the learning contract involved self- and teacher assessment.

Results at the end of the programme indicated that the predominant approach to learning was deep or transformative. Seventeen students reported having a 'constructive' conception of learning, that is, at levels four, five or six in the framework of conceptions of Marton *et al.* (1993). One had increased by three levels, three by two levels, and six by one level. Four had decreased by one level, and eight had not changed. Support for improvement in the quality of learning through the development of relational understanding was evidenced in a number of instances. In all of these areas, the results require students to be proficient in the use of metacognitive thinking.

The findings of the studies referred to provide directions for teaching for improved learning. The adoption of deep and/or achieving approaches to learning, by older students, both of which require metacognitive behaviour on the part of the learner can be facilitated by teaching approaches and course designs that:

1. Help develop students' knowledge about learning through emphasising that learning is about seeking meaning and understanding and seeing things in a different way. This can be complemented through the provision of learning activities that require accessing different information resources; the use of collaborative learning groups to explore different perspectives; and assessment procedures congruent with this conception of learning (for example, negotiated learning contracts in which understanding and application in appropriate contexts are the focuses).

2. Require students to become aware of and understand their own learning processes through activities that demand analysis, application, evaluation and reflection. Sharing learning experiences with peers can assist this development as can the maintenance of a learning journal which serves the purpose of stimulating reflection on these experiences.

3. Ensure that students attain the necessary learning strategies, cognitive (particularly Elaboration) and metacognitive, to successfully accomplish the tasks of the subject of study. The successful acquisition of these strategies in context will empower students in task analysis and in planning, monitoring and evaluating their learning.

4. Provide opportunities for students to experience autonomy and self-direction in their learning through being actively involved in the learning process (for example, through the use of collaborative learning groups and negotiated learning contracts).

5. Identify how the material being learned is important both now and later for the professional development of the student.

6. Foster intentions for learning the material of the subject in terms of interest and challenge. That is, teach in ways and provide learning activities that arouse in students the need to know and understand.

7. Provide models of desirable learning behaviours (processes) and outcomes (products).

References

Baird, J (1991) 'Individual and group reflection as a basis for teacher development' in *Teachers' Professional Development*, P Hughes (ed.), Australian Council for Educational Research, Hawthorn, Victoria.

Baird, J, Fensham, P, Gunstone, R and White, R (1989) 'A Study of the Importance of Reflection for Improving Science Teaching and Learning'. Paper presented at the annual meeting of the National Association for Research in Science Teaching, San Francisco.

Beyer, B (1987) *Practical Strategies for the Teaching of Thinking*, Allyn and Bacon, Boston.

Biggs, J (1987) *Student Approaches to Learning and Studying*, Australian Council for Educational Research, Hawthorn, Victoria.

Biggs, J (1988) The role of metacognition in enhancing learning, *Australian Journal of Education*, 32(2), 127–38.

Biggs, J and Moore, P (1993) *The Process of Learning* (3rd edn), Prentice-Hall, New York.

Brown, A (1978) 'Knowing when, where, and how to remember' in *Advances in Instructional Psychology*, Vol. 1, R Glaser (ed.), Lawrence Erlbaum, Hillsdale, New Jersey.

Brown, A (1988) Motivation to learn and understand: on taking charge of one's own learning, *Cognition and Instruction*, 5(4), 311–21.

Burnett, P (1991) Decision-making style and self-concept, *Australian Psychologist*, 26(1), 55–8.

Cohen, J (1969) *Statistical Power Analysis for the Behavioral Sciences*, Academic Press, New York.

Dart, B C (1994a) A goal-mediational model of personal and environmental influences on tertiary students' strategy use, *Higher Education*, 28, 453–70.

Dart, B C (1994b) 'Teaching for Improved Learning in Small Classes in Higher Education'. Paper presented at the annual conference of the Australian Association for Research in Education, Newcastle.

Dart, B C and Clarke, J A (1991) Helping students become better learners: a case study in teacher education, *Higher Education*, 2, 317–35.

Fisher, R (1915) Frequency distribution of the values of the correlation coefficient in samples from an indefinitely large population, *Biometrika*, 10, 507–21.

Glass, G V (1976) Primary, secondary, and meta-analysis of research, *Educational Researcher*, 5(10), 3–8.

Hayes, E (1992) Students' perceptions of women and men as learners in higher education, *Research in Higher Education*, 33(3), 377–93.

Jonassen, D (1994) Toward a constructivist design model, *Educational Technology*, 34(4), 34–7.

Kasworm, C E (1990) Adult undergraduates in higher education: a review of past research perspectives, *Review of Educational Research*, 60(3), 345–72.

King, A (1993) From sage on the stage to guide on the side, *College Teaching*, 41(1), 30–35.

Marton, F, Dall'Alba, G and Beaty, E (1993) Conceptions of learning, *International Journal of Educational Research*, 19(3), 277–300.

Prawat, R and Floden, R (1994) Philosophical perspectives on constructivist views of learning, *Educational Psychology*, 29(1), 37–48.

Resnick, L (1987) Learning in school and out, *Educational Researcher*, 16, 13–20.

Richardson, J T E (1993) Gender differences in responses to the approaches to studying inventory, *Studies in Higher Education*, 18(1), 3–13.

Roby, T (1988) 'Models of discussion' in *Questioning and Discussion: A Multidisciplinary Study*, J Dillon (ed.), Ablex, Norwood, New Jersey.

Tarule, J (1988) 'Voices of returning women: ways of knowing' in *Addressing the Needs of Returning Women*, L Lewis (ed.), 19–33, Jossey-Bass, San Francisco, California.

Taylor, P (1994) *Tertiary Students' Conceptions of Learning*, unpublished manuscript, School of Learning and Development, Queensland University of Technology, Australia.

Van Rossum, E and Schenck, S (1984) The relationship between learning conception, study strategy and learning outcome. *British Journal of Educational Psychology*, 54, 73–83.

Zimmerman, B (1990). Self-regulated learning and academic achievement: an overview, *Educational Psychologist*, 25, 3–17.

LEARNING AND EDUCATION

CHAPTER 4

Epistemological Approaches to Cognitive Development in College Students

Paul Hettich

The only person who is educated is the person who has learned how to learn; the person who has learned how to adapt and change; the person who has realised that no knowledge is secure, that only the process of seeking knowledge gives a basis for security. (Adapted from Carl Rogers.)

What assumptions about knowing do college students possess as they approach a body of knowledge? What changes occur developmentally in the process of seeking knowledge? This chapter focuses on a qualitatively derived, evolving model of cognitive development that facilitates our understanding of these issues.

Pascarella and Terenzini (1991) identify four clusters of developmental models that describe change in college students: typological models; person–environment interaction models; psychosocial theories; and cognitive–structural theories. Briefly, typological models emphasise 'distinctive but relatively *stable* differences among individuals' (p.36) and categorise people by groups according to those differences. An example is Kolb's learning styles. Person–environment interaction theories emphasise the ways in which behaviour is influenced by specific aspects of the environment and the individual's interaction with it. An example is Holland's theory of career choice.

Although the cognitive–structural approach is the focus of this chapter, readers should be aware of the larger context in which cognitive behaviour occurs interactively with social development. Chickering and Reisser (1993) maintain that psychosocial development is a journey of increasing complexity. During development, maps (vectors) are provided that 'describe major highways for journeying toward individuation – the discovery and refinement of one's unique way of being – and also toward communion with other individuals and groups' (p.35). Students journey differently through the vectors at different rates, but they always move from a lower to a higher level of complexity within the vector.

In the vector of *developing competence*, students move from lower to higher levels of intellectual, physical, and interpersonal competence. Intellectual competence includes mastering content, building skills in comprehension, analysis and synthesis, and developing intellectual and aesthetic sophistication. Interpersonal skills include listening, responding and aligning personal with group goals.

In *managing emotions*, students progress from lower to higher levels of: (a) control over disruptive emotions (eg anxiety, aggression, depression); (b) awareness of feelings; and (c) ability to integrate feelings with action. *Moving through autonomy toward interdependence* requires students to learn self-sufficiency, accept responsibility for pursuing self-chosen goals, and become less influenced by others. In *developing mature interpersonal relationships*, students progress from lower to higher levels of interpersonal and intercultural tolerance of differences and from having nonexistent, short-term or unhealthy relationships to a greater capacity for intimacy and commitment. *Establishing identity* is a journey from discomfort to comfort with one's appearance, gender, family, social/cultural roots, roles and lifestyles. *Developing purpose* enables students to articulate their interests, goals and plans with respect to vocation, personal interests and commitments to relationships. *Developing integrity* is closely related to the two previous vectors. At this point, a student's values are transformed from being dualistic, rigid and self-centred to values that are humanising (considering other people's interests), personalising (affirming one's core values while respecting those of others) and congruent (matching one's personal values with socially responsible behaviours).

Chickering and Reisser (1993) contend that the developmental process applies to students of virtually all ages. Also, the fundamental themes contained in their model are compatible with specific research studies they cite of women, non-white students, and homosexual students. Chickering and Reisser maintain that 'Institutions that emphasize intellectual development to the exclusion of other strengths and skills reinforce society's tendency to see some aspects of its citizens and not others' (p.41). Although the model has been criticised for its lack of specificity, Pascarella and Terenzini regard it as the most influential of the psychosocial models of student development.

Cognitive-structural theories of development

Included in the Pascarella and Terenzini (1991) synopsis of cognitive–structural theories are Perry's forms of ethical and intellectual development; Kohlberg's theory of moral development; King and Kitchener's reflective judgement model; Gilligan's different voice model; and Loevinger's theory of ego development. This chapter addresses an evolving epistemological model of intellectual development begun by Perry in the 1950s (Perry, 1970) and extended by Belenky and her associates (1988), King and Kitchener (1994) and Baxter Magolda (1996) from the late 1970s to the present. The populations sampled for the Perry and Baxter Magolda studies are exclusively young adult, primarily white, middle- and upper-class American college students. Belenky *et al.* and King and Kitchener also included diverse samples of college and non-college students The Baxter Magolda and King and Kitchener findings are derived from ongoing longitudinal research on men and women. The methodology used by each investigator was primarily qualitative.

Perry's 'scheme of intellectual and moral development' (Perry, 1970) is well known to most readers. His interviews yielded a nine-stage sequence of 'positions' that provided a developmental framework for understanding the meaning of students' educational experiences. The scheme reflects the increasingly complex epistemological assumptions that students bring to a learning situation. Perry reduced the nine positions to three clusters: dualism modified; relativism discovered; and commitment in relativism developed. However, King and Kitchener (1994) and others group the nine positions into four categories: dualism (positions 1–2); multiplicity (positions 3–4); relativism (positions 5–6); and commitment in relativism (positions 7–9).

Perry discussed the implications of his findings for curriculum development, and encouraged teachers 'to introduce our students, as our greatest teachers introduced us, not only to the orderly certainties of our subject matter but to its unresolved dilemmas. This is an art that requires timing, learned only by paying close attention to students' ways of making meaning' (Perry, 1981, p.109). Although Perry has been criticised for insufficiently defining and measuring change in the nine positions, his ideas have met with considerable enthusiasm and have been applied by many educators including Moore (1994) and Nelson (1989).

Noting the absence of research on the intellectual development of women, Belenky *et al.* (1986) integrated Gilligan's research on moral development and identity in women with Perry's scheme of epistemological development. They grouped their 135 participants' ways of knowing into five categories: silence; received knowledge; subjective knowledge; procedural knowledge; and constructed knowledge. Just as Perry contended that his scheme of development applied to both genders, Belenky *et al.* do not claim that the five patterns of knowing are exclusive to women. Readers interested in this model should consult other chapters in this book.

King and Kitchener's reflective judgement model

In the late 1970s, King and Kitchener began formulating a model that somewhat incorporates Perry's framework and John Dewey's concept of reflective thinking as the evaluation of potential solutions to ill-structured problems. A reflective thinker understands that problem solving involves uncertainty but formulates a solution based on evidence and critical inquiry. From cross-sectional and longitudinal studies of collectively large samples of men and women diverse in age (16 to mid 50s) and education (high school to graduate school), have emerged a refined methodology and the reflective judgement model. The seven-stage model describes 'changes in assumptions about sources and certainty of knowledge and how decisions are justified in light of those assumptions' (Kitchener and King, 1990, p.160). The stages are organised into: pre-reflective thinking (stages 1–3); quasi-reflective thinking (stages 4–5); and reflective thinking (stages 6–7) (King and Kitchener, 1994).

In Stage 1, knowledge is assumed to be absolute and concrete; it is obtained with certainty by direct observation of the knower. This stage represents 'cognitive simplicity' and was found in some of the youngest high school students. For individuals in Stage 2, knowledge is regarded as absolute and certain, or certain but accessible only to authorities. Beliefs are acquired by direct observation or from authorities. Beliefs are justified by comparing them with what authorities believe. Similar to Perry's dualism, this stage is typical of young adolescents and some college students. In Stage 3, knowledge is either certain or temporarily uncertain in some areas; it resides in authority. This stage characterised the assumptions of students during their last two years of high school or first year of college. The first three stages are called pre-reflective because individuals do not acknowledge uncertainty and, consequently, cannot distinguish between well-structured and ill-structured (real life) problems.

In Stage 4, knowledge is regarded as abstract, not concrete; it is uncertain due to limitations of the knower and of authorities. Because there is no certainty, all views are equally valid, ie, idiosyncratic. Beliefs can be justified through reasoning and evidence, but they remain idiosyncratic. The acceptance of uncertainty by the knower indicates an ability to distinguish well-structured from ill-structured problems; the basis for reflective judgements. Stage 4 thinking is characteristic of college seniors. Knowers in Stage 5 begin to view knowledge as contextual and subjective. They realise that beliefs are filtered through one's perceptions and interpretations of evidence acquired in particular situations or contexts. Knowers may avoid viewing problem solutions as 'right' or 'wrong', given that knowing is contextual. This form of reasoning is typical of graduate students; most persons were in the aged 26-to-35 category. Stages 4 and 5 are called quasi-reflective thinking: while knowers acknowledge uncertainty and can distinguish well-structured from ill-structured problems, they remain unable to compare and evaluate alternative views.

In Stage 6, knowledge is uncertain, contextual, and constructed (knowledge is not a given) into individual conclusions for the solution of ill-structured problems. The conclusions are based not on subjective judgements but on interpretations and evaluations of evidence derived from different sources. In addition, some alternatives can be judged better than others. This stage was found in advanced graduate students, most of whom were over 30 years of age. In Stage 7, solutions to ill-structured problems are constructed through critical inquiry and evaluated and re-evaluated in terms of what is most reasonable, given the evidence. Kitchener and King believe this stage is rare among graduate students, but it can be found in some mature, educated adults in their thirties or older. Stages 6 and 7 represent true reflective thinking as described by John Dewey.

King and Kitchener (1994) discuss the results of a ten-year longitudinal study ($N = 200$) begun in 1977 and several cross-sectional studies that collectively validate the reflective judgement model. More than 1700 men and women have participated in the reflective judgement interview. Overall, the findings revealed that people who are involved in educational activities tend to improve their reasoning about ill-structured problems. Development proceeds in a 'slow but steady' pattern, but it follows the stages of the model and is facilitated by educational settings. Age alone was not predictive of differences in reflective thinking, but, for adult students, age is related to factors such as readiness to learn and openness to challenge and divergent views. Traditional age and non-traditional age students did not differ significantly from each other either as freshmen or as seniors, although there was less variability in scores among non-traditional age students. The authors conclude that gender is not a factor significantly differentiating reflective thinkers, although some differences may exist in the 'timing' of developmental changes between men and women. King and Kitchener (1994) offer several suggestions for promoting reflective thinking in students, which include:

- show respect for students as people regardless of the developmental level(s) they may be exhibiting; (p.231)
- familiarise students with ill-structured problems within your own discipline or areas of expertise; (p.233)
- create multiple opportunities for students to examine different points of view on a topic reflectively; (p.237)
- create opportunities and provide encouragement for students to make judgements and to explain what they believe; (p.238)
- acknowledge that students work within a developmental range of stages, and target expectations and goals accordingly; (p.242)
- provide both challenge and supports in interactions with students; (p.244)
- recognise that challenges and supports can be grounded emotionally as well as cognitively. (p.246)

Baxter Magolda's epistemic reflection model

The most recent contribution to the epistemological model of intellectual development is that of Baxter Magolda. Incorporating concepts, methodology and findings from Perry, Belenky *et al.* and King and Kitchener, Baxter Magolda has established a framework for knowing, investigated gender-related patterns and conducted follow-up studies in workplace and post-baccalaureate settings.

Baxter Magolda interviewed 101 randomly selected, traditional age freshmen (51 female, 50 male) who enrolled at Miami University of Ohio in 1986. Her methodology included taped interviews and the MER (measure of epistemological reflection), which addressed six domains of knowing: the nature of knowledge; decision making; evaluation of learning; and the roles of the learner, instructor and peers. From her analysis of the data, Baxter Magolda constructed four levels of knowing: absolute knowing; transitional knowing; independent knowing; and contextual knowing. Gender-related patterns of knowing were found in the first three levels.

'Absolute knowers view knowledge as certain. They believe that absolute answers exist in all areas of knowledge. Uncertainty is a factor only because students do not have access at the time to absolute knowledge' (Baxter Magolda, 1992, p.36). According to students, the learner's role is to obtain knowledge from an all-knowing instructor who uses teaching methods that promote the acquisition and retention of information, mainly through memorisation. The purpose of evaluation and assessment is to show the instructor that the student can reproduce the knowledge acquired. The role of peers in learning is minimal, given that their knowledge of the topic is limited to what the instructor has provided.

Baxter Magolda discerned two patterns of knowing among absolute knowers that are opposite ends of a continuum. Receiving-pattern learners describe their role in terms of listening and note taking and take a private approach to learning. They expect little or no interaction with instructors, view peers as sources of support in note taking and listening and regard assessment as a tool for demonstrating what they know. Receiving-pattern students in the study tended to be women, but some were men.

Mastery-pattern learners describe their role as assertive and public in the classroom; interacting and sometimes arguing with instructors whose job is to challenge students to master knowledge. Peers are but partners in the interaction process. Mastery-pattern students tended to be men, but some were women. Baxter Magolda observed that absolute knowing characterised 68 per cent of the freshmen, 42 per cent of the sophomores, 11 per cent of the juniors, and 2 per cent of the seniors in her sample. To engage absolute knowers, teachers should try to be helpful, use active teaching strategies, promote peer interaction, help students understand the grading system and provide opportunities for students to know them in and out of the classroom.

Transitional knowing serves as a transition stage between the certainty of absolute knowing and the uncertainty of independent knowing. 'Although transitional knowers still believe that absolute knowledge exists in some areas, they have concluded that uncertainty exists in others' (p.47). If there are discrepancies among authorities, it is because authorities do not know the answers. The role of instructors is not only to communicate information but also to use methods that help students understand and apply information. Evaluation should measure understanding, not simply rote memory. Peers can help by participating in discussions and activities that promote understanding.

Two bipolar, gender-related patterns of knowing observed in transitional knowers were interpersonal and impersonal. Interpersonal pattern knowers, predominantly women in Baxter Magolda's sample, view learning as a process of exchanging ideas with other students and the instructor; evaluation lets students express creatively what they understand. Uncertainties about knowledge are reduced by making personal judgements. Impersonal pattern students (predominantly men) seek challenge through debate, prefer evaluation that is fair and practical and reduce uncertainties through reason and research. Transitional knowing characterised 32 per cent of the freshmen, 53 per cent of the sophomores, 83 per cent of the juniors, 80 per cent of the seniors and 31 per cent of the sample in the year following graduation. Baxter Magolda recommends that teachers who work with transitional knowers should: (a) demonstrate a caring attitude that promotes student–teacher interaction; (b) use teaching strategies that involve students in course material and with each other; and (c) promote understanding and thinking over memorisation.

'Independent Knowing represents a shift to assuming that knowledge is mostly uncertain. Viewing knowledge as uncertain changes substantially the learning process and the sense of where knowledge resides' (p.55). The fact that authorities differ is mainly a reflection of the range of views that exist in an uncertain world. Independent knowers view themselves as equal to authorities, thus their ideas are as valid as those of their teachers. Independent knowers believe that students must think for themselves and create their own perspectives. Instructors should create an environment that promotes an interchange among students who are now valued as sources of ideas.

The bipolar, gender-related patterns observed in independent knowers are interindividual and individual. In the former, predominantly female group in the study, students tend to think for themselves but also seek the perspectives of others. Teachers should promote an exchange of views and include students in the evaluation process. Individual pattern knowers in the sample tended to be men who focused on their own independent thinking and expected peers to do the same. They prefer instructors who allow students to define their own learning goals and expect assessment to focus on independent thinking. As the characteristic mode of learning, independent knowing was found in none of the freshmen, 1 per cent of the sophomores, 5 per cent of the juniors and 16 per cent of the seniors, but it dominated the knowing of

57 per cent of the sample in the year following graduation. Baxter Magolda's advice for instructors who work with independent knowing students includes the following: (a) use teaching strategies that connect classroom learning with real life, promote independence, develop critical thinking and encourage peer collaboration; (b) develop a genuine relationship with students; and (c) treat them with respect and as equals.

Baxter Magolda believes that contextual knowledge is rarely evident in college, based on the sample of young adults she interviewed. Contextual knowledge was first observed during the junior year in 1 per cent of the students. It doubled to 2 per cent in seniors, and characterised knowing of 12 per cent of the sample participants in the year following college. In contextual knowing, 'The nature of knowledge remains uncertain... but the "everything goes" perspective is replaced with the belief that some knowledge claims are better than others in a particular context' (p.69). Individuals resolve the uncertainty of knowing in a particular context by judging the available evidence. The role of the learner is to think through issues, compare differing perspectives, integrate existing with new knowledge and apply it to new contexts. Students expect their professors to create an environment that facilitates these processes; one which allows mutual critique of students with each other and with the instructor. In contextual knowing, the gender-related patterns merge.

The post-college interviews examined changes in knowing that occur in job and post-baccalaureate settings (Baxter Magolda, 1994). Thirty-seven women and 33 men participated in the fifth year of the study; 29 women and 22 men consented to a sixth-year interview. After graduation, the participants entered such occupations as insurance, sales, accounting, teaching, mental health, advertising, retail management, airline attendance and government. Thirteen participants entered graduate or professional programmes.

One obvious change was the sharp decline in transitional knowing 'from 80 percent in the senior year to 31 percent the fifth year and to 8 percent the sixth year' (p.31). In contrast, independent knowing increased sharply from 16 per cent in the senior year to 57 per cent in the fifth year and declined slightly to 55 per cent in the sixth year. Three themes that characterised the post-college experiences of independent knowers help explain the changes. First, participants were expected to function independently in their settings. As one woman noted, 'It's up to me how, what approach I take to do it, and different angles for things. It's expected of me to improve, but a lot of... the way I do it is my choice' (p.32). Second, participants learned by gathering information from others. Gone was the transitional knowing assumption that peers are not essential to the learning process. Third, participants recognised that learning occurs through direct experience. As one corporate employee noted, 'I learned how to become very clear and concise.... I learned to be prepared. I learned that you don't call someone when you don't know what you're talking about. You learn those things in school, but you don't really experience them. You don't experience the consequences or you don't experience the reality' (p.33). Independent knowers also noted the importance of acting assertively and reducing the influence that others have on them.

Contextual knowing increased from 2 per cent during the senior year to 12 per cent in the fifth year and 57 per cent in the sixth year. Three major themes contained in contextual knowers' remarks may explain this increase: they made subjective decisions in their work; they frequently acted in the role of authority; and they collaborated with others in the exchange of ideas. In discussing the implications of the post-college study for higher education, Baxter Magolda (1994) observed that, 'Participants in the post-college study reported experiences that, in their perspective, affected ways of knowing that were different from ways they reported during the college study. It was the nature of these experiences – the independence and responsibility – not the context of the experiences (work or school) that was important to them' (p.39). In addition, she noted that 'Study participants found themselves in work and academic settings in which they were expected to be authorities or to find out what they needed on their own with minimal guidance' (p.40). In view of these observations, transitional knowers would be forced to make drastic changes in their epistemic assumptions and behaviour from classroom to job or post-baccalaureate settings in order to succeed. Baxter Magolda (1994) recommends that courses for advanced students should require them to analyse and evaluate knowledge acquired in lower-level courses, develop their belief systems about it, and perform the tasks of their discipline to the extent possible in the college setting. To promote independent and contextual knowing, teachers should design learning environments that provide students with independence, direct experience in decision making, accountability for their actions and interaction with other students; in short, an environment in which students are able to construct their knowing. This writer notes that strategies that can promote independent and contextual knowing include research projects, internships, independent study and group projects in which students are responsible for planning, decision-making, execution and follow-up.

How are assumptions about knowing influenced by post-baccalaureate education? Of the 70 students interviewed after graduation, 25 enrolled in post-baccalaureate education, full-time or part-time, immediately or within one year of graduation. Analysis of the interview and MER data revealed five interrelated themes that indicate the central importance of knowledge construction to contextual learning (Baxter Magolda, 1996).

First, students valued opportunities to think for themselves; to develop opinions supported by evidence and to struggle with new ideas. Second, students appreciated opportunities to form connections between the ideas they learned in coursework and their beliefs, values and identity. Third, they valued environments where they were encouraged to incorporate their own knowledge and experiences into course topics and assignments. Fourth, students appreciated environments characterised by mutual respect between teachers and students. Fifth, students valued collaboration with peers that promoted sharing experiences, discussing different perspectives and processing ideas. In short, the five themes are extensions of contextual knowing observed in undergraduate settings.

Baxter Magolda maintains that these findings provide challenges to teachers who strive to promote contextual knowing. For example, instructors and students could jointly determine the kind of personal experiences that can be incorporated into classroom discussion. Although some students are willing to share relevant experiences, others may not understand the value of their particular experiences or be willing to share them. A technique successfully used by this writer and others is the use of journals in which students record the connections between course-related concepts and their experiences (Hettich, 1992). Another challenge is to teach students that 'the ongoing construction of knowledge involves balancing experience and evidence outside one's experience. Thus teaching involves helping students analyze their own experience in light of existing perspectives' (Baxter Magolda, 1996).

Discussion

The works of Perry, Belenky *et al.*, King and Kitchener, and Baxter Magolda, essentially and collectively represent a single *model* of epistemological knowing that has evolved over the past four decades but with different points of emphasis. That the different populations sampled yielded generally similar structures is testimony to the robustness of the model, the methodologies used and the basic theoretical assumptions proposed. Differences exist among theorists in their emphasis, characteristics of stages, scope of knowing, and other issues; but the similarities are more numerous than the differences. There are, however, issues to be raised. For example, what are the limitations of a constructivist approach to knowing? What is the external validity of the research performed, given that the studies were based on predominantly white, middle-class, American college students? What impact do the recommendations for teaching have on learning in various settings? Studies that are as thoughtful and informative as these are going to raise several issues, which should be addressed.

Earlier it was asserted that cognitive development in college students proceeds within the broader context of psychosocial development. A comparison of the psychosocial approach of Chickering and Reisser (1993) with the epistemological approaches presented reveals agreement that the course of growth is a process of developing increasing complexity. Furthermore, progress in specific vectors is reflected in changes observed in studies reported above. Specific comparison between Chickering and Reisser and the four approaches is possible, but the primary implication to be drawn is that educators are not merely improving students' *intellectual* skills. Regardless of age, maturity and background, students are on a journey toward complexity, and all dimensions of their beings are involved. They travel through several interacting vectors, but teachers interact with them primarily in the intellectual vector of *competence*.

The implications for teachers who work with students in various stages of epistemological development were addressed by Kitchener and King and Baxter Magolda. If their recommendations do not surprise adult educators, at least we understand the theoretical and methodological contexts from which they were derived. Of special interest are Baxter Magolda's findings regarding her graduates' experiences in workplace and post-baccalaureate settings. Not only are these the situations to which students aspire, but they are also where many adult students currently operate. Teachers may benefit from learning about different workplace and post-baccalaureate settings and integrating the relevant skills and procedures practised there into instructional strategies. The writer has suggested (Hettich, 1992) that study skills (eg time-management, listening, reading) represent 'job' requirements at college that subsequently connect to job settings. Recall the increase in independent and contextual knowing that students experienced with their post-college experiences. Note also the themes reflected by Baxter Magolda's independent knowers: learn independently; learn by using others; learn by direct experience; learn by acting assertively; and learn by thinking for yourself. The post-college themes of contextual knowers included: learn by making subjective decisions; learn by acting in the role of authority; and learn through collaboration. Many correlates of these themes are common classroom practices such as individual and group projects, internships and independent study. Similarly, co-curricular activities involving leadership, service, team work and other forms of personal and group development are rich opportunities for developing the higher levels of knowing. Baxter Magolda (1992) and King and Kitchener (1994) discuss the implications of their findings for student service personnel. What would be the effects on the development of independent and contextual knowing if more aspects of the workplace and post-baccalaureate education were incorporated into classroom and co-curricular activities?

Finally, what place might theories of college student cognitive development occupy in the classroom? Every student who completes a course in introductory psychology is introduced to Piaget and Erikson, but how many students know how their own cognitive and social development proceeds during college? When this writer discusses Perry, Belenky *et al.* and Baxter Magolda in advanced courses, students grasp essentials of the theories, participate in class discussion and write about the theories in their journals. Students at all levels are nearly unanimous in asserting that exposure to the epistemological theories helps them understand their personal growth. Some students express regret that they were not exposed to such theories earlier in college. Perhaps these students are wiser than we know. They seem aware, like Carl Rogers, that the *process* of seeking knowledge, not necessarily knowledge itself, is the basis for a secure education.

References

Baxter Magolda, M B (1992) *Knowing and Reasoning in Students: Gender-related Patterns in Students' Intellectual Development,* Jossey-Bass, San Francisco, California.

Baxter Magolda, M B (1994) Post-college experiences and epistemology. *Review of Higher Education*, 18(1), 25–44.

Baxter Magolda, M B (1996) Epistemological development in graduate and professional education. *Review of Higher Education,* 19(3), 283–304 (in press).

Belenky, M F, Clinchy, B M, Goldberger, N R and Tarule, J M (1986) *Women's Ways of Knowing,* Basic Books, New York.

Chickering, A W and Reisser, L (1993) *Education and identity,* Jossey-Bass, San Francisco, California.

Hettich, P (1992) *Learning Skills for College and Career,* Brooks/Cole, Pacific Grove, California.

King, P M and Kitchener, K S (1994) *Developing Reflective Judgment: Understanding and Promoting Intellectual Growth and Critical Thinking in Adolescents and Adults,* Jossey-Bass, San Francisco, California.

Kitchener, K S and King, P M (1990) 'The reflective judgment model: transforming assumptions about knowing' in *Fostering Critical Reflection in Adulthood: a Guide to Transformative and Emancipatory Learning,* J Mezirow (ed.), Jossey-Bass, San Francisco, California.

Moore, W S (1994) 'Student and faculty epistemology in the college classroom: the Perry scheme of intellectual and ethical development' in *Handbook of College Teaching: Theory and Applications,* K Prichard and R McLaran Sawyer (eds), Greenwood Press, Westport, Connecticut.

Nelson, C E (1989) 'Skewered on the unicorn's horn: the illusion of the tragic trade-off between content and critical thinking in the teaching of science' in *Enhancing Critical Thinking in the Sciences,* L W Crow (ed.) 17–27, Society for College Science Teachers, Washington DC.

Pascarella, E T and Terenzini, P T (1991). *How College Affects Students: Findings and Insights from Twenty Years of Research,* Jossey-Bass, San Francisco, California.

Perry, W G (1970) *Forms of Intellectual and Ethical Development in the College Years,* Holt, Rinehart and Winston, New York.

Perry, W G (1981) 'Cognitive and ethical growth: the making of meaning' in *The Modern American College,* A W Chickering *et al.,* 76–116, Jossey-Bass, San Francisco, California.

CHAPTER 5

Personality Factors that Influence a Student's Choice of Learning Tactics

Ronald R Schmeck

This chapter is written for teachers who want to conceptualise the individuality of their students. Techniques and theories of personality research are used to elaborate the descriptions of student learning tactics that we began in 1977 (Schmeck *et al.*, 1977). These descriptions were revised extensively in 1991 (Schmeck *et al.*, 1991) and again in 1995 (Geisler-Brenstein and Schmeck, 1996). The chapter is prepared from a perspective stated by Biggs (1970); 'study behaviour is regarded as the translation in the context of study, of certain enduring personality characteristics into a series of operations or strategies' (p.163).

Much of the chapter will centre upon Table 5.1. The reader is urged to consult the two table notes in order to fully understand it. It has three columns. The first lists scales of the Inventory of Learning Processes: Revised version (ILP-R) (Geisler-Brenstein and Schmeck, 1996). The second provides a partial list of tactics assessed by the ILP-R scales. The third column provides a list of personality descriptors, or qualities, associated with the learning tactics listed in column two. This information is derived from several data sets that enabled us to correlate scales of the ILP-R with personality tests. Most emphasis is given to the 30 facets of the revised Neuroticism, Extraversion and Openness (NEO) personality inventory (NEO-PI-R) (Costa and McCrae, 1992), but the table also includes typological labels from the Myers-Briggs type indicator (MBTI) (Myers and McCaulley, 1985), as well as the differential aptitude tests (DAT) (Bennett *et al.*,1989) and several academic self-concept scales that are part of the ILP-R itself (Geisler-Brenstein and Schmeck, 1996). The emphasis throughout is on listing qualities rather than quantification.

Personality and learning tactics

We begin with the first two rows of Table 5.1. *Agentic* learning tactics are generally work-oriented. Success is assumed to result from hard work, from the completion of tasks. Tactics specifically assessed by the ILP-R scale *agentic analytic* (row one) all involve pragmatic, tough-minded problem solving. These tactics include logical decomposition of problems and logical generation of solutions. Students who prefer agentic analytic tactics judge the quality of a class according to the number of problem solutions required by the syllabus and the number of solution techniques taught by the teacher. These students expect a class to teach them the way; the skills involved in deriving solutions in a particular area of content specialisation. They enjoy teachers who are self-assured and masterful. The person preferring agentic analytic tactics tends to believe that mastery and control are the direct result of focused application of logical analysis (knowing 'the way'). It is no surprise that confidence, labelled self-efficacy on the ILP-R, is high among individuals preferring agentic analytic tactics.

The personality descriptors associated with agentic analytic tactics in Table 5.1 include the MBTI-STJ designation. The MBTI-S designation indicates attention to detail. The MBTI-T affirms this student's commitment to demonstrations of competence and use of systematic logic. Beyler and Schmeck (1992) found the MBTI-T classification to be indicative of tough-mindedness in students. The MBTI-J designation coupled with not being open to novel actions (Table 5.1) suggests a conservative preference for tried and true procedures ('if it isn't broke, don't fix it'). NEO-PI anger and mistrust are also prominent in the list, and perhaps these are necessary components of determination. In any case, this is all combined with a strong sense of personal responsibility and a strong sense of duty. The list also includes high confidence and openness to feelings.

The other agentic cluster of ILP-R tactics in row two is *agentic serial*. Again work is expected. Without work, without tasks to complete (eg homework), there is assumed to be no learning, and course evaluations tend to reflect this attitude. Agentic serial tactics specifically involve an emphasis upon plodding; completing tasks in serial order without jumping from one to another until the previous one is complete. Tasks are listed, scheduled, and completed one by one. Closure is important, as it was in the case of agentic analytic tactics.

The list of personality descriptors associated with agentic serial tactics in Table 5.1 is marked by orderliness and avoidance of gregariousness. Thus, when employing these tactics, students would tend to be 'loners', focused on their work. Modesty and low anxiety are also in the list. The MBTI-SJ classification (without the T present with agentic analytic tactics) was identified by Beyler and Schmeck (1992) as a 'pure' left-brained, or serialist, profile. Agentic serial tactics are associated with high ILP-R motivation effort (as is the other agentic cluster). Finally, comparing the three abilities assessed by the

Table 5.1 ILP-R scales, learning tactics and personality.

ILP-R Scales	Learning tactics*	Personality descriptors**
1. Agentic analytic	working; goal-directed; problem centred; task analysis or decomposition; ratiocination; rationally controlling; pragmatic; toughminded	angry hostility (N5); not trusting (A1); not blaming of others (ILO-R motivation: responsibility); not open to novel actions (O4); open to feelings (O3); dutiful (C3); high self-efficacy (ILP-E self-efficacy); MBTI-STJ, DAT: spatial not mechanical
2. Agentic serial	working; focusing on one thing at a time; competing tasks; plodding; programmatic	not gregarious (E2); modest (A5); orderly (S2); not anxious (N1); MBTI-SJ, DAT: spatial not mechanical
3. Reflective: deep thinking	inquiring; scientific; cycling from evidence to conclusion to evidence to conclusion; comparing theories; questioning assertions	modest (A5); open to feelings (O3); straightforward (A2); warm (E1); self-conscious (N4); dutiful (C3); not blaming of others (ILP-R motivation: personal responsibility); MBTI-IN
4. Reflective: deep semantic memory	interpretive; construing; interrelating different sources to extract gist or essence; hierarchising meanings	modest (A5); dutiful (C3); warm (E1); self-conscious (N4); open to feelings (O3); compliant (A4); not blaming of others (ILP-R motivation: personal responsibility); high self-efficacy (ILP-R self-efficacy); MBTI-N
5. Reflective: elaborative self-actualisation	activities that lead to unfolding or becoming a person; search for self-knowledge; interested in the meaning of life; intuitive	modest (A5); dutiful (C3); not gregarious (E2); not assertive (E3); not dogmatic (O6); straightforward (A2); playful (E6); disciplined (C5); MBTI-N, DAT: abstract
6. Reflective: elaborative episodic memory	narrative approach to learning; imagination; associating learning to events; free associative	not anxious (N1); open to feelings (O3); warm (E1); playful (E6); dutiful (C3); MBTI-N, DAT: highest spatial of all tactics
7. Self-assertion	expressing opinions; learning by hearing oneself talk	not deliberative (C6); not self-disciplined (C5); excitement-seeking (E5); aesthetic (O2); warm (E1); open to feelings (O3); modest (A5); not depressed (N3); high self-esteem (ILP-R self esteem); high self-efficacy (ILP-R self-efficacy, especially self-efficacy: critical thinking); not blaming others (ILP-R mot: responsibility); MBTI-EN, DAT: mechanical
8. Literal memorisation	rote learning usually through literal repetition; routinising complex ideas and processes into recitations	not trusting (A1); not compliant (A4); angry hostility (N2); tough-minded (A6); not open to feelings (O3); blaming others for school difficulties (ILP-R motivation: personal responsibility); low self-esteem (ILP-R self-esteem); MBTI-S
9. Methodical study	external study methods of the type in old how-to-study manuals (keep desk neat, use library, use dictionary, keep study schedule)	not warm (E1); not gregarious (E2); not trusting (A1); angry hostility (N2); not altruistic (A3); not compliant (A4); not impulsive (N5); not straightforward (A2); not modest (A5); MBTI-J, DAT: spatial
10. Conventionality	following instructions; orthodox; establishmentarian	not straightforward (A2); lonely and easily discouraged (N3); anxious (N1); not assertive (E3); does not blame others for school difficulties (ILP-R motivation: personal responsibility); low self-esteem (ILP-R self-esteem); MBTI-SJ

* The first two columns of Table 5.1 provide the categories of learning tactics presented by Schmeck *et al.* (1991) and Geisler-Brenstein and Schmeck (1996) resulting from extensive factor analyses. The first six rows present the most effective learning tactics. The first two rows are agentic, and rows three to six are reflective. Agentic tactics operate on the assumption that learning is something earned, the result of hard work; and reflective tactics operate on the assumption that learning is something discovered, the result of insight.

The first two rows of Table 5.1 divide agentic tactics into (1) agentic analytic (pragmatic and problem-centred) and (2) agentic serial (sequential, plodding and persistent). The next six rows all deal with reflective tactics which are first divided into two major categories and then two subcategories each. Thus, the two deep categories of reflective are: (3) deep thinking (scholarly, scientific, theoretical) and (4) deep semantic memory (scholarly, hierarchised meanings). The two elaborative categories are: (5) elaborative self-actualisation (search for unity, or identity, in experience) and (6) elaborative episodic memory (storage of raw experience).

Rows seven to ten in Table 5.1 are tactics that are more or less useful depending on whether and how they are combined with the others presented in the first two rows of the table. Thus, we have: (7) self-assertion (learning from one's own expressions); (8) literal memorisation (concerned with recitation); (9) methodical study habits concerned with appearance more than substance); and (10) conventionality (concerned with the maintenance of orthodoxy).

** The personality descriptors listed in the third column of Table 5.1 come mainly from the NEO-PI-R (Costa and McRae, 1992). This instrument measures five general dimensions of personality, and each dimension is assessed in terms of six facets. Thus, we have:

- neuroticism (N1, anxiety; N2, hostility; N3, depression; N4, self-consciousness; N5, impulsivity; N6, vulnerability);
- extroversion (E1, warmth; E2, gregariousness; E3, assertiveness; E4, activity; E5, excitement-seeking; E6, positive emotions);
- openness (O1, fantasy; O2, aesthetics; O3, feeling; O4, action; O5, ideas; O6, values);
- agreeableness (A1, trust; A2, straightforwardness; A3, altruism; A4, compliance; A5, modesty; A6, tendermindedness); and
- conscientiousness (C1, competence; C2, order; C3, dutifulness; C4, achievement striving; C5, self-discipline; C6, deliberation).

The third column also contains labels from the Myers-Briggs type indicator (MBTI: Myers & McCaulley, 1985). The MBTI types are:

- extroversion (E, attention to outer world);
- introversion (I, focus on private inner world);
- sensing (S, attention to details);
- intuition (N, attention to impressions);
- thinking (T, decide with cool logic);
- feeling (F, decide with emotions);
- judging (J, decisiveness); and
- perceiving (P, exploring possibilities).

The table also contains information from the differential aptitude tests (DAT: Bennett, Seashore & Wesman, 1989). The present version of the DAT includes subtests that measure spatial, abstract and mechanical reasoning.

DAT (ie spatial, mechanical and abstract reasoning), both agentic scales are differentially high on spatial ability compared with the other two abilities.

Turning now to the *reflective* learning tactics in rows three to six, we begin with the *deep* cluster labelled *deep thinking* (row three). These tactics encompass the scientific method. When focused on deep thinking tactics, students expect a university class to demand inquiry. They expect to be required and coached to think scientifically about issues. They expect a source of data, and they expect to derive and revise their own conclusions while learning. They do not expect to be told 'answers' for purposes of memorisation. These tactics involve cycling from evidence to conclusions to evidence in a continuing progression that some have called the hermeneutic circle (Lincoln and Guba, 1985).

The personality description associated with deep thinking tactics includes modesty, dutifulness and openness to feelings. There is also a strong sense of personal responsibility as opposed to a tendency to blame other people (similar to the other deep tactics in row four and the agentic analytic tactics in row two). In addition, there is warmth, straightforwardness and self-consciousness. Warmth and self-consciousness seem to distinguish the two categories of deep tactics from all others. The MBTI-IN designation (introverted and intuitive) indicates impressionistic attention to one's private thoughts.

The other cluster of deep tactics is in row four of Table 5.1. *Deep semantic memory* involves one of the two types of memory discussed by Tulving (1989), ie semantic and episodic. Semantic memory (concerned with symbolic representation of meanings) is considered deep on the ILP-R, while episodic memory (concerned with actual, raw, uninterpreted memories of experiences) is considered elaborative (row six). Deep semantic tactics involve construing, or interpreting, meanings of symbolic representations of knowledge and integrating them into hierarchically organised structures (trees). When using these tactics a student renders bodies of knowledge, extracting gist, comparing essence to essence to extract higher levels of meaning which are then also symbolically represented. It should be emphasised that students might use these tactics implicitly rather than explicitly, especially when they first begin to develop the approach. Most importantly, such a student does not simply memorise abstractions but rather *builds* them through comparison and contrast.

The list of personality descriptors associated with deep semantic tactics in Table 5.1 includes modesty, dutifulness, and openness to feelings. Also, there is a strong sense of personal responsibility and high confidence (similar to agentic analytic tactics). The list also includes warmth and self-consciousness (similar to deep thinking). The MBTI-N designation once again indicates intuition and originality, but the MBTI-I designation present with deep thinking (and indicating special attention to private thoughts) is absent in this case.

Rows five and six contain reflective tactics labelled *elaborative* on the ILP-R, and they generally concern the actual experiences of the person or self.

Elaborative self-actualising tactics integrate life experience as the person's identity develops. When using these tactics, students seem to be searching for meaning in life, trying to make intuitive sense of things. This can involve pursuit of a career as well as generally asking 'what does it all mean?' Course content is personalised and identity issues predominate. These tactics can include *identifying with* course content and instructor. Students who prefer elaborative self-actualisation tactics have high scores on DAT abstract reasoning (as compared to spatial and mechanical reasoning), and this finding is unique to this cluster of tactics.

The personality descriptors associated with elaborative self-actualisation tactics in Table 5.1 include modesty and dutifulness, also present with the other reflective tactics, but the list uniquely includes positive emotion or playfulness. Elaborative self-actualisation tactics were also associated with *low* gregariousness and *low* assertiveness suggesting that one is a 'loner' while using these tactics. The personality descriptors in Table 5.1 also include straightforward, self-disciplined, and not dogmatic. Detailed analyses revealed that *angry* students interested in self-actualisation included literal memorisation (row eight) in their arsenal of tactics, while students focusing on *hard work* included agentic tactics (these latter individuals also seem to see *career* as central to self-actualisation). In either case, the underlying global or holistic tendencies of the self-actualiser may be hidden behind obsessive-looking, serialist, detailed tactics when the individual is doing school work. The MBTI-N designation confirms their true holistic nature (Schmeck and Geisler-Brenstein, 1989; Beyler and Schmeck, 1992).

The other elaborative category in Table 5.1 is *elaborative episodic memory* (row six). Narration, giving accounts, and creating scenarios are among tactics in this category, eg they learn the principles of evolution by conjuring up a scenario of natural evolutionary events rather than by memorising phyla, etc. Course material is associated with real or fictional events. Students preferring such tactics enjoy a good story, whether in writing, film or personal fantasy. Tactics frequently involve intuitive free association and creativity.

As row six indicates, the personality description associated with elaborative episodic memory tactics includes dutifulness, openness to feelings and positive emotion or playfulness. These individuals are also warm and not anxious. Playfulness was of course presei. in the other elaborative category and absent from all others. The *difference* between the two elaborative categories lies in the avoidance of gregariousness in the self-actualising category, indicating that students are 'loners' when pursuing self-actualisation. The MBTI-N, or intuitive, classification is present again for elaborative episodic as it was for all other reflective tactics. It is also interesting that the elaborative episodic cluster of tactics was associated with the highest of all scores on the spatial reasoning test of the DAT (even higher than the agentic tactics).

It is interesting to note similarities and differences between the personality descriptions associated with the clusters of tactics in the first six rows of Table

5.1. Generally, agentic clusters are distinguished from reflective ones by their association with ILP-R motivation: effort, indicating a special commitment to work. Also, although deep and elaborative tactics are all reflective, the elaborative tactics are associated with playfulness and deep tactics are associated with warmth and self-consciousness. Furthermore, the two types of deep and the two types of elaborative tactics can be distinguished one from the other by a desire for solitude (introversion or low gregariousness). The person engaging in deep thinking tactics prefers solitude. Likewise, one using self-actualisation tactics also prefers solitude.

Virtually all clusters of *reflective* tactics were distinguished by their association with modesty and others of the more 'gentle' personality characteristics (eg warmth, self-consciousness, playfulness). It is possible that one generally has to have 'a good attitude' in order to use reflective tactics. To some extent, attitudes are under the control of the students themselves. Students need to see that getting angry at a particular subject matter or a teacher may make a bad situation worse than it already is. Anyone familiar with *The Fourth Way*, a programme for intellectual improvement based on the work of P D Ouspensky (Ouspensky, 1971), will recognise one of his primary rules; never, ever, let negative emotion drive your thoughts, because negative emotion sabotages intellectual growth (reflective tactics in the present case).

The only cluster of effective tactics to involve anger and mistrust is agentic analytic. Students preferring these tactics include strong components of conscientiousness and personal responsibility in their list of personality descriptors. They channel their anger into their work and they don't blame others for their difficulties.

Agentic tactics include faith that the completion of tasks assigned by teachers leads to learning. Students preferring these tactics compliment a good class by saying, 'it really made me *work*'. Reflective tactics on the other hand include faith that contemplation is the road to learning. Students preferring these tactics compliment a good class by saying, 'it really made me *think*'. The highest quality learning occurs when agentic and reflective tactics are used by the same student.

The other categories of tactics in Table 5.1 have a place in school, but they should not be used to the exclusion of agentic and reflective ones. These other tactics are self-assertion, literal memorisation, methodical study and conventionality. Each of these latter categories shares personality features with the six agentic and reflective categories. However, it is a peculiar mix of personal qualities in each case that seems to distinguish it from the more effective agentic and reflective tactics.

Self-assertion (row seven) basically involves learning by 'hearing oneself talk'. Expressions of the mind reveal the contents of the mind to the mind itself. The following quotation is a perfect example: 'How do I know what I think until I see what I say?' (Biggs, 1988, p.205). These are excellent tactics when combined with others in the first six rows of Table 5.1. Lease and

Schmeck (1990) report that the *interaction* between the student's and the teacher's personalities is one of the main factors influencing the use of self-assertion tactics on the part of students. Lease and Schmeck found that female teachers elicited the greatest overall amount of student assertion or expression.

Personality descriptors associated with self-assertion are excitement-seeking, not deliberative, and not self-disciplined *but* nevertheless warm (friendly extroverts). The MBTI-EN classification means extroverted and intuitive. These tactics were associated with the highest of all scores on ILP-R self-esteem. The personality descriptors also include openness to feelings, modest, and not depressed as well as particularly high scores on ILP-R self-efficacy critical thinking (which suggests that students employing self-assertion enjoy a good argument). High scores on ILP-R motivation : personal responsibility indicate those using self-assertive tactics avoid blaming others for their problems (as do most of the other tactics in the first six rows of Table 5.1). Inter-correlation among ILP-R scales also revealed that students using self-assertion tactics are quite happy to include deep semantic and elaborative episodic tactics (especially the former) along with their usual tactics. It is very interesting that, in general, all of the best learning tactics were related to low mechanical reasoning on the DAT *except* this one. Self-assertion learning tactics were associated with differentially *high* mechanical aptitude scores when compared to scores on spatial and abstract reasoning.

Literal memorisation anchors the surface end of the deep-surface continuum of learning tactics (Schmeck, 1988a). Of course, literal memorisation is a legitimate learning tactic, but it can be a problem if used to the exclusion of other tactics. Routinising complex ideas and processes into recitations is a very old and honoured learning tactic. However, if one technifies recondite concepts into sets of recitations, transfer may be minimised and teachers will have no way of knowing whether real understanding has been achieved. Literal memorisation is most appropriate when tests or work call for repetition or iteration.

Table 5.1 indicates that students who use literal memorisation to the exclusion of, rather than in conjunction with, reflective tactics are angry and mistrusting, noncompliant, not tender, not open to feelings and, most important of all, especially low on personal responsibility (ie prone to blame others for difficulties experienced in their school work). One of the items on the ILP-R motivation : personal responsibility scale is, 'It's the teacher's job to tell me the answers'. Students who prefer literal memorisation are also low on anxiety, yet they have the lowest self-esteem of any of those described in Table 5.1. The predominant Myers-Briggs descriptor is S, or sensing, indicating pragmatic attention to detail.

Detailed analyses of the data indicated that the tendency to blame others coupled with anger and mistrust distinguished literal memorisation from all other tactics. The personality characteristics associated with literal memorisation are similar to those associated with agentic analytic tactics *except* for the tendency to blame. Perhaps the message is, if you are going to be angry, be sure you *channel* your anger into your work and *don't blame* others for your difficulties.

Methodical study (row 9) is the ILP-R cluster of transparent, externalised learning tactics commonly called 'study methods'. Frequently, the student adhering to these tactics is described as a 'good student'. 'Good study methods' are those listed in traditional how-to-study manuals (eg Hettich, 1992). Exteriorised tactics are often emphasised in such a list. These tactics include turning in work on schedule or ahead of schedule without grammatical or spelling errors and without coffee stains. This is good. Any problems with these tactics again concern using them to the exclusion of deep and elaborative ones. The problem again concerns routinising or technifying complex ideas.

Generally, the personality of students who prefer methodical study tactics is similar to those preferring agentic analytic and literal memorisation tactics. They are angry, mistrustful and confident, similar to those using agentic analytic tactics, but the dutifulness present with agentic analytic tactics is absent here, and there is a presence of qualities that suggest a willingness to *use people* to achieve one's goals; not straightforward, not warm, not gregarious, not altruistic, not compliant. The personality associated with methodical study differs from literal memorisation in that methodical study includes more willingness to take responsibility and more confidence. However, it is informative that students preferring methodical study tactics were the only ones to score systematically *low* on modesty (indicating narcissism). Interestingly, we also have low self-esteem and high anxiety in this category. Also, the absence of assertiveness in the presence of the other qualities might suggest that students using these tactics are willing to dissimulate if necessary to achieve school goals. The Myers-Briggs descriptor that best fits this individual is J, or judging (in contrast to the simple S designation which predominated in the case of literal memorisation). This J designation indicates decisiveness.

More detailed analysis led to the discovery that students preferring methodical study tactics were especially high on ILP-R motivation: academic interest and ILP-R self-efficacy: fact retention. These two ILP-R subscales are correlated, and the relationship is best expressed by one of the self-efficacy: fact retention items, which states, 'I understand and am good at "playing the school game"'. The view that school is a 'game' which one can 'win' seems to be particularly strong in the student preferring methodical study. Also, moderator analyses revealed that when NEO-PI anger and ILP-R self-efficacy: fact retention were both high (an angry person playing the game), then the student preferring methodical study was also prone to use agentic analytic tactics, but when a tendency to blame (low responsibility) was systematically added to the mix, then they tended toward literal memorisation.

The final ILP-R cluster of learning tactics in row ten of Table 5.1 is called *conventionality*. Conventional tactics involve following instructions. The individual preferring conventional tactics is orthodox and establishmentarian. These individuals expect to be given instructions (as opposed to 'instruction'). They want a lot of guidance and mentoring, and they expect teacher and syllabus to tell them quite clearly what to do. They are disappointed if left to their own devices. They are not good candidates for independent study or self-directed learning.

The personality descriptors associated with conventional tactics include high anxiety, low esteem and low assertiveness coupled with being not straightforward and yet taking personal responsibility. This seems to be the individual who is afraid of hurting the feelings of other people. They are also lonely and easily discouraged. Those familiar with the MBTI will not be surprised to learn that the typological descriptors that best describe this individual are MBTI-SJ (sensing and judging), the pre-eminent keepers of orthodoxy.

Adult learning tactics

Since the inception of the current research project in 1977, we have found only one dimension of the ILP to vary when older and younger learners are compared. This dimension is academic self-efficacy, the most influential aspect of academic self-concept. While self-efficacy is not a learning tactic, it is very influential in a student's *choice* of learning tactics. Furthermore, multivariate analyses have revealed that changes in self-efficacy are related to experience, not to age *per se*. Not surprisingly, successful coping with the demands of school raises self-efficacy. In turn, higher self-efficacy increases the chances that more effective learning tactics will be chosen by students ('success breeds success').

Interviews with adult learners have yielded the following conclusions. When a learner is absent from school for a prolonged period, forgetting of school procedure and changes in school procedure (eg increased use of computers) coupled with *beliefs* regarding the effects of ageing frequently lower the adult's self-efficacy. Lowered efficacy, in turn, presses the individual to employ learning tactics listed toward the bottom of Table 5.1 (rows eight, nine and ten). These are less effective tactics and serve to further lower the individual's academic self-efficacy.

One type of adult learner seems to resent the circumstances that either led to their absence from school or that led to the demand that they return to school (job requirements); they are angry, jealous or envious, with or without awareness. In these individuals, literal memorisation (row eight) seems to predominate. If anger diminishes, the reflective tactics (rows three to six) are more frequently chosen. If anger remains but the learners 'forgive' circumstances or blame themselves instead of others for missed opportunities, then the road is open for the development of agentic analytic tactics (row one).

The teacher can help in all of this by providing reassurance and extra help. It seems that a reduction in anger and the tendency to blame others is easier once returning students start to believe that they can still succeed ('all is *not* lost').

Another type of adult learner is one who feels he or she *never was* competent in school. In other words, ILP-R self-efficacy was always low, and after an absence from school the student's efficacy is lower than ever. In this case, the most frequent choice of learning tactic seems to be conventionality (row ten). This type of student is fully 'syllabus-bound' (Parlett, 1970); looking to be told what to do and fearful of deviating from the prescribed path. Once again, the teacher can help by trying to raise self-efficacy. Often, the student who prefers tactics labelled conventionality in Table 5.1 will gravitate toward agentic serial tactics (row two) as self-efficacy increases. Regardless of whether agentic analytic or agentic serial tactics are the point of entry into successful school performance, their arsenals of tactics subsequently tend to expand into the deep or elaborative tactics as self-efficacy continues to increase along with success.

Either of the above approaches to coping with the demands of school (literal memorisation or conventionality) can easily metamorphose into methodical study (row nine), especially if methodical tactics have proved effective for the individual in the world outside school. In this case, the student is once again 'syllabus-bound' (Parlett, 1970) but often for manipulative reasons. The underlying belief seems to be that one has to 'look like' a co-operative, interested student in order to get what one wants; success. In this case, a potential remedy is for the teacher to encourage self-expression (row seven). This can be done both through oral and written assignments. If the student expresses his or her true self and still experiences success, then the road to reflective intellectual development can be opened.

It is important to emphasise that once the impact of detrimental experience is overcome, underlying preferences for learning tactics appear to relate to personality in adult learners just as tactic preferences relate to personality in younger learners. Costa and McCrae (1992) have demonstrated that personality is very stable across the lifespan, with 50 per cent of it genetically determined. Ultimately, the task for the student remains that of finding his or her most comfortable niche with regard to learning (cf. Schmeck, 1988b).

Teachers of adults are all familiar with the thrill of watching the aftermath of renewed confidence in adult students as they begin to let go of insecurities and unfold as individuals within the school setting. Whether the unfolding leads in the direction of the more academic, deep tactics or the more personal, elaborative and self-assertive ones, past impediments are quickly forgotten and enthusiasm takes centre stage. This enthusiasm is often contagious and is very rewarding to the teacher as well as the student.

References

Bennett, G K, Seashore, H G and Wesman, A G (1989) *Differential Aptitude Tests: Perceptual Abilities Test*, The Psychological Corporation, New York.

Beyler, J and Schmeck, R R (1992) Assessment of individual differences in preferences for holistic-analytic strategies: evaluation of some commonly available instruments, *Educational and Psychological Measurement*, 52, 709–19.

Biggs, J (1970) Faculty patterns in study behaviour, *Australian Journal of Psychology*, 22, 161–74.

Biggs, J (1988) 'Approaches to learning and to essay writing' in *Learning Strategies And Learning Styles*, R R Schmeck (ed.), Plenum Press, New York.

Costa, P T and McCrae, R R (1992) *The Revised NEO Personality Inventory (NEO-PI-R) and NEO Five-Factor Inventory (NEO-FFI) professional manual*, Psychological Assessment Resources, Odessa, Florida.

Geisler-Brenstein, E and Schmeck, R R (1996) 'The revised inventory of learning processes: a multifaceted perspective on individual differences in learning' in *Alternatives in Assessment of Achievements, Learning Processes and Prior Knowledge – a European Perspective*, M Birenbaum and F J R C Dochy (eds), Kluwer Publishing, London.

Hettich, P I (1992) *Learning Skills for College and Career*, Brooks/Cole, Pacific Grove, California.

Lease, S H and Schmeck, R R (1990) The relationship of gender and gender identification to classroom participation, *College Student Journal*, 24, 392–8.

Lincoln, Y S and Guba, E G (1985) *Naturalistic Inquiry*, Sage, Beverly Hills, California.

Myers, I B and McCaulley, M H (1985) *Manual: A Guide to the Development and Use of the Myers-Briggs Type Indicator*, Consulting Psychologists Press, Palo Alto, California.

Ouspensky, P D (1971) *The Fourth Way*, Vintage Books, New York.

Parlett, M R (1970) 'The syllabus-bound student' in *The Ecology of Human Intelligence*, L Hudson (ed.), Penguin, Harmondsworth, England.

Schmeck, R R (1988a) *Learning Strategies and Learning Styles*, Plenum Press, New York.

Schmeck, R R (1988b) 'Individual differences and learning strategies' in *Learning and Study Strategies: Issues in Assessment, Instruction, and Evaluation*, C Weinstein, E Goetz and P Alexander (eds), Academic Press, San Diego.

Schmeck, R R and Geisler-Brenstein, E (1989) Individual differences that affect the way students approach learning, *Learning and Individual Differences*, 1, 85–124.

Schmeck, R R, Ribich, F and Ramanaiah, N (1977) Development of a self-report inventory for assessing individual differences in learning processes, *Applied Psychological Measurement*, 1, 413–31.

Schmeck, R R, Geisler-Brenstein, E and Cercy, S P (1991) Self-concept and learning: the revised inventory of learning processes, *Educational Psychology*, 11, 343–62.

Tulving, E (1989) Remembering and knowing the past, *American Scientist*, 77, 361–7.

CHAPTER 6

Behaviourist Approaches to Adult Learning

Glyn Owens

Behaviourism today

It is perhaps unfortunate that for many people the term 'behaviourism' is still synonymous with a rather simplistic caricature of the approach proposed by Watson (1919). This approach, which has been termed 'methodological behaviourism', centred on the notion of restricting the field of psychology to observable behaviour. Perhaps unsurprisingly, an approach to psychology which de-emphasised unobservable aspects of human experience soon came to be regarded as excessively limited, and by the 1940s methodological behaviourism was seen as untenable.

Somewhat oversimplifying, such disillusionment can be seen to have had two alternative effects. The first was a judgement that the approach had failed because it led to a psychology that was *too* behaviourist, and approaches diametrically opposed to behaviourism (eg Rogers, 1969) began to appear. The second was a judgement that the approach had failed because it had been *insufficiently* behaviourist, and that what was needed was a psychology that concerned itself with the whole of human experience from the viewpoint of behaviour (Skinner, 1948). This approach, which has come to be known as 'radical' behaviourism, has since grown to be the dominant approach within behaviourism today.

Radical behaviourism today

The dominant figure, at least in terms of theoretical development of radical behaviourism, has undoubtedly been the Harvard psychologist Burrhus Frederick Skinner (1904–1990). Although much of his early writing was concerned with reporting the results of experimental research (eg Skinner, 1938) he was quick to recognise the broader implications of research findings, and theoretical accounts illustrating how human behaviour could be understood in terms of the experimental findings of behaviourism, soon began to appear (Skinner, 1953). One of the most striking aspects of radical behaviourism, and one which is often not realised by non-behaviourists, is the explicit extension of the subject matter to include areas not considered by methodological behaviourists, in particular those aspects of experience not amenable to direct observation; thoughts, wishes, dreams, etc. Generally discussed under the broad heading 'private events', such phenomena have been seen as 'the heart of radical behaviourism' (Skinner, 1974) and have been the subject of much discussion in the behavioural literature. Realising, as Skinner put it (1974), that 'the skin is not that important as a boundary', behaviourists have recognised that perceiving, thinking, dreaming etc can all be conceived as things that people *do*, that is to say as behaviours, subject to the same kinds of parameters as more overt behaviours. Such an extension of behaviourism from its original methodological constraints has permitted the development of a substantive and powerful theoretical infrastructure.

Behaviourism and adult learning

Although behaviourism has traditionally centred on the study of learning, it is important to note that learning as conceived by behaviourism differs somewhat from more commonplace notions. To the casual observer learning may be seen to be about acquiring some new skill or knowledge. A behaviourist, however, asks what are the signs that learning has taken place? Generally we know that someone has learned something if they now do something that, prior to some 'learning experience', they did not do. Thus a person who cannot solve a quadratic equation can be taught a simple formula and, having learned the formula and the principles of its use, will now be able to solve it. One way of looking at this is to say that the probability of particular behaviours has changed; prior to the learning experience the probability of solving the quadratic equation was zero (or at least very low), whereas after the learning the probability is 1 (or at least very high).

Within behaviourism it has been recognised that such a concept of learning is excessively restrictive; a transition from a response probability of around zero to a response probability of around 1 represents only a special case. Clearly, one might also consider learning to have occurred if, following the learning experience, a probability changes from, say, 0.3 to 0.8, or from 0.1 to 0.2. Thus a behaviourist concept of learning might encompass all changes in the probability of a behaviour that take place as a result of experience (the latter element being necessary to exclude changes in behaviour that are the result of maturation, fatigue, intoxication and similar factors). Note that this concept also subsumes those cases in which the probability of a behaviour *reduces*, so that 'weakening' of a behaviour is also seen as a learning process.

It should also be noted that there is no obvious equivalent in a behavioural analysis of the distinction sometimes made between performance and competence. The notion that someone has 'learned how to do something' but is not actually doing it can be restated as an observation that the probability of their doing it has changed in some circumstances but not others. That is to say, a radical behaviourist analysis explicitly recognises the importance of the context on the occurrence of behaviour.

Conventionally behaviourists note three basic processes in learning, which together are seen as the building blocks for learning in general. The first is the process of habituation, by which individuals learn *not* to respond to particular events. Most complex organisms show some form of 'orienting response' when a novel stimulus is presented, typically involving increases in sensitivity of sensory organs, orientation towards the stimulus, musculature and vegetative changes and changes in brainwave patterns. Clearly if the organism were to respond in this way to every stimulus presented, it would soon become incapable of doing anything else. The process of habituation therefore provides a mechanism whereby the individual can learn *not* to respond to repeated occurrences of a stimulus if it has no significance for the individual. Habituation processes are dependent on a number of factors including pattern of presentation of the stimulus, the significance of the stimulus for the individual, and so on. A summary of the factors involved can be found in Lynn (1966).

The second type of learning is that first demonstrated by Pavlov involving the pairing of a neutral stimulus with one that elicits some form of autonomic response from the individual. After repeated pairings the originally neutral stimulus may come to take on some of the properties of the original stimulus, eliciting the same kinds of physiological response. Such learning is, of course, widely discussed and has been variously known as 'Pavlovian conditioning', 'classical conditioning' or 'respondent conditioning'.

The third type of learning, and that which accounts for the bulk of research in modern behaviourism, is that demonstrated most clearly by Skinner (1938) and known as 'operant conditioning' or 'instrumental learning'. In a simple experiment a rat in an experimental chamber presses a lever on the wall; when the lever is pressed, food is delivered. The delivery of the food is said to *reinforce* the behaviour of pressing the lever, strengthening or maintaining the behaviour. Although the importance of habituation and of Pavlovian conditioning must be acknowledged, there is no doubt that it is the study of operant conditioning that has dominated modern behaviourism and has led to the most important theoretical and empirical breakthroughs. It is therefore important to look at some of the elements of operant conditioning in a little more detail.

Important issues in operant conditioning

The shaping of behaviour

Having recognised the value of a broad concept of learning (concerned with all changes in probability of behaviour, not just those from 0 to 1), operant conditioning has tended to take little interest in the specifics of 'acquiring' new behaviours. In the laboratory situation (and in many applied settings) the production of a new behaviour can be routinely achieved by the process of 'shaping', whereby reinforcement is delivered first for any behaviour that might be seen as a 'first step' towards the final objective, then gradually requires the behaviour to approximate more and more closely to its final form before reinforcement is delivered. A consequence of this has been the realisation that 'speed of learning' – for example, how long it takes for a new behaviour to be established – is not a useful or meaningful dependent variable, being a function of the complexity of the behaviour, its similarity to existing behaviours, the skill with which the new behaviour is shaped, and so on. The issue relates to old debates about whether learning is a gradual or an 'all-or-none' process. If a complex behaviour of several elements is considered, then even if each element is learned on an all-or-none basis, the impression will be of gradual learning. Skinner (1938) demonstrated elegantly the acquisition of a bar-pressing response in a rat as an all-or-none process. Once the various associated elements had been learned, there was an effectively instantaneous transition from hardly any pressing of the bar to pressing at a high, steady rate.

The contingency of reinforcement

The description of the experiment above implied that there was a simple relationship between the behaviour and the reinforcement to the effect that each time the lever was pressed, food was delivered. In practice such a relationship would be uncommon in the experimental laboratory and, more commonly, the reinforcement stands in a more or less complex relationship to the behaviour (eg reinforcement might be delivered only after a certain number of responses have occurred, or only following the first response during a specified time interval). The precise relationship between the behaviour and the reinforcement is termed the reinforcement contingency, and a considerable body of research has shown that different reinforcement contingencies may have markedly differing effects on behaviour (Ferster and Skinner, 1957).

The nature of reinforcement

One of the important aspects of behaviourist thinking that has escaped many observers has been the emphasis on considering variables from a *functional* viewpoint. In the case of reinforcement, this means that definitions are not in terms of the physical or procedural properties but rather in terms of effects on behaviour. Thus, an event can be said to reinforce a particular behaviour if and only if it has specific effects on that behaviour, in this case maintaining or increasing the probability of the behaviour. It would make no sense in behavioural terms to say something like 'we reinforced the behaviour but it had no effect'. Certain distinctions within the topic of reinforcement are of importance. A major distinction is between *positive* and *negative* reinforcers. While both of these serve to reinforce behaviour, the two have traditionally been distinguished in terms of their mode of delivery; positive reinforcers being those that have their effect if *presented* contingent on behaviour (eg food) and negative reinforcers being those that have their effect if *withdrawn* contingent on behaviour (eg distressing noise). A better criterion for distinguishing the two is probably in terms of their relationship to escape; contingencies of positive reinforcement reinforce only the specified behaviour, whereas those of negative reinforcement reinforce either the specified behaviour or escape from the situation. Thus, under conditions of negative reinforcement, the individual can obtain success by leaving the specific environment where the reinforcer occurs (eg moving to a place where there is no distressing noise). Other distinctions between types of reinforcement should also be noted. In particular it is useful to distinguish *intrinsic* reinforcement (eg the relief experienced by relinquishing a hot object) and *extrinsic* reinforcement (eg payment for performing some task). It is also useful (Ferster, 1967) to distinguish *arbitrary* reinforcement (eg a therapist giving a sweet to a handicapped child to reinforce social behaviour) and *natural* reinforcement (eg friendly responses from others that serve to reinforce social behaviour). Note that no value judgements should necessarily be associated with these; a reinforcer is not necessarily better if it is, say, intrinsic and natural than if extrinsic and arbitrary. There may be times (eg in developing new skills) when arbitrary reinforcement is necessary to bring a behaviour to a level that will trigger the natural contingencies (social behaviour is an example here; unskilled social behaviour may need to be maintained by arbitrary contingencies until it has become sufficiently well developed that the community at large will deliver sufficient reinforcement to maintain the behaviour). It can also be useful to distinguish *conditioned* reinforcers, which owe their properties to some prior learning experience, from *unconditioned* reinforcers whose properties do not depend on such learning.

The use of functionally defined concepts

As highlighted above, a reinforcer is defined not by its physical properties (topographical definition) or by procedural features (operational definition) but rather by its effect on the behavioural system under consideration (functional definition). This use of functional definitions extends throughout behaviourist approaches (Skinner, 1957; Owens and Ashcroft, 1982) and applies equally well to behaviours and to stimuli. In particular it is important to note that phenomena (behaviour, stimuli or reinforcers) may be regarded as *functionally equivalent* if they have equivalent effects within the system (and, by extension, functionally similar to the extent that their effects are similar). It follows that two physically different behaviours that are functionally similar will have similar probabilities of occurrence. This can have important implications. For example, if a student's only reason for studying a particular topic is to obtain a passing grade, then under some circumstances the behaviours of, say, writing an original essay and plagiarising the work of someone else may be functionally equivalent. It is therefore necessary to ensure that some contingencies apply to one of the behaviours and not to the other (eg recognition and downgrading of plagiarism) in order that the two are no longer seen as functionally similar. Although the functional approach is not without its problems (see, for example, Jones and Owens, 1992) it can nevertheless be argued that this, more than anything, separates a behaviourist approach from other perspectives within psychology. A failure to recognise the importance of adopting a functional perspective can make it extremely difficult to understand modern behaviourism.

The role of stimuli in operant conditioning

In a Pavlovian paradigm, a stimulus holds a central role, *eliciting* a reflexive action. In an operant paradigm, by contrast, there need be no specific stimulus associated with a behaviour; the rat in a box pressing the lever has no prompt to do so, but simply does so, we might say, 'whenever it feels like it'. This is not, however, to say that stimuli do not play an important role in operant conditioning, and it is possible to arrange matters so that particular stimuli exert a greater or lesser degree of control over particular behaviours. Thus, if one adds to the experimental situation originally described a particular tone that is sounded whenever the food dispensing mechanism is switched 'on', leaving a silence when the mechanism is 'off', it can be demonstrated that the subject will learn to show a high pattern of responding in the presence of the tone and little if any responding in its absence. This phenomenon is known as *stimulus control*, and subsumes earlier learning theory concepts of discrimination (equivalent to a high degree of stimulus control) and generalisation (equivalent to a low degree of stimulus control).

Adult learning from a behavioural viewpoint

From what has been said already, it will be apparent that a behavioural programme aims to provide an understanding of adult learning using the processes already referred to as basic units or 'building blocks' in such analyses. At
first glance this might seem far from simple, the phenomena of adult learning
appearing to be aeons away from the (apparently) simple laboratory experi-
ments of the behaviourists. However, just as a finished building need bear no
obvious resemblance to the bricks of which it is composed, so there is no
reason to conclude from the appearance of adult learning that behavioural
processes are not operating. In this light it is useful to examine some of the
phenomena of human adult learning and consider how a behavioural perspective might shed some light on the underlying processes.

The role of language

Clearly not all adult learning depends on the use of language. A person with
whom I have no common language may still be able to demonstrate to me
certain skills and techniques. Nevertheless, it is probably fair to say that the
overwhelming majority of adult learning draws at least to some extent on the
use of language. Language, of course, has the effect of permitting extremely
rapid learning. Instead of an individual spending a long period of time,
having behaviour shaped by a process of 'trial and success' (rather than trial
and error) learning, it is possible to acquire new skills by the simple expedient
of following instructions.

In considering the behavioural processes involved, the use of language can
be seen as a particular kind of stimulus control. Just as the rat's lever pressing
becomes more likely in the presence of a tone in the experiment described
earlier, so particular behaviours of humans may become more likely following exposure to particular sets of verbal stimuli. In particular, this provides a
powerful means of generating novel behaviours. If individual stimuli (words,
phrases, sentences, etc) make particular behaviours more likely, then it
follows that novel combinations of such stimuli will make novel behaviours
likely.

The importance of language in developing new behaviours has been recognised in behaviourist theory with distinction between behaviours that are
largely or entirely shaped by exposure to the relevant contingencies, hence
known as *contingency-shaped* behaviours, and behaviours that result from
following verbal guidelines or rules, and hence known as *rule-governed*
behaviours (Skinner, 1968). Although in practice skilled performance will
normally involve elements of both, there are circumstances in which each is
of particular value. This is especially true, of course, when learning by
exposure to the contingencies would be dangerous, for example in dealing

with high voltage circuitry. Simply leaving individuals exposed to the contingencies would result in most being electrocuted before learning the relevant precautions, whereas giving initial instructions can minimise risk. It is not just in the area of immediate safety, however, that rules can be of value in learning. Sometimes the contingencies may be too temporally remote to permit effective learning through exposure (eg in learning the correct procedures for the handling of radioactive materials). In most cases the advantage of verbal instruction will simply be one of speed. The use of rules provides a valuable 'shortcut', eliminating the need for slow learning through experience.

There are, of course, also problems with rule-governed behaviour. First, of course, the rules have to be appropriate; to the extent that the rules fail to describe (and hence produce) appropriate behaviour they will fail to facilitate learning. Indeed, under such circumstances there may well be an influence on the broader process of stimulus control. For example, words originating from that source (eg a particular teacher) may lose control; 'it's no use listening to him, he's hopeless'. Second, even when the rules are appropriate, they will only rarely specify the whole of the complex contingencies operating with respect to some behaviour. In practice, rule-governed behaviour will be such as to permit safe and effective interaction with the natural contingencies, but the fine details of these contingencies will then, over time, further refine the behaviour. Thus, a person may be given instruction on effective lecturing – how to modulate the voice, how to maintain eye contact with an audience, and so on – but these skills might then be expected to be further refined as direct experience of lecturing exposes the individual to the natural contingencies that shape the details of the behaviour. In this example, too, it is interesting to note how the person who is highly anxious about lecturing may show no improvement; here 'following the rules' may be reinforced by removal of the anxiety, a process of negative reinforcement ('as long as I follow the instructions to the letter, I'll be OK'). Under these circumstances the negative reinforcement involved in controlling anxiety might be such as to overwhelm any other contingencies, 'locking' the individual into a pattern of rigid rule following, and avoiding any deviation from the instructions.

Learning by imitation

In many respects, learning by imitation (sometimes termed 'modelling' – see, for example, Bandura, 1969) can be seen to have parallels with learning through the medium of language. Indeed, to some extent one could argue that the major difference between the two is that in verbal teaching the stimuli do not have the same physical form as the desired behaviour (although there may be close *functional* similarities) whereas in modelling the two are as closely topographically matched as possible. Learning by imitation is, of course, often used in the teaching of physical skills, and shares many of the properties of rule-governed behaviour. It permits rapid, safe teaching and the behaviour produced may later be further refined through exposure to the contingencies. In general, modelling will have advantages over verbal teaching to the extent that the degree of stimulus control is stronger. For example, a judo student being taught to throw an opponent by 'spinning on the ball of the left foot until one is underneath the opponent, tucking the right elbow under the opponent's right armpit' is likely to find that a whole range of behaviours, some successful and some less so, fit the description equally. However, a demonstration of the throw by an expert coach carries little ambiguity and permits rapid learning (which, like verbal learning, is then refined as the individual is exposed to the natural contingencies when practising the technique).

Thinking and problem-solving

Once it is recognised that new behaviours can arise as a result of exposure to verbal rules generated by others, it follows that rules generated by individuals themselves can also generate novel behaviours. Clearly, when individuals generate rules for themselves, it is not always necessary to produce these in any kind of overt form. Producing the same verbal behaviour internally may be just as effective in producing the desired result. This kind of 'talking to oneself' is what we normally describe as 'thinking', and such talk directed towards solution of a problem of course becomes 'problem solving'. Such self-talk is valuable in many different contexts, as a means of increasing the probability of some particular behaviour. For example, the pole vaulter who, during the run up to the vault, repeats to herself 'early and high' is taking action to increase the probability of planting the pole in the box in the manner described and thereby producing a successful vault.

When thinking is directed towards the production of novel behaviour (rather than, as in the last example, increasing the probability of an existing behaviour) it shares many of the advantages of other rule-governed behaviours; differing strategies can be described, and in doing so the consequences 'seen'. (Remember that 'seeing', like other private events, can be considered a behaviour. Although normally under very strong stimulus control – we usually see what is there – such seeing may also occur in the absence of the stimulus seen, as in imagining, dreaming, visualising, etc.) Being generally more rapid than overt behaviour, there is the possibility of running through several possible 'solutions' more quickly than would otherwise be possible and, of course, where a mistake could be disastrous, possible solutions can be attempted in imagination without the risk of dreadful consequences.

The process can be continued to a higher level, for example in producing rules about how to go about solving problems (an example of such principles in mathematics is given by Polya, 1957). That is to say, it is possible to create rules about how to generate rules. Examples of such rules (of differing valid-ity according to context) might include: 'consider a simplified version of the problem' (a common strategy in mathematics); 'identify similar problems to which solutions are known' (a strategy of general usefulness); 'list the avail-able options' (a general strategy for decision-making), and so on. In this way, problem solving can be seen as an aspect of rule-governed behaviour, which itself can be seen as an aspect of stimulus control.

Attention

The concept of attention is, in many ways, central to notions of human (and animal) learning. We only learn, it can be argued, if we are paying attention. From a behavioural perspective, however, attention can be seen as merely another name for stimulus control (Terrace, 1966). To the extent that a behaviour is influenced by some stimulus (words, demonstration, etc) then the individual can be said to be paying attention to it. Conversely, the stimulus that fails to have any influence on behaviour can be described as one to which the individual was paying no attention. The shift of emphasis is not simply a linguistic nicety to mollify diehard behaviourists who object to unobservable entities. The reconceptualisation also has several advantages. First the proc-esses that give rise to stimulus control are well understood, reflecting the extent to which different stimuli are associated with different patterns of reinforcement. Second, apparent puzzles and anomalies are eliminated, as when a person has clearly 'attended' to instructions in the sense of being able to repeat them verbally but fails to change behaviour accordingly. It seems likely that such circumstances reflect association with reinforcers linked to verbal behaviour (knowing the 'right' answer if asked) but lack of apparent association with reinforcers linked to the desired behaviour ('this sounds like a total waste of time').

Difficulties in learning and remembering

It is commonly believed that learning is a more difficult process for adults than for children. Indeed, there have been attempts to suggest that, for some kinds of learning at least, there exist 'critical periods' during which learning is much easier than subsequently. However, although it is hard to believe that such widely held beliefs have no foundation at all, there is at the same time no evidence that conditioning procedures are less effective in adults. How then might the apparent difficulties in adult learning be explained?

Arguably there are at least two important issues here. The first concerns the problem of acquiring the new responses. In many respects the difficulties experienced by adults seem anomalous from a behavioural viewpoint. After all, with so much knowledge and skill already, surely any new behaviour is likely to relate to other behaviours already in the repertoire, making acquisition of a new response easy.

Unfortunately this plethora of existing responses in the individual's repertoire can, under certain circumstances, work against the individual as much as with him or her. In particular it is clear that developing a new behaviour can be problematic if there are already within the individual's repertoire other behaviours that already have a high probability in the same kinds of situation. Thus, in learning a new language, the adult has the problem that under the circumstances under which it would be appropriate to utter, say, the word 'poisson', there is already a long history of successfully uttering the word 'fish'. The adult thus has two tasks; one is to increase the probability of uttering the French word, the other is to decrease the probability of uttering the English. The problem may be confounded when, besides learning new words, the individual also has to learn new grammatical structures (as in German) or new alphabets (as in Welsh, Greek, Russian and Japanese – the first three particularly so as in some cases like 'F' in Welsh, 'X' in Greek or 'P' in Cyrillic, the letters may appear identical but require different responses). In many cases, then, adults may, relative to children, appear to have difficulty learning simply because they have, at the same time, a considerable amount of *unlearning* to do.

The second important issue here is that of forgetting. While it is tempting to think of forgetting (as did many early learning theorists) in terms of the decay over time of some 'memory trace', such a viewpoint is difficult to maintain. First, we know from studies of memory problems among older people that it is commonly early memories, those that have had the longest time to 'decay', that are in fact best remembered. Second, we know from experimental research that conditioned responses can be demonstrated after a gap of many years.

From a behavioural viewpoint, forgetting can be seen as a function of several processes. Especially important is the process of *extinction*. If we return to the original description of the basic operant conditioning experiment, it is unsurprising that if the mechanism responsible for delivering the food fails, then over time the response will weaken and eventually the animal will cease responding, ie the process of extinction. It should be noted that when such extinction is demonstrated experimentally, it is common to detect later a period of *spontaneous recovery*; a further period of responding, not as strong as the original and eventually fading out permanently unless reinforcement occurs. Thus, it follows that if a behaviour that has been learned fails to produce the desired reinforcement, it is likely to become weaker, less likely to occur; the signs by which we recognise that something has been forgotten.

Extinction can also relate to forgetting in another way, of especial relevance in considering adult learning. Remember that one problem in adult learning can be that adults may have to unlearn one response at the same time as learning another. Unfortunately, the phenomenon of spontaneous recovery can mean that an unlearned competing response may resurface after a period of time. Thus, the person who has successfully replaced the response 'fish' with the word 'poisson' may find that after a time it is difficult to remember the word 'poisson' because the word 'fish' has regained some strength as a response through the process of spontaneous recovery.

Of course, the issues discussed above far from exhaust those important to adult learning, and inevitably the analyses presented oversimplify for the purposes of clarity. A detailed presentation of behavioural analyses of these and other topics would require considerably more space than is available. The above should therefore be regarded not as definitive behavioural theoretical positions on the topics but rather as an introduction to the way in which such issues might be addressed by behaviourists.

References

Bandura, A (1969) *Principles of Behavior Modification*, Holt, Rinehart and Winston, New York.

Ferster, C B (1967) Arbitrary and natural reinforcement, *The Psychological Record*, 17, 341–7.

Ferster, C B and Skinner B F (1957) *Schedules of Reinforcement*, Appleton Century Crofts, New York.

Jones, R S P and Owens, R G (1992) Applying functional analysis, *Behavioral Psychotherapy*, 20, 37–40.

Lynn, R (1966) *Attention, Arousal and the Orienting Reflex*, Pergamon, Oxford.

Owens, R G and Ashcroft, J B (1982) Functional analysis in applied psychology, *British Journal of Clinical Psychology*, 21(3), 181–90.

Polya, M (1957) *How to Solve It*, Princeton University Press, New Jersey.

Rogers, C R (1969) *Freedom to Learn*, Charles E Merrill, Columbus, Ohio.

Skinner, B F (1938) *The Behavior of Organisms*, Appleton Century Crofts, New York.

Skinner, B F (1948) *Walden Two*, Macmillan, New York.

Skinner, B F (1953) *Science and Human Behavior*, Macmillan, New York.

Skinner, B F (1957) *Verbal Behavior*, Appleton Century Crofts, New York.

Skinner, B F (1968) *Contingencies of Reinforcement: a Theoretical Analysis*, Appleton Century Crofts, New York.

Skinner, B F (1974) *About Behaviorism*, Jonathan Cape Ltd, London.

Terrace, H S (1966) 'Stimulus control' in *Operant Behavior; Areas of Research and Application*, W K Honig (ed.), Appleton Century Crofts, New York.

Watson, J B (1919) *Psychology From the Standpoint of a Behaviourist*, Lippincott, Philadelphia.

CHAPTER 7

Experiential Learning and Constructivism:

Potential for a Mutually Beneficial Synthesis

Peter Sutherland

Introduction

Within adult learning, experiential learning has been a very influential idea in recent years. It is argued by its advocates such as Kolb (1984) that mature adults have much to offer to the educational process from their life experiences. Within the school age range constructivism has been a very influential idea over the past decade. The movement argues that children bring many valuable experiences to the classroom. On the lines of Ausubel's (1968) dictum, teaching should start with the teacher having an exact knowledge of what each student knows.

This chapter argues that these movements can be blended into a fruitful union. To some extent experiential learning is constructivism in an adult context. It is argued that carrying out this analysis will prove of value to both schools. By comparing and contrasting each with the other, it is hoped that the scope of each can be more clearly defined and understood; what each is and what each is *not*. If, in the final analysis, the differences are regarded as minimal and a union of the two is achieved, the new school should be all the stronger from the contribution of its two separate root systems. Whether it is decided that the two schools should be united or not, this analysis may be of benefit both to theory and to practice; the application to actual classroom teaching.

Some founders of the experiential learning tradition

There are many different definitions and traditions, for which there is only space to consider a few here. For instance, Kolb (1984) defined experiential learning as 'the process whereby knowledge is created through the transformation of experience.' Two of the leading figures behind the historical development of experiential learning have been Lewin (1951) and Dewey (1963).

Lewin evolved the strand of experiential learning where students are deliberately given planned experiential learning as part of their course. This may take the form of work experience or role playing of some aspect of the job the person is training for. The idea is now at the peak of its influence with emphasis on relevant vocational training for a tough job market. Lewin's conception of experiential learning was within a group setting. He was, of course, one of the founders of social psychology and his conception of experiential learning was that of a group of trainees, led by an expert. This evolved out of his T-group (training group) concept. The trainees were to evolve their attitudes to the work situation, under the leadership of a trainer.

On a residential, work-training exercise, some of the trainees approached the trainers with a view to being allowed to participate in the evaluation of their own performances. Until that moment, the pattern of the 24 hours had been one of daytime interaction between the trainees and trainers, followed by evening self-segregation by the trainers in order to evaluate the performance of the trainees. At this point (a turning point in the ethos of training groups), Lewin bowed to the pressure of the trainees. This established a new, more democratic ethos. Mature adult trainees were allowed to use their experiential learning of life to assist in their own evaluation.

However, there are problems with Lewin's conception of experiential learning groups. There is a distinction between the 'here-and-now' involvement of the group and effective 'there-and-then' reflection on what has been learnt from the experiential learning situation. The new British programme for training student nurses, Project 2000, uses the idea of an experiential learning group. Student nurses and midwives meet their mentor on Friday afternoons to reflect on the week's experiential learning. One problem is that the group sometimes becomes so involved in the 'here-and-now' mode (eg an encounter group) that it does not wish to switch to the reflective one.

These Lewinian concepts of experiential learning cannot be seen as common to constructivism, which has, until now, not seen learning within a group context. Its model has been one of an individual child learning, probably under the influence of constructivism's founding father, Piaget.

The recent experiential learning tradition

In the past decade or so the argument for appreciating the importance of experiential learning has been put forward in the USA by, amongst others, Knowles (1984) and by Brookfield (1986), who linked it with self-directed learning. There is certainly a very strong element of self-direction in the learning of the Brazilian street children studied by Carraher *et al.* (1985) in a classic study of the constructivist movement. However the Brazilian children did not have the luxury of Brookfield's American adults of *deciding* to learn. They had to learn in order to survive.

A critical reaction has followed the initial enthusiasm for experiential learning. Its limitations have been pointed out by Miller (1964), among others, who pointed out that some older mature learners may tend to pre-judge and are unable to attain the necessary objectivity to learn. They approach their experience too passively. Miller also noted a tendency to focus on differing and limited aspects of experience. These learners knew neither how to frame questions that can be asked about experience, nor how to look for connections and interrelationships that might be relevant to inter-pret experience.

Smith (1983) likewise urges educators to ask mature adult learners to ask themselves the following.
1. What assumptions are they making?
2. What biases do they bring to the endeavour?
3. Are they getting confused between their own experiences and their for-mal learning in an educational setting?

However, 1. and 2. are very difficult for young adults to realise. In 1. and 2. it is very helpful if the teacher first tries to make the young adult aware of the problem and, second, gives assistance to the learners in trying to solve the problem.

Knowles (1984) made certain assumptions about andragogy (the teaching of adults, as opposed to pedagogy, which is the teaching of children) and experiential learning. Most of these seem to apply to constructivism too.
1. As a person matures, his or her self-concept moves from one of depend-ence towards being self-directed.
2. The maturing person becomes a resource for learning.
3. The mature person's readiness to learn is oriented to the demands of social roles such as parent, employee, committee member, and so on.
4. The application of knowledge is immediate and therefore problem cen-tred rather than subject centred.

Tennant (1988) criticised Knowles's ideas; in particular how Knowles's model can be interpreted in a number of ways.
1. That students need to be weaned away from a traditional way of learn-ing to a self-directed one. There may be a degree of patronage on the part of the educator in doing this.
2. The learner controls the content of learning, but the educator controls the process. The overall operation is then not being genuinely self-directed.
3. There may be an incompatibility between the experiential self-directed learning of the student and the institution's goals. This implies that a learning contract should be established between the two. How much freedom does the student have in establishing this contract? If not enough, then the learning can no longer be held to be self-directed.

Tennant regards Knowles's andragogical model of a teacher as an incompatible blend of the humanistic, Rogerian and behaviourist traditions.

Kolb (1984) lists the essential characteristics of experiential learning. These will be checked for their applicability to constructivism.

1. Learning is a *process* model of learning, as opposed to a product one.
2. Learning is a continuous process grounded in experiences.
3. The process of learning requires the resolution of conflicts between diametrically opposed modes of adaptation to the world; for example, an adult learning a foreign language where the rules of grammar are diametrically opposed to those of the home language.
4. Learning is a holistic process of adaptation to the world.
5. Learning involves transactions between the person and the environment.
6. Learning is the process of creating knowledge.

In all six of Kolb's characteristics there would seem to be, *a priori*, a fit with constructivism.

The implications of experiential learning for teaching

As a result of the seminal contributions of Kolb (1984) and Knowles (1984), the main impact on teaching has been that of Kolb's andragogy. In other words there is a style of teaching adults that involves utilising their experiential learning. This is distinct from pedagogy, in which the teacher instructs the students, but does not take their experiential learning into account in any way.

Andragogy involves the building-in of experiential learning into the learning cycle, as illustrated in Figure 7.1. Students are then encouraged to reflect on these experiences and come to conclusions that modify their cognitive structures. They are then ready for the next cycle of experiential learning.

This is a short-term concept of experiential learning. Utilising this concept,

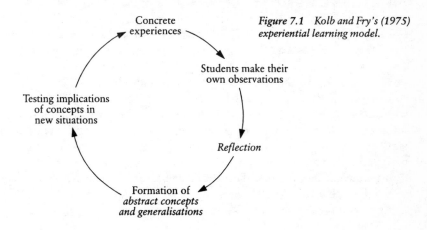

Figure 7.1   Kolb and Fry's (1975) experiential learning model.

planned sessions of experiential learning are built into curriculum planning. For instance, in Project 2000 for the education of student nurses, the course commences with regular planned experiences that are seen by the teachers to be relevant to nurses, such as a visit to a nursery, visits to various sorts of wards in hospitals, etc.

However there is also a long-term conception of experiential learning. This values what mature students bring to a course from the time they enter. Mothers and fathers bring experiences of raising children that are relevant to preparing for jobs such as teaching. In business studies, mature students can make worthwhile contributions as a result of the experiences from the jobs they had. Even if there is no direct application of the experience to the future job, adults bring experiences of adult life and maturity.

Coleman (1976) pointed to the inadequate ability of experiential learners to generalise the principle learnt from experience. This puts much of the responsibility for optimising experiential learning on to the teachers. They should provide experiential learning situations for their students. A degree of trial-and-error learning (or 'the school of hard knocks') then ensues. The teachers should encourage the learners to realise the consequences of their experiences.

The constructivist tradition

Constructivism is defined by Child (1993) as the learner actively constructing both the knowledge acquired and the strategies used to acquire it. An alternative definition is given by Sutherland (1992) as the child constructing 'his own version of reality from his own unique experiences. It is this construction he then uses to deal with any new experiences in that field'. In other words, Kelly's (1963) use of interpreting constructs as a basis for categorising an adult's personality is *not* included in the scope of this article.

The idea has evolved out of Piaget's pioneer work. However, not all of Piaget's ideas are acceptable to constructivists. They accept his theory of knowledge, but not his stages. What constructivists accept most powerfully from Piaget and take as their fundamental axiom is that people construct their own real knowledge from their own experiences and that this is not necessarily the same as what they have been taught at school.

Once a particular idea has been truly integrated into the person's consciousness (eg that the sun goes around the earth), this knowledge and understanding is difficult for teachers to alter. If a new idea is taught (eg that the earth goes around the sun), the person tends to regress back to the earlier one, particulary when under pressure.

If these points apply to children, the age group on which constructivists have up to now mainly concentrated, how much more strongly must they apply to adults who have integrated and consolidated their cognition for so much longer than children? The same argument would apply even more strongly to older adults than to younger.

Driver *et al.* (1985) list three essential qualities of constructivism.

1. The ideas are personal to the learner. Students internalise their experiences in a way which is at least partly their own.
2. Students' individual ideas may be incoherent. There may be contradictions in the conceptualisation. Hopefully this would apply to 'normal' adults to a much lesser extent, although reflection may be needed to resolve some of the contradictions.
3. The ideas learnt are stable within students' cognitive structure. Students tend to ignore counter evidence and tend to regress back to their original conceptualisations.

Within school-based studies constructivism has had its most radical influence on the learning of (and consequently the teaching of) science and mathematics. A very influential strand of constructivism within school science has been Driver's (1983) distinction between academic understanding of a subject, on the one hand, and a 'gut' understanding, on the other. This is illustrated by children who bring understanding to school from their experiences of parks, zoos, home science kits, watching television and reading books. This is a similar level of understanding to what Piaget (1955) called the intuitive stage. Children make a common-sense interpretation of their experiences.

A very influential study is that of Carraher *et al.* (1985). This was carried out among the children of migrant workers in a Brazilian city. Children aged 9–15 years ran a market to sell their goods. Carraher *et al.* discovered that these children had learnt for themselves remarkable mental algorithms for multiplying the cost of items, adding different items together and subtracting the change from the amount given to them. They had not been taught any formal paper-and-pencil techniques at school. In fact they had little formal schooling. Here again an argument can be made for analogous experiences in adults.

There are many experiences that adults gain in their jobs and leisure pursuits that lead, in a similar way, to strongly established learning. This can be built upon in later normal academic study. In the case of clerical work in an office, an improvement on the basic school-leaving levels of reading, writing and typing skills is often demanded. This progress in basic academic skills should in turn prove useful should the adult return to academic study.

Related to the constructivist position is the perspective transformation position of Mezirow. His initial three areas of cognitive interest evolved out of Habermas: technical/instrumental (task-related); communicative (social-related); and emancipatory (self-related). These have later been synthesised (1989) into two areas: the emancipatory area operates in both the self- and social domains or the technical domains. In the course of this emancipatory learning, perspective transformation takes place. As Mezirow (1990) stated,

'Perspective transformation is the process of becoming critically aware of how and why our presuppositions have come to constrain the way we perceive, understand and feel about our world: of reformulating these assumptions to permit a more inclusive, discriminating, permeable and integrative perspective; and of making decisions or otherwise acting upon these understandings.'

His very latest views are found in Chapter 1.

Mezirow has, however, been criticised (eg by Collard and Law, 1989) for being too individualistic and not emphasising the social context and the social implications of perspective transformation/change. However, in this book we are considering individuals in Sections I and II, so Mezirow's ideas fit within the framework of Section II.

Compared to the school-based constructivist movement, Mezirow puts far more emphasis on self-reflection, personal decision-making and personal responsibility for learning. The school-based constructivists stress the need for the initial learning to be in an informal, practical context, whereas Mezirow emphasises change and the need for change. There is a shared stress in both the school-based constructivists and Mezirow on the learner formulating his own constructs, and another on the vital importance of *understanding* everything that is learnt. There is also a common thread in the focus on the learner himself determining his own learning destiny with the pedagogue/andragogue cast in the role of an enabler. For example, Mezirow (1985, p.148) advises adult educators 'to help learners make explicit, elaborate and act upon the assumptions and premises... upon which their performance, achievement and productivity are based'.

However, Mezirow's version of constructivism is a complicated one that applies only to mature adults. Certain applications of reflective learning and reflective judgement do not appear to be fully developed even in young adults. Mezirow's conception is at the opposite end of the spectrum from the naïve constructivism of children.

A common experiential learning–constructivism tradition

Perhaps the most influential educationist who belongs unambiguously to both schools is Freire (1970). He emphasises the desirability of making use of the peasants' own experiences; experiential learning. Simultaneously, there is an element of constructivism: the teachers build upon the informally learnt concepts and strategies that the peasants bring to the classroom (which may well be a hut in a slum). According to Freire, the peasants' consciousness should be raised and this consciousness utilised in the political education that follows.

Another educationist who spans both traditions is Piaget, if rather more ambiguously. There is no ambiguity about his contribution to constructivism;

he is its founding father. However influential members of the movement later rejected his stage theory, while accepting his theory of knowledge.

It is more surprising to find Kolb (1984, p.15), one of the leading exponents of experiential learning, calling Piaget one of 'the foremost intellectual ancestors of experiential learning theory'. Kolb's inclusion of the original constructivist among his three fundamental experiential learning theorists is the most powerful validation encountered of the argument being put in this chapter.

The experiential ideas of Dewey are also compatible with constructivism. He represented very much the same progressive roots as does the constructivist movement. In many ways he is an embodiment of the theme of this chapter, that the education of children and adults should be based on the same principle. The experiential learning of both should be appreciated by their teachers. In most cases adults will have more experience to offer than children, but teachers should build on such informal learning experiences as the learners have, whether they be children or adults.

Miller (1964) argued that some experiential learners tend also to approach their experience too passively, a criticism that can also be applied to many constructivist learners. This is in the metacognitive sense of not being sufficiently consciously aware of the learning and therefore of not making use of it.

Of Smith's (1983) list, 1. and 2. would seem to be equally desirable to ask constructivist learners.

1. What assumptions are they making?
2. What biases do they bring to the endeavour?
3. Are they getting confused between their own learning experience and their formal learning in an educational setting?

Number 3. would seem as difficult for constructivist as for experiential learners.

The way in which adults from a non-academic work background bring learning to bear on formal education is similar to this. The common features are that the experiences have made a deep impression on the adults and become part of their internalised thinking. For instance the knowledge a parent gains from bringing up children can be used in the subsequent study of education and in a career in teaching. However, if we pursue this analogy, adults have to be weaned away from 'gut' understanding if they are to understand the subjects they are studying from *within* the conceptual framework of the subject.

Schön (1983) is also seen as belonging to both traditions in this chapter. Experiences of teaching should be organised for the teacher (ie experiential learning is essential in teacher education). Teachers should then reflect on these experiences. In doing this they build up their own concepts of education (ie by constructivist learning.)

Kolb recommends experience-based curricula for school pupils of science and maths and for first- and second-year undergraduates in social studies.

However, there is a conflict in the advocacy of experience-based curricula for adults. In Piagetian stage terms, it is implied that higher education should be carried out on an abstract level (Piaget's 'formal operational' stage). Yet experiential-based curricula imply that the adult students are still at Piaget's concrete operational level.

Knowles (1982) pointed out, however, that life experiences can be an obstacle to new learning eg negative prejudices, old ways of doing things. This disadvantage probably also applies to the constructivist model, where the informally learnt skill, concept or fact prevents further development. Perhaps a perspective transformation has become necessary or else a concrete model needs to be dropped in order to integrate a more abstract, theoretical model.

Differences between experiential learning and constructivism

The constructivists probably put more emphasis on the learning of *strategies* than do the adherents of experiential learning (whereas both stress the learning of concepts). Adherents of experiential learning such as Knowles (1982) tend to accentuate the reflective aspect of this type of learning more than supporters of constructivism do.

In addition proponents of experiential learning emphasise the rich emotional associations (rather than just the cognitive aspects) of experiential learning in a way in which proponents of constructivism do not. The rich emotional associations provide a source within the student which the teacher should draw on. For example, an adult may have had emotionally charged experiences of heterosexual love or of the trauma of divorce, which the educator can use as a basis for creative writing.

Kidd (1983) emphasised the importance for adults (as opposed to children and adolescents) of experiences. He pointed out that adults have more experiences and different kinds of experiences (eg sexual, job, political or war) than the young. In addition, adults organise their experiences in a cognitively different way, compared to the young.

Discussion, conclusions and implications for teaching

It is not clear whether the type of analysis carried out in this chapter could be based on empirical evidence (in any practical sense). Hence the analysis has instead been based on ethos, principles and concepts.

It is argued that there is a high degree of concordance between the principles of experiential learning and constructivism. They have quite distinctively different (if recent) historical origins, as pointed out in the introduction.

Hence the ethos of each is quite distinct. It is from the complementarity of ethos that each movement may gain in studying the other. For instance, constructivism may gain from putting more emphasis on self-reflection. This would fit well with its recent alliance with the metacognition movement. Experiential learning may gain from addressing Driver's (1983) distinction between 'gut' and academic learning. This would have considerable implications for mature students coming into formal higher education. Do teachers need to wean such students away from a 'gut' level of understanding?

Is this always possible? Is it always desirable? Or, put another way, are there any subjects in which a 'gut' level of understanding is acceptable? Adult educators need an answer to these many questions. Adult researchers should carry out the empirical investigations required to provide the answers.

References

Ausubel, D (1968) *Educational Psychology; A Cognitive View*, Holt, Rinehart & Winston, New York.

Brookfield, S (1986) *Understanding and Facilitating Adult Learning*, Open University Press, Milton Keynes.

Carraher, T, Carraher, D and Schliemann, A (1985) Mathematics in the streets and in the schools, *British Journal of Developmental Psychology*, 3, 22–39.

Child, D (1993) *Psychology and the Teacher* (5th ed.), Cassell, London.

Coleman, J (1976) 'Differences between experiential learning and classroom learning' in *Experiential Learning: Rationale, Characteristics and Assessment*, M. Keeton *et al.* (eds), Jossey-Bass, San Francisco, California.

Collard, S and Law, M. (1989) The limits of perspective transformation: a critique of Mezirow's theory, *Adult Education Quarterly*, 39(2), 99–107.

Dewey, J (1963) *Experience and Education*, Collier-Macmillan, London.

Driver, R (1983) *The Pupil as Scientist*, Oxford University Press, Oxford.

Driver, R, Guesne, E and Tiberghien, A (1985) 'Children's ideas and the learning of science' in *Children's Ideas and the Learning of Science*, R. Driver (ed.), Open University Press, Milton Keynes.

Freire, P (1970) *Pedagogy of the Oppressed*, Herder & Herder, New York.

Kelly, G (1963) *A Theory of Personality: The Psychology of Personal Constructs*, Norton, New York.

Kidd, J R (1983) *How Adults Learn* (rev. ed.), Associated Press, New York.

Knowles, M (1982) *The Modern Practice of Adult Education: From Pedagogy to Andragogy* (2nd ed.), Cambridge Books, New York.

Knowles, M (1984) *The Adult Learner: a Neglected Species,* (3rd edition), Gulf, Houston.

Kolb, D (1984) *Experiential Learning*, Prentice-Hall, Englewood Cliffs, New Jersey.

Kolb, D and Fry, R E (1975) 'Towards an applied theory of experiential learning' in *Theories of Group Processes*, C Cooper (ed.), John Wiley, London.

Lewin, K (1951) *Field Theory in the Social Sciences*, Harper & Row, New York.

Mezirow, J (1985) Concept and action in adult education, *Adult Education Quarterly*, 35(3), 3–27.

Mezirow, J (1989) Transformation theory and social action: a response to Collard and Law, *Adult Education Quarterly*, 39(2), 170–76.

Mezirow, J (1990) 'Conclusion: toward transformative learning and emancipatory education' in *Fostering Critical Reflection in Adulthood: A Guide to Transformative and Emancipatory Education*, J Mezirow *et al.* (eds), Jossey-Bass, San Francisco, California.

Miller, H (1964) *Experience and Learning in Adult Learning*, Collier-Macmillan, London.

Piaget, J (1955) *The Origins of Intelligence in Children*, Routledge & Kegan Paul, London.

Schön, D A (1983) *The Reflective Practioner: how professionals think in action*, Harper Collins, New York.

Smith, R (1983) *Learning How to Learn*, Open University Press, Milton Keynes.

Sutherland, P (1992) *Cognitive Development Today: Piaget and his Critics*, Paul Chapman Publishing, London.

Tennant, M (1988) *Psychology and Adult Learning*, Routledge, London.

Acknowledgements

Professor Alan Rogers of Reading University, Professor Ian Stronach of Manchester Metropolitan University, Dr Mike Osborne of the Department of Educational Policy and Development, Stirling University, Jean Barr of Glasgow University and Jill Moore, formerly of St Mary's College, Strawberry Hill are thanked for their comments on an earlier draft.

ADULTS LEARNING
IN SMALL-GROUP SITUATIONS

CHAPTER 8

Learning in Small Groups

Ian Mowatt and Gerda Siann

Introduction

Over the past four decades, many movements within education have stressed the pedagogic advantages of groups. It has been suggested that locating learning within a group situation aids the movement away from student passivity to students actively structuring their own learning (Rogers, 1969); that working collectively stimulates and accelerates cognitive growth (Gruenfeld and Hollingshead, 1993); that the experience of learning in a group situation enhances social and communicative skills (Cassels, 1990) and serves as a means of enhancing creativity (Hare, 1982); and, finally, that teaching students in groups utilises scarce teaching resources effectively (Griffiths, 1994).

The theoretical underpinning for such claims ranges widely from traditional learning theory, which stresses the social reinforcements gained from group interaction (Diamond, 1964); through cognitive approaches, which stress the enhancement to sociocognition provided by the opportunities for discussion and brainstorming (Connolly *et al.*, 1993); to more psychodynamically oriented approaches, which emphasise the personal growth aspects of group work (Smith, 1980).

However, group work also has its critics, who argue that there is a dearth of evidence indicating that group work consistently promotes learning (Topping, 1992) and also that groups may be an ethically unacceptable form of social control and may disadvantage certain types of learner, notably those who are socially reticent (Abson, 1994). But the general consensus with respect to learning in groups, particularly adult learning in groups, is that the benefits it conveys far outweigh its disadvantages, particularly when it is conducted within a cooperative ethos (Millis, 1991).

In this chapter we consider adult learning in the context of group work, taking as a definition of group work 'two or more individuals in face-to-face interaction, each aware of his or her membership in the group, each aware of the others who belong to the group, and each aware of their positive interdependence as they strive to achieve mutual goals' (Abson, 1994, p.153). This definition aside, it is obvious that group learning takes place in a number of different formats, for example, seminars, workshops, student presentations to small groups, buzz groups, snowballing, brainstorming, group consideration of case studies, role play, joint projects, and so on (Griffiths, 1994). We are concerned, primarily, with small groups (under about 18 participants) although we are aware that continuing economic pressure on tertiary education in particular, has had the effect of greatly increasing the size of 'small groups'.

Although, as the list above suggests, the range of learning activities possible in groups is wide, there are certain commonalities in the optimum organisation of such groups for adult learners. Perhaps the chief of these is the need to help the group emerge from the collection of individual learners of which it is composed. Rogers (1986) suggests that this is best promoted by encouraging frequent face-to-face interchanges. He also proposes that some initial cooperative action (for example on a short-term task) facilitates the involvement of all group members in the social interaction of the group and helps to prevent dominance of the group by the tutor.

Positive social interactions can be promoted to some extent by the seating arrangements provided for group meetings. As is well known, circular seating helps to promote free discussion and reduce hierarchy and, according to Rogers, ideally the seating should consist of individually placed chairs rather than the formality imposed when chairs are arranged around a table.

Rogers notes that although such physical arrangements are easy for a tutor to put in place, it may be far more difficult for a tutor accustomed to more formal teaching to develop the social sensitivities required to facilitate easy communication within the learning group. These sensitivities include awareness of the group members' non-verbal as well as verbal interactions; awareness of group tension and its release symptoms (jokes, laughter, etc); and awareness of the signs of individual emotional tone (eg the way a group member sits nervously on the edge of a chair).

Whereas some tutors take to small group teaching with facility and find the social sensitivity required by such teaching easy, others may need to increase their awareness of the subtle social processes operating in small groups by explicitly watching and monitoring the social interaction in the group they are leading.

In recent years, researchers have come increasingly to take gender into account in the consideration of adult learning and other chapters in this book (notably Chapters 11 and 12) are concerned with this issue. With respect to learning in small groups, most of the gender-related research in academic institutions concerns children. Research centring on gender aspects of adult learning in groups has largely been in the area of management. Studies in this area have tended to indicate that when female consultants lead learning groups, participants report higher levels of learning than they do with male consultants although this is sometimes accompanied by greater levels of stress (Wilson, 1995). In general, however, we would argue (see Siann, 1994) that in task oriented learning groups, gender probably plays a relatively minor part with the possible exception of learning associated with computers, where women may benefit particularly from single-sex groups (Stockdale, 1987).

As we noted above, the kind of teaching that takes place in small groups varies considerably, but it is possible to group the underlying processes of learning in small groups into two broad substantive areas, cognitive and social, and in the next two sections of this chapter we consider each of these in turn. We follow this by a consideration of two factors impinging on adult learning in small groups; the nature of the discipline/task and its assessment and the effect on the type of learner.

Cognitive and social aspects of learning in groups

A basic premise of all groups is that their members interact. It has frequently been suggested (eg Kaye *et al.*, 1984) that in the analysis of such interaction, it is helpful to consider two potentially conflicting objectives.

1. Defining and working towards goals. For the purpose of this chapter, the chief of such goals is the acquisition of cognitive skills and growth.
2. Remaining together as a group and. For the purpose of this chapter, the learning that is associated with this objective is the enhancement of social and communication skills.

We turn now to the first of these.

Cognition in groups

A great deal of adult teaching is carried out in group settings, particularly in the educational settings of universities and colleges. Much of this teaching is carried out without a great deal of formal analysis of either the processes or the products that result from such teaching. By this we mean that the teaching staff concerned seldom step back to consider the extent to which the learning and cognitive growth that takes place in such settings differs from their students' other learning experiences, for example in lectures, laboratories and individual study.

There is, however, one particular aspect of cognition resulting from learning in small groups that has been subjected to a great deal of analysis, and this is with respect to problem solving. One technique that has been widely used has been the brainstorming technique originally formulated by Osborn (1957). He proposed that small groups working interactively and using the principles of quantity not quality, no censorship or evaluation, and building on each other's ideas would produce more and better ideas than individuals working alone. Dubrin (1994) suggests that the optimum size of group for brainstorming should be 5–7 individuals.

While brainstorming was initially greeted with a great deal of enthusiasm, empirical studies have not substantiated the initial claims that the technique produced concepts and solutions superior to individuals working alone (Connolly *et al.*, 1993) and current research suggests that both nominal groups (see below) and electronic brainstorming are more productive techniques.

Electronic brainstorming is a problem-solving method in which group members simultaneously enter their suggestions in a computer and these are distributed to other group members' screens. Evaluation of electronic brainstorming indicates that, particularly with large groups, it tends to be more productive of acceptable solutions than conventional social groups (Dubrin, 1994). It has been suggested (Connolly *et al.*, 1993) that the size effect may be due to declining levels of apprehension about being individually evaluated as group size is increased, as well as the possible motivating effect of presenting individual ideas to a large audience without the inhibiting effects of needing to speak out in public.

Although, as indicated above, electronic brainstorming appears to be more effective than conventional brainstorming, there is a group size effect in that electronic brainstorming with small groups does not compare well with small social groups utilising what have been called 'nominal group' techniques. (Dubrin, 1994). The nominal group technique was devised in the 1960s by Delbecq and Van de Ven (see Korhonen, 1991). The group is called 'nominal' because people present their ideas initially without interacting with each other, as they would in most social groups. Initially a six-stage process was suggested. Subsequently a number of modifications of this six-stage process were developed but all these retain the following stages.

1. The problem to be solved is clearly defined at the outset.
2. Individuals in the group work independently to formulate written responses to the problem.
3. Written responses are presented to the group by the individuals concerned and the ideas generated are shared and discussed by the group (round robin stage).
4. The group then decides on a form of ranking of the solutions generated. It should be stressed that consensus in this technique derives from the ranking of individual solutions rather than from the changing and integrating of individual input.

The advantages and disadvantages of nominal group techniques have been ably summarised by Korhonen. From the point of view of utilising this technique in the instruction of adults it has some strong advantages. The chief of these is that it satisfies the need expressed by many adult learners for group interaction while imposing on the group a degree of closure in that the problem is well defined initially and in that the technique specifies a final decision-making process. The technique also reduces the influence of dominant group members, which is especially advantageous if the group contains reticent learners whose level of confidence is easily threatened. By also minimising the role of the group leader, it restricts the tendency often found in tutors to overmanage learning groups and can, in addition, be utilised by students working in groups without formal tutors. The technique also exposes learners to a breadth of ideas and, consequently, it is particularly well suited to groups whose members come from differing academic backgrounds or disciplines.

The disadvantages of the technique lie in the fact that the final stage is competitive rather than consensual and that while it may provide a platform for normally reticent learners to put forward their ideas, the final ranking may prove demotivating for members with the solutions that have been ranked as least acceptable. But perhaps the chief disadvantage of nominal groups is the extent to which it emphasises the exchange of individual solutions rather than the integration of idea and concepts.

Research on the output of nominal groups has tended to indicate that on most cognitive tasks (eg those requiring logic, judgement or problem-solving skill) groups outperform the level of their best member (Gruenfeld and Hollingshead, 1993) and as a result research on cognitive processes in small groups has, until recently, tended to focus chiefly on how group activity affects individual cognition.

More recently, however, interest in the general area of social cognition has influenced a reappraisal of cognition in groups. This interest in social cognition, together with the perception that nominal groups (see above) have tended to emphasise competition rather than consensus, has led to attention being turned away from individual cognition in group interaction and towards the collective aspects of cognition in groups. New research paradigms ('sociocognition', Levine and Resnick, 1993; 'transactive memory', Wegner *et al.*, 1991; 'group culture and socialisation', Levine and Moreland, 1991) have begun to be applied to group interaction. These paradigms suggest that cognition is a product of social interchange and is constructed, shared and distributed among groups of individuals during the course of social interaction.

The theory underpinning this proposition and the research that is being currently carried out from this perspective support the idea that individuals in social interaction do not simply exchange or replace cognitions. Rather, while they may do this to some extent, they are more likely to engage in active reconciliation and integrative processes, leading to the emergence of unique, collectively produced conceptualisations, including ideas, representations, solutions and arguments that no individual had at the outset (Gruenfeld and Hollingshead, 1993).

The implications of this orientation for learning in groups is that, while it might be appropriate to follow the first three stages of nominal group techniques (ie the formulation of the problem, individual production of solutions and individual presentation of solutions), these first three stages should be followed by group collaboration in the sharing, discussion, modification and integration of individual solutions rather than by the evaluation and ranking of individual solutions. This modification of nominal group techniques fits well with recent research on minority and majority influence (eg Nemeth, 1986), attitude change (eg Petty and Cacioppo,1981) and cognitive development (eg Doise and Mugny, 1984), which suggest that social interaction is not characterised only by convergent influences such as imitation and conformity but is also characterised by divergent cognitive responses to the views of others, and that such divergence when shared leads to novel thoughts and interpretations that are unlikely to be generated by group members working on an individual basis. In short, the cognitive tasks and processes of groups cannot be divorced from their social and communicative contexts and we now turn to this aspect of learning in groups.

Social learning and communication in groups

Anyone working in groups with adult learners is soon aware that there are strong social forces operating in small groups. These social pressures acting on group members are immediately obvious, in that no matter how structured the task the group is gathered to carry out, most individual group members tend to be apprehensive of evaluation by others and clearly monitor their own and others' social behaviour. Further it is always clear that in any group there are very marked individual differences in the extent to which group members are prepared to speak out, especially initially. These social and interpersonal pressures undoubtedly affect group members but the extent to which such changes enhance (or indeed detract from) members' social or communicative skills is more difficult to monitor or evaluate.

Indeed, in general, there is a dearth of material relating to evaluations of such learning outcomes in adult groups. There is, however, one exception to this general statement and this is with respect to the large numbers of studies conducted in the 1960s, 70s and 80s of groups that were specifically set up to teach such skills. These groups tend to be grouped generically as sensitivity or T-groups, and the major areas in which they are conducted are in training for the caring professions and (more commonly in the recent past than at the moment) in management training.

The rationale for such groups lies largely in the work of psychodynamic theorists, notably in the psychoanalytic approach of Bion (1961) and the person-centred approach of Rogers (1969).

Within these psychodynamic perspectives it is suggested that small groups move through a number of discrete phases throughout their life history and that the social dynamics of these phases impinge powerfully on group members. The model most often referred to with respect to these phases was outlined by Tuckman (1965), who suggested that, not only in T-groups, but in all small groups there are four stages of group development: 'forming'; 'storming'; 'norming'; and 'performing'. By this he implied that, after an initial stage of establishment (forming), groups experience a phase of confusion (storming). This is followed by a more harmonious phase in which members begin to interact positively and to share values about the nature of the group and the task the group is engaged on (ie the group members begin to develop group norms). The final phase is one in which the group ideally begins to achieve its objectives (performing).

At the close of training, the desired outcomes of sensitivity or T-groups are the following.

1. Members should feel more favourably towards themselves with respect to their interpersonal and social skills.
2. Members should feel more able to control their actions, be more open to new experiences and be more concerned with giving and receiving affection.
3. Members' social and interpersonal behaviour should be perceived by others as changed for the better, particularly with respect to improved communication skills (Smith 1980).

There has been a large number of evaluations of the social and interpersonal learning in small sensitivity or T-groups. One of the most comprehensive of these was carried out by Lieberman *et al.* (1973). This study compared reports of the learning mechanisms felt to be most important by members of small groups with independent measures by others of what group members had learnt. The most endorsed sources of learning were feedback from others, learning that one's problems were not unique, receiving advice or suggestions, understanding areas of oneself previously unknown and feeling positively about the cohesion of the group. Smith (1980) suggests that this and other similar studies indicate that the more fruitful formulations of the change process are those that incorporate some reference to the warmth and acceptance of the group and some understanding of or thinking about one's behaviour.

Smith himself (1987) collected data from 154 professionals who had participated in ten human relations sensitivity workshops. Outcome was assessed in terms of reported self-benefit and in terms of one's relations with others not present. The maximum gain on the self-benefit criterion was found when the principal learning group in the workshop focused on sharing feelings arising from life and past experiences. The greatest gain on the relationship benefit was when workshop sessions were relatively undifferentiated and when the trainers interpreted or clarified what was taking place.

Controlled studies in tertiary education are scarce, but in one study

McConnell (1971) studied the use of four-day groups with 120 masters degree students in a business school setting, comparing them to doctoral degree students and also to students on an introductory degree. After the group training experience, the masters students rated themselves as significantly more at ease with their new environment, more satisfied with their peers and more aware of themselves, whereas the two control groups indicated no such improvements. These effects did not last, however, when the masters students rated themselves after a period of two months. McConnell discusses these negative findings with respect to learning in the small group to the nature of the masters degree programme rather than the failure of small group techniques. However, his findings are not dissimilar to a number of others which have found sensitivity or T-group training to confer more short- than long-term benefits.

T-groups were widely used in organisational training in the 1970s and in general were found to be most effective when embedded in a context of organisational support that endorsed the values of such groups (Smith, 1980). As noted above, such groups are now relatively uncommon except in areas of interpersonal training in the caring professions, particularly in social work.

Explanations of why changes in social and communication skills may arise from taking part in small groups vary widely and include those deriving from social learning theory that stress the reinforcement provided by positive feedback from group members and group leaders and explanations drawing on the insight and understanding provided by the interpretations of group trainers. Psychodynamic accounts tend to identify learning as occurring where two paradoxical messages impinge on the learner, the messages centring on support on the one hand and confrontation on the other. When this occurs it is suggested that learners are able to move on to a phase where they can take more personal responsibility for their actions and are therefore able to sustain changes following the group experience (Smith, 1980).

Providing group learning for changes in social and interpersonal behaviour is a task that requires considerable effort from the viewpoint of the trainer. Klein (1970) suggests that trainers need three skills: an understanding of the relevant theory; a knowledge of the application of such theory in practice; and trained experience in its use. These are demanding requirements and it is not surprising, in view of them, that the explicit use of groups for social and communication learning is largely within the caring professions, where trainers with such skills are to be found.

Factors impinging on adult learning in groups: the nature of the task and its assessment

As the discussion above indicates, the nature of group learning depends crucially on the nature of the task. In the section above we have indicated that small groups are commonly used to enhance cognitive skills with repect to problem solving.

A vocational/occupational area in which particular use has been made of group work is computing, and in a recent review article of 35 studies, which covered childen as well as adult learners, Stephenson (1994) concludes that these studies indicate that computer training courses can be as effective as individual courses and that there may be some benefit for these being single sex. He also concludes that there is no clear consensus as to whether the small groups should be homogeneous in aptitude in that the aptitude grouping issue in computer training courses is probably highly interactive with software focus, subject material, ability differential and course length.

Another area where group work would appear to be particularly suitable and where it is commonly used is in the completion of group or laboratory projects (Kolmos, quoted in Callaghan *et al.*, 1994). Kolmos suggests that learning can be particularly enhanced in such groups if tutors specifically and explicitly draw attention to metacognitive skills. However, although the pedagogic and cost-effective benefits of using groups for group projects in tertiary education may seem clear, problems frequently arise in practice in the assessment of such work. This is because students often report grievances when group work is jointly assessed, in that more conscientious students frequently believe that less motivated students benefit unfairly from the former's hard work.

The present authors (Callaghan *et al.*, 1994) investigated these issues in a recent study of the use of a non-assessed group project on a media studies course. Thirty-one students working on non-assessed joint projects filled in a questionnaire at three stages: at the commencement of the project; at the end of the project; and three months after the end of the project. A number of questions concerned their attitudes to assessed versus non-assessed group projects. The results indicated that, following the group experience of their non-assessed projects, students rated non-assessed group work as preferable from the point of view of group dynamics but assessed group work as preferable from the point of view of learning outcomes. Extended comments and interviews reinforced this in that these students who had had experience of assessed group projects in the past, reported enjoying group projects more when these were non-assessed but felt that if such projects were assessed they learned more because they felt the need to work in a more task-oriented manner. Some students also indicated that they had felt considerable resentment when working on assessed group projects in the past when certain group members had been 'freeloaders', and they argued that if group projects were to be jointly assessed, safeguards against such individuals benefiting unfairly had to be built in.

Evaluation of small group working can be problematic but some form of independent analysis is essential if group methods are to be perceived as being superior to traditional learning approaches. Jacques (1991) presents a comprehensive review of current techniques in the evaluation of groups in his excellent book on learning in groups. He concludes that 'Evaluation works best if it is seen as a continuous process engaged in by all those who contribute to the setting up and participating in the group.'

Although detailed evaluations of the comparative advantage in utilising small group learning across different academic and vocational areas is scanty, it does seems clear that diverse subject and vocational areas will continue to utilise small group learning in different ways and that the manner in which use is made of small groups depends on a large number of factors, including type of learner as well as subject area. With respect to this consideration there is one particular group of adult learners who, in our opinion, are most likely to benefit from small group learning and this group is considered below.

Small groups in adult literacy and basic education

The use of small groups in adult literacy and basic education has been stimulated by a desire to provide a more learner-centred and collaborative learning environment than is provided by formal tertiary education, where the emphasis is, of necessity, far more likely to focus on learning that can be formally and individually assessed from the point of view of issuing diplomas, certificates and degrees. Adult literacy courses, on the other hand, can concentrate on student-centred learning that is not only enhancing from the point of view of the learner but also freed from the constraints of formal assessment.

For this sector, Imel (1992) suggests that the major advantages of the small group are that it: allows for integration of critical thinking; permits learners to expand their repertoire of learning strategies; breaks down isolation and provides peer support; enhances learners' self-esteem; and provides a cooperative participative environment. She believes, however, that there are three major associated disadvantages: difficulty in accommodating a wide range of needs and abilities; negotiation of a learner-centred curriculum; and more preparation time.

She proposes that such groups should be small in size (5–15 individuals) and that the tutor should act as a facilitator of learning and leader, rather than as a person conveying information. She also recommends that tutors should be prepared to adjust their leadership style to the developmental stage of the group. For example, the early stages may require a more directive style than the later stages.

Imel's survey of group learning and adult literacy points to the necessity, in facilitating group learning with adults, of taking the total context of the learning situation into account. This emphasis on the learning context is one, we believe, that should be extended into all aspects of group learning as we indicate below.

Concluding remarks

In conclusion we propose, following on from the work of Korhonen (1991) that the choice of group as a vehicle for adult learning should take the following considerations into account:

1. the appropriateness of the particular group method chosen in relation to the knowledge, ability and skill of the participants;
2. the purpose to which the desired learning is directed;
3. the institutional context in which the learning takes place;
4. the extent to which needs of the individual members are met by the internal dynamics of the group;
5. an understanding that the utilisation of the group is as an instructional or problem-solving method and not as a recreational activity.

References

Abson, D (1994) 'The effects of peer evaluation on the behaviour of undergraduate students working in tutorless groups' in *Group and Interactive Learning*, H C Foot, C J Howe, A Anderson, A K Tomlin and D A Warden (eds), 153–8, Computational Mechanics Publications, Southampton.

Bowen, H C (1907) *Froebel and Education by Self Activity*, Heinemann, London.

Bion, W R (1961) *Experiences in Groups: and Other Papers*, Tavistock Publications, London.

Callaghan, M, Knox, A, Mowatt, I and Siann, G (1994) 'Empirical projects and small group learning' in *Group and Interactive Learning* H C Foot, C J Howe, A Anderson, A K Tomlin and D A Warden (eds), 165–70, Computational Mechanics Publications, Southampton.

Cassels, J (1990) *Britain's Real Skill Shortage*, Sage, London.

Connolly, T, Routhieaux, R L and Schneider, S K (1993) On the effectiveness of brainstorming: test of one underlying cognitive mechanism, *Small Group Research*, 24(4), 490–503.

Diamond, M J (1964) From Skinner to Satori? Towards a social learning analysis of encounter group behavior change, *Journal of Applied Behavioral Science*, 10, 133–48.

Doise, W and Mugny, G (1984) *The Social Development of the Intellect*, Pergamon, Oxford.

Dubrin, A J (1994) *Applying Psychology: Individual and Organizational Effectiveness* (4th edn), Prentice-Hall, London.

Griffiths, M (1994) The use of study packs in small groups as a form of learning: a qualitative study of student opinion, *Psychology Teaching Review*, 3(2), 118–24.

Gruenfeld, D H and Hollingshead, A R (1993) Sociocognition in work groups: the evolution of group integrative complexity and its relation to task performance, *Small Group Research*, 24(4), 383–405.

Hare, A P (1982) *Creativity In Small Groups*, Sage, London.

Imel, S (1992) *Small Groups in Adult Literacy and Basic Education*, Office of Educational Research and Improvement, Washington, DC.

Jacques, D (1991) *Learning in Groups* (2nd edn), Kogan Page, London.

Kaye, T, Wolfe, R and Fletcher, C (1984) *Adult Learning, Individual, Group and Community*, 3rd level course, Open University, Milton Keynes.

Klein, J (1970) *Working with Groups*, Hutchinson, London.

Korhonen, L J (1991) 'Nominal group technique' in *Adult Learning Methods*, M W Galbraith (ed.), 247–60, Krieger, Malabar, Florida.

Levine, J M and Moreland, R L (1991) 'Culture and socialization in work groups' in *Perspectives on Socially Shared Cognition*, L B Resnick, J M Levine and S D Teasley (eds), 257–79, American Psychological Association, Washington DC.

Levine, J M and Resnick, L B (1993) Social foundations of cognition, *Annual Review of Psychology*, 44, 585–612.

Lieberman, M A, Yalom, I D and Miles, M B (1973) *Encounter Groups: First Facts*, Basic Books, New York.

McConnell, H K (1971) Individual differences as mediators of participant behavior and self-descriptive change in two human relations training programs, *Organizational Behavior and Human Performance*, 6, 550–72.

Millis, B J (1991) Enhancing adult learning through cooperative small groups, *Continuing Higher Education*, 55(3), 144–54.

Nemeth, C (1986) Differential contributions of minority and majority influence, *Psychological Review*, 93, 23–32.

Osborn, A (1957) *Applied Imagination*, Scribners, New York.

Petty, R E and Cacioppo, J T (1981) *Attitudes and Persuasion: Classic and Contemporary Approaches*, William C Brown, Dubuque, Iowa.

Rogers, A (1986) *Teaching Adults*, Open University Press, Milton Keynes.

Rogers, C R (1969) *Freedom To Learn*, Merrill, Ohio.

Siann, G (1994) *Gender, Sex and Sexuality: Contemporary Psychological Perspectives*, Taylor and Francis, London.

Smith, P B (1980) *Group Processes And Social Change*, Harper & Row, London.

Smith, P B (1987) The laboratory design and group process as determinators of the outcome of sensitivity training, *Small Group Behavior*, 18(3), 291–308.

Stephenson, S D (1994) The use of small groups in computer-based training: a review of recent literature, *Computers in Human Behavior*, 10(3), 243–59.

Stockdale, J E (1987) *Desexing Computers*, Proceedings of the Fourth GASAT Conference, vol. 1, University of Michigan, Ann Arbor, Michigan.

Topping, K (1992) Cooperative learning and peer tutoring: an overview, *The Psychologist*, 5, 151–7.

Tuckman, B W (1965) Developmental sequences in small groups, *Psychological Bulletin*, 63, 384–99.

Wegner, D M, Erber, R and Raymond, P (1991) Transactive memory in close relationships, *Journal of Personality and Social Psychology*, 61, 923–39.

Wilson, F M (1995) *Organizational Behaviour and Gender*, McGraw-Hill, London.

CHAPTER 9

Peer Tutoring for Flexible and Effective Adult Learning

Keith Topping

Introduction

Research on teaching and learning in further and higher education is much less voluminous than that on teaching and learning in schools. Although there have been a number of books on the topic of adult learning, both the quantity and quality of research in this area is surprisingly limited, considering the vast resources expended on the tertiary sector.

However, the quality and cost-effectiveness of teaching and learning in the sector is increasingly coming under the microscope. There has long been concern that traditional curricula, delivered and assessed in traditional ways, promote a surface approach to learning rather than a deep or even a strategic approach (Entwistle, 1992). Teaching quality assessment exercises consistently result in criticism of departments for failing to promote the development of transferable skills in their students (Barnett, 1992). At the same time, increased student numbers coupled with reduced resources have often resulted in larger class sizes, thus encouraging a reversion to a traditional lecturing style of delivery and a reduction in small group and tutorial contact; in short, less interactive teaching and learning.

The dual requirement to improve teaching quality while 'doing more with less' has recently increased interest in peer tutoring in higher and further education. However, it would be unwise to seize upon peer tutoring as a universal, undifferentiated and instant panacea.

Definitions of peer tutoring

Peer tutoring is a very old practice, traceable back at least as far as the ancient Greeks. Archaic definitions of peer tutoring perceived the peer tutor as a surrogate teacher, in a linear model of the transmission of knowledge, from teacher to tutor to tutee. Later, it was realised that the peer tutoring interaction was qualitatively different from that between a teacher and a student, and involved different advantages and disadvantages. At this point of development, a widely accepted definition might have been 'more advanced learners helping less advanced learners to learn in co-operative working pairs or small groups carefully organised by a professional teacher'.

However, as development and research in different formats of peer tutoring proceeded apace in more recent years (Topping, 1992), it became clear that peer tutoring is not necessarily about transmission from the more advanced (who already have the knowledge and skills) to the less advanced (who are yet to acquire them). The traditional assumption of cross-ability matching in peer tutoring was often taken to imply cross-year or cross-age matching too, and this latter assumption has been even more comprehensively dispelled.

As peer tutoring has become much more various, defining it becomes more difficult and a current definition seems so broad as to be rather bland; 'people from similar social groupings who are not professional teachers helping each other to learn and learning themselves by teaching'. However, this flexible definition for the new millennium does have the benefit of including reference to the gains accruing from the tutoring process to the tutor.

Increasingly, peer tutoring projects target gains for both tutors and tutees; not only added value but double added value. Peer tutoring is characterised by specific role taking; at any point someone has the job of tutor while the other (or the others) are in the role of tutee(s). Peer tutoring typically has a high focus on curriculum content. Although participants do tend to 'feel good' about learning, curriculum mastery is targeted, and not the 'feel good factor'. Peer tutoring projects usually also outline quite specific procedures for interaction, in which the participants are likely to have training which is generic or specific or both. In addition, their interaction may be scaffolded to a greater or lesser extent by the provision of structured materials, among which a degree of student choice may be available.

Peer tutoring can be additionally defined by exclusion. To be a peer tutor is not to act as a surrogate professional teacher. Nor is it merely having a student make a short presentation to the group. Many developments in teaching and learning in higher education have connections with peer tutoring, but can be differentiated from it. These include 'mentoring', 'peer counselling', 'cooperative learning' (in higher education sometimes designated as group project or syndicate learning) and 'peer assessment'. Other related learning methods which can be found in association with peer tutoring (but should be differentiated from it) include games and simulations, learning contracts, learner managed learning and study skills training.

A typology of peer tutoring

A typology of peer tutoring could include many dimensions, but for current purposes eleven different parameters will suffice.

1. The first and most obvious way in which peer tutoring projects differ is with reference to the content or the curriculum to be covered. This may be knowledge or skills oriented, or a combination. The scope of peer tutoring is very wide. Projects are reported in the literature in: adult literacy; anatomy; biology; business studies; chemistry; computer science; dentistry; engineering; English; geography; interpersonal skills; law; languages; mathematics; medicine; nursing; organisational behaviour; physics; psychology; social work; sociology; statistics; and study skills. The applications are growing all the time.

2. The contact constellations of peer tutoring can also vary considerably. Echoing traditional teacher practice, some projects operate with one tutor working simultaneously with a small group of tutees. However, the size of this group can vary from two to three tutees right through to thirty or more. Less traditional, and more intensive, is peer tutoring in pairs, arguably likely to maximise commitment and time on a task, provided there is a clear structure and the pair can relate to each other.

3. The third parameter in a typology of peer tutoring is the year of study or age of the tutors and tutees. In higher education, the year of study is not well correlated with the chronological age of a student, especially as the intake of mature students increases. It is usual, therefore, to refer to 'same-year' tutoring or 'cross-year' tutoring (rather than cross-age or same-age, as one would in schools).

4. More important than the issue of year membership is the fourth parameter of participant ability, achievement or advancement in the content area to be tutored. Whereas many projects operate on a cross-ability basis (even if they are same year), increasingly there is interest in same-ability tutoring (where the tutor perhaps has superior mastery of only a very small portion of the curriculum, or the tutor mastery is insignificantly different from that of the tutee but the pair are to work towards a shared, deeper and hopefully correct understanding).

5. Role continuity is the fifth parameter. Especially in same-ability tutoring, the roles of tutor and tutee need not be permanently assigned to particular individuals. Structured switching of roles at strategic moments (reciprocal tutoring) has the advantage of building in greater novelty and a wider boost to self-esteem, in that all participants get to be tutors.

6. Peer tutoring projects vary enormously in location of operation. Some occur in regular teaching rooms, some in less formal rooms within the institution, some in domestic homes and some in other places such as community centres.

7. The situation is similar with the seventh parameter; time of tutoring. Whereas some projects schedule peer tutoring within regular class-contact times, other projects designate it as a supplementary activity to occur outwith this time. Contact times may be carefully pre-specified or left to the judgement of the participants, or may be a combination of both. Some projects operate outside ordinary office hours, and tutoring can occur in the evenings, at weekends or at summer schools.

8. Peer tutoring projects also differ in terms of the characteristics of the tutees (eighth parameter) and tutors (ninth parameter) on which they are targeted. Many projects operate on a mixed ability basis for all students within a course, module or year group. However, other projects target particular tutee groups; perhaps the especially able or gifted where there is concern that they are not being extended intellec-tually, or other groups of students who are construed as being at risk of failure or drop out or underachievement. Projects have been targeted on ethnic, religious and other minorities, in an attempt to positively dis-criminate by improving the quality of such groups' teaching and learn-ing experiences. Students identified as having low levels of relevant skills on entry to courses can likewise be targeted.

9. Traditionally, there was an assumption that tutors should be among the 'best students' (ie those who are most like the professional teachers). A problem here can be that a very large differential in levels of ability and interest in such a situation can prove understimulating for the tutor, who is unlikely to gain cognitively from the interactions. Recently there has been a great deal more interest in deploying tutors whose capabili-ties are nearer to those of the tutees, so that both members of the pair find some cognitive challenge in their joint activities. As tutoring is in-tended to be 'learning by teaching', it is necessary to ensure that tutors gain intellectually as well as in other ways.

This also implies that students who are merely average (or even less) should be seriously considered as potential tutors. Although the quality of tutoring they offer may not be as good as that of the high flyers, if both tutor and tutees are learning, the aggregate gain is bound to be greater than if only the tutee is learning. Additionally, tutors of more proximate ability may be more effective models and show greater empathy.

10. It will be clear from the foregoing that peer tutoring projects can have many different objectives, and this is the tenth parameter on which they strikingly differ. Projects may target intellectual gains, formal academic achievement, affective and attitudinal gains, social and emotional gains, self-image and self-concept gains or any combination of all these and more. Organisational objectives might include reducing drop out, increasing access and so forth.

11. Finally, peer tutoring may be motivated entirely by intrinsic reward, or

forms of extrinsic reward may be involved, such as course accreditation, other certification or personal references for the tutors. Monetary reward is not unusual in North America, although it is rare in Europe.

Theoretical advantages of peer tutoring

The cognitive processes involved in peer tutoring have been explored by various writers over the years, many of whom emphasised the value of verbalisation and questioning (eg Gartner *et al.*, 1971). A neo-Piagetian interpretation of individual development through the cognitive conflict and challenge inherent in many forms of peer-assisted learning is offered by Doise and Mugny (1984).

However, peer-assisted learning is more fully understood through the social interactionist (or sociocultural or social constructivist) view of cognitive development, which can be traced at least as far back as Vygotsky, whose centenary of birth was celebrated on 5 November 1996. Supported (or 'scaffolded') exploration through social and cognitive interaction with a more experienced peer in relation to a task of a level of difficulty within the tutee's 'zone of proximal development' remains a theoretical cornerstone of peer-assisted learning (Vygotsky, 1978).

This theme has been further developed by Rogoff (1990) under the label 'apprenticeship in thinking'. Peer tutoring is often promoted on the grounds that, for the tutors, it is 'learning by teaching'. This view is expanded in the old saying 'to teach is to learn twice', a view shared by many professional teachers.

Simply preparing to be a peer tutor has been proposed to enhance cognitive processing in the tutor, by increasing attention to and motivation for the task, and necessitating review of existing knowledge and skills. Consequently, existing knowledge is transformed by re-organisation, involving new associations and a new integration. The act of tutoring itself involves further cognitive challenge, particularly with respect to simplification, clarification and exemplification.

An excellent study by Annis (1983) compared three groups of students: one that merely read the material to be studied (history); one that read the material in the expectation of having to teach it to a peer; and a third that read the material with the expectation of teaching it to a peer and then actually carried this out. Allocation to conditions was random. A 48-item test of both specific and general competence was the outcome measure. The 'read only' group gained less than the 'read to teach' group, who in turn gained less than the 'read and teach' group. The tutors gained more than the tutees.

A similar study by Benware and Deci (1984) compared the relative effectiveness of reading to learn for a test and reading for learning to teach a peer. Subjects were randomly assigned to conditions and the outcome measure was a 24-item test of both rote memory and conceptual understanding. Although both groups performed equally well on rote learning, the 'learn to teach' group performed better on higher order, conceptual understanding. Furthermore, on a questionnaire regarding motivation and learning experiences, the learn to teach group perceived their experience as more active and interesting.

Many other advantages have been claimed for peer tutoring and related forms of peer-assisted learning (eg Greenwood *et al.*, 1990). Pedagogical advantages include active and participative learning, immediate feedback, swift prompting, lowered anxiety with correspondingly higher self-disclosure, and greater student ownership of the learning process. The pupil-to-teacher ratio is much reduced (although so, perhaps, is the quality of teaching) and engaged time on task increased. Opportunities to respond are high, and opportunities to make errors and be corrected similarly high.

In addition to immediate cognitive gains, improved retention, greater metacognitive awareness and better application of knowledge and skills to new situations have been claimed. Motivational and attitudinal gains could include greater commitment, improved self-esteem, self-confidence and greater empathy with others. Much of this links with work on self-efficacy and motivated learning (Schunk, 1987), leading on to the self-regulation of learning and performance (Schunk and Zimmermann, 1994). Modelling and attributional feedback are important here. Perhaps peer tutoring can go some way towards combating the dependency culture associated with superficial learning.

From a social psychological viewpoint, social isolation might be reduced, the enthusiasm for and the application of the subject modelled, and aspirations raised, while combating any excess of individualistic competition between students.

Economically, it might prove possible to teach more students more effectively, freeing staff time for other purposes. Politically, peer tutoring delegates the management of learning to the learners in a democratic way, seeks to empower students rather than de-skill them by dependency on imitation of a master culture and might reduce student dissatisfaction and unrest. Whether these theories and claims are supported by hard evidence is another matter.

Effectiveness of peer tutoring within higher education

Previous reviews and surveys of peer tutoring in higher and further education include those of Goldschmid and Goldschmid (1976), Cornwall (1979), Whitman (1988), Lee (1988), Lawson (1989), Maxwell (1990) and Moore-West *et al.* (1990). All of these are well worth reading, but tend to be discursive rather than conclusive. An exception is Lee's (1988) comparison of the cost-effectiveness in reducing student drop-out of peer tutoring, peer counselling and funded remediation programmes with professional staff. The latter were concluded to be 'very cost-ineffective' by comparison. A more recent review of the literature is found in Topping (1996), and this is briefly summarised below.

Peer tutoring is already widely used in further and higher education, in a variety of different forms. Surveys suggest several hundred institutions deploy this interactive method of teaching and learning. Of course, the existence of one small pilot project at a time in an institution does not constitute peer tutoring on a large scale across the curriculum which is quality controlled and embedded within the organisational culture. Of the different formats and methods, the personalised system of instruction (PSI) and supplemental instruction (SI) have been the most extensively implemented in recent years.

Cross-year small-group tutoring, the format least disparate from traditional methods, can work well. Studies of achievement gains almost all indicate outcomes as good as, or better than, group tutoring by faculty, and student subjective feedback is generally very positive.

PSI involves independent learning from programmed texts followed by peer assessment. It has been widely used and evaluated in the USA. Two-thirds of studies found PSI involvement associated with higher class marks and 93 per cent of studies found PSI associated with higher final examination performance, compared to control groups. PSI also improved longer term retention of the material learnt.

SI adopts a very different model of operation (cross-year process support) and has become more popular outside the USA than PSI. There is persuasive evidence of impact on drop-out rates, course grades and graduation outcomes. Graduation outcomes tend not to be increased to the same extent as by PSI, but SI targets 'difficult' courses so the two cannot be directly compared.

Same-year, dyadic, fixed-role tutoring has been the subject of several studies over the years, research of mixed quality yielding mixed results. However, two good quality studies found improved achievement from this format, and three others found achievement the same as with faculty teaching. Same-year, dyadic, reciprocal tutoring has been the focus of fewer studies, but these were of high quality (eg Goldschmid and Goldschmid, 1976, Fantuzzo *et al.*, 1989b). Increased attainment was demonstrated by all four studies. There was also evidence of reduced student stress. The degree of structure in the programme was also related to outcomes. Cross-year, dyadic, fixed-role tutoring has been the subject of three studies of poor quality. Same-year group tutoring has yielded positive subjective feedback in four studies, but no harder evidence on achievement outcomes.

Nine studies of peer-assisted writing or co-composition have shown generally favourable outcomes in terms of subjective feedback. The process can be scaffolded to a greater or lesser degree, but usually includes an interactive framework for ideas generation, drafting, reading, editing, best copy and evaluating, the latter stage often through peer assessment. Gains in writing competence were shown in two or three of the four studies examining this, despite the inherent difficulty of this kind of research. There is little evidence that peer assistance in distance learning improves achievement outcomes, although there is evidence of positive subjective feedback, but this area is even more difficult to research.

In summary, three methods of peer tutoring in further and higher education have already been widely used, have been demonstrated to be effective, and merit wider use in practice. These are cross-year, small-group tutoring, the PSI and SI. Same-year, dyadic, reciprocal tutoring has been demonstrated to be effective, but has been little used, and merits much wider deployment. Same-year, dyadic, fixed-role tutoring and peer-assisted writing have shown considerable, but not necessarily consistent, promise and should be the focus of continuing experimentation and more research of better quality. In three areas there are barely the beginnings of a satisfactory body of evaluation research: cross-year, dyadic, fixed-role tutoring, same-year group tutoring and peer-assisted distance learning. It is essential that subsequent research strives to achieve adequate quality in design and execution, and addresses issues of achievement gain and parameters of successful course completion as well as subjective participant feedback. If achievement gains can be demonstrated that go beyond the narrow confines of the institutional assessment system and endure in the longer term, so much the better. This implies that impact upon wider cognitive abilities and transferable skills should also be measured. However, peer tutoring is always likely to be a relatively small component of the whole higher education experience, so the extent to which it is realistic to expect associated gains to be widespread, maintained, generalised and measurable is debatable.

Two recent studies of peer tutoring within higher education

A same-year, dyadic, peer tutoring in undergraduate mathematics was reported by Topping et al. (1996a), related to the work of Fantuzzo and his colleagues (1989a, 1989b). The project was located in a calculus class of 45 students and tutoring occurred bi-weekly for a whole academic year, substituting for some traditional teaching. Although fixed role in intention, some reciprocal tutoring occurred spontaneously.

Better degree examination results were evident in the experimental year, compared to the previous year, but the experimental and comparison years were not identical in terms of composition and initial ability, and the apparent gains could not definitely be attributed to the impact of peer tutoring. However, the conservative interpretation that tutoring results in no deterioration in degree exam outcomes, even when substituted for more traditional forms of teaching, was supported by the data. Poor attenders had worse outcomes, but causality was difficult to attribute. Drop-out rates did not change significantly, continuing at low levels.

However, subjective but specific and structured post hoc feedback from experimental students indicated that tutoring had added value in terms of improvements in a variety of transferable skills, most notably: filling of gaps in knowledge; confidence; oral communication; writing; presentation; problem-solving; improvisation/innovation; collaboration; awareness of one's strengths and weaknesses; awareness of one's own learning style; and awareness of how others learn. Notable social benefits included improvements in peer relations, student–staff relations and better student integration in the course group. Thus peer tutoring appeared to add value to teaching and learning.

The exam results of the (possibly weaker) non-mathematics major students in this project showed the most striking increase (notwithstanding the non-equivalence of the comparison year), but those with the poorest attendance (possibly the weakest) did much worse than the rest. Perhaps peer tutoring can help weaker students differentially, but only if they attend.

A majority of the studies in the literature evaluated relatively short-term tutoring interventions, unlike this project, which lasted for a full academic year. More longer-term project evaluations, preferably with post-project follow-up, are needed. A larger related study was reported by Topping *et al*. (1997). A same-year, dyadic, reciprocal peer tutoring experiment was undertaken with 125 undergraduates in a year-long class in mathematical economics, initially on a supplementary basis and latterly on a substitutional basis. The innovation affected only 7 per cent of the total original contact time of the course.

Training and both verbal and written instructions and two peer assessment checklists were provided. Participants were expected to plan, prepare, present, give feedback and question, tutor, engage in teamwork and check correctness on their chosen topic and material. Supervision and support from staff were available on request.

In the first supplementary phase, when matching of pairs was random and supervision not close, difficulties were encountered with accommodation, timetabling, and other organisational and contextual problems. Attendance declined, and low rates of student planning, preparation, time on task and requests for staff help were evident. The substitutional phase featured closer supervision by staff, and higher rates of attendance, time on task and completion of self-recording. Activity patterns differed over time and according to supervisor, and this appeared to have an effect (albeit not statistically significant) on summative outcomes. Subjective process questionnaire feedback from participants identified few major problems but noted low rates of preparation and planning and time on task, a substantial proportion of time working alone and low usage of the materials provided to help structure the process of tutoring.

On summative assessment for the course, the experimental and previous comparison years seemed very similar early in the academic year. Overall final class marks were also very similar, except for a small number of economics majors taking BSc degrees, who performed significantly better in the experimental year. Likewise, there were no significant differences on mean degree exam marks, although the experimental BScs again did better than in the comparison year.

Those students attending substitutional peer tutoring regularly attained significantly higher class marks and degree exam marks than those attending irregularly. Early in the academic year, the high attenders already had significantly higher mean attainment than low attenders on class examinations, but not on essay marks. Student drop-out was substantially lower in the experimental year, but not statistically significantly.

Participants also gave subjective questionnaire feedback on the extent to which the peer tutoring had yielded cognitive, affective, social and transferable skill gains for them. Overall, cognitive and affective gains were reported by a minority. Better remembering, filling of gaps in knowledge and greater confidence were reported by about a third of respondents, and half reported improved awareness of their own strengths and weaknesses. Social effects were more frequent. Almost half reported better relations with academic staff and feeling more integrated in the course group, and a substantial majority felt their peer group relations had improved. Effects on transferable skills were also evident; almost half reporting better oral and problem solving skills, and more than half better collaborative skills. A third reported better writing, presentation and questioning skills. Regular attenders at peer tutoring sessions also showed significantly better outcomes than irregular attenders for a number of gains, including understanding, remembering, writing skills and problem solving.

Despite some initial difficulties in the supplementary phase, the peer tutoring project met many of the objectives set for it, particularly in improved communication, interpersonal and teamwork skills and awareness of strengths and weaknesses. Peer tutoring on a substitutional basis was again found to cost-effectively add value to teaching and learning in higher education.

Peer tutoring in adult basic education

Peer tutoring is not restricted to clever people. Everyone can be a tutor; everyone has something to give. Peer tutoring can also be found among adults with literacy difficulties. Volunteer tutoring has a long tradition, but volunteers tend to come from one sector of society and students from another, so the aura of Victorian altruism can be hard to escape. Alternative projects seek to deploy adults of restricted literacy to tutor other adults of even more restricted literacy, within the context of group or class meetings. Beyond this, training family, friends and workmates as tutors within the tutee's natural community context has shown encouraging results (Scoble *et al.*, 1988).

The literacy problems in less-developed countries around the world are of a scale unimaginable to the average UK teacher, and there will never be enough resources to solve these problems. Some form of low-technology, cost-effective self-help through peer tutoring is one of the few interventions viable in such contexts (see Topping, 1995).

Peer tutoring and mentoring in training and the workplace

Mentoring may be defined as 'an encouraging and supportive one-to-one relationship with a more experienced student or worker (who is not a line manager or assessor) in a joint area of interest.' Mentoring is characterised by positive role modelling, raising aspirations, positive reinforcement, open-ended counselling and joint problem solving. It is often cross-age, always cross-achievement, always fixed role (although mentees can become mentors themselves later), often cross-institution and often targeted on disadvantaged groups.

Both peer tutoring and mentoring can be found in day release courses in further education colleges, within youth training and employment training schemes and within the workplace. Both can occur on an informal, spontaneous basis, or be part of a structured scheme. Tutoring has focused on direct job skills and also on background transferable skills such as literacy and numeracy. However, mentoring is intrinsically extremely difficult to evaluate satisfactorily, and tutoring in the workplace has also generated mainly descriptive literature.

Organising peer tutoring

Like everything else in life, peer tutoring does not work well if organisation is poor or absent. When seeking to organise peer tutoring, seven basic questions must be answered (Topping, 1988). Who is going to do what to whom, why, when, where and how? The local context and its idiosyncrasies should inform the objectives for the initiative, which themselves should be realistic, or failure is inbuilt. Of course the typology of peer tutoring should be considered and a form of tutoring chosen that is most appropriate to local needs and resources. Do not assume that either colleagues or students will welcome the initiative, however much they used to complain about the old ways of doing it!

Units of curriculum need to be targeted that are particularly suitable for this purpose. Recruitment, selection and matching of tutors and tutees will need considerable thought; errors here can prove fatal. Initial introduction must be carefully managed. Contact logistics will need thinking through;

synchronising timetables can be a big problem. In addition to time, how are the participants to find a suitable place and space? Will they need particular materials, are these to be differentiated, and if so how are they accessed and individual progression criteria determined? How much planning and preparation will be required of students before tutoring sessions, and what action is possible if it is not done? Another possibility to consider is to require partners to generate and administer tests for each other. How is non-attendance to be managed?

What are the structured procedures for interaction to be, and how can they be modelled as part of proper training for tutors and tutees? Will the training be generic or specific to the curriculum and its tasks, or both? During training, partners should be introduced and information given in large groups followed by demonstration and practice of structured procedures for interaction in smaller groups, preferably in the room where tutoring will take place. Verbal and/or written information should not be expected to be effective by itself.

How can you be sure the tutors are not teaching wrong information or methods? What self-checking or reference to a master source is to be operated? What other monitoring and support (or quality assurance) arrangements can be provided within existing resources, and can you be sure the students will use them? It is obviously important that academic staff monitor closely the correctness of what pairs are doing, especially with weaker students, even if their help is not requested by the pair, who may be erroneously convinced that they are already correct or unwilling to request help. Student requests for staff help need to be strongly encouraged.

What form of assessment of learning outcomes will there be, and will it be in a form that relates to the interactive tutoring experience? Will the tutoring be accredited in any way? Finally, how is the tutoring project to be evaluated?A greater degree of structure is associated with better outcomes in the literature (eg Fantuzzo et al., 1989a, 1989b). Project planning should thus include measures to increase the degree of structure promptly should this prove necessary.

Conclusion

Peer tutoring, both informal and structured, will undoubtedly continue to spread in the world of adult learning. Small experimental initiatives are already leading to large-scale projects embedded within institutions, such as faculty-wide accredited cross-year tutoring (Topping et al., 1996c).

The implications for the role and function of teachers of adult learners are considerable, as peer tutoring appears to be at least as effective as traditional curriculum delivery through lectures, etc. In peer tutoring projects, academic staff remain essential to successful teaching and learning, but instead of

117

directly transmitting curriculum content they function as organisers, quality controllers and assessors of learning. Of course, there is no suggestion here that peer tutoring is other than one additional useful tool in the repertoire of university teachers. However, exploration in different curricular areas of the most cost-effective balance of the wider variety of teaching and learning methods now available is long overdue.

Even where the dominant culture is resistant to the introduction of structured peer tutoring, there is much that learners can do informally through their own enterprise. To facilitate this, a self-help guide to peer assisted learning for students has recently been produced (Donaldson and Topping, 1996), set in the context of the new movement toward learner-managed learning and learner empowerment.

References

Annis, L F (1983) The processes and effects of peer tutoring, *Human Learning,* 2(1), 39–47.

Barnett, R (1992) *Improving Higher Education,* Open University Press, Buckingham.

Benware, C A and Deci, E L (1984) Quality of learning with an active versus passive motivational set, *American Educational Research Journal,* 21(4), 755–65.

Cornwall, M G (1979) *Students as teachers: peer teaching in higher education,* COWO, University of Amsterdam, Amsterdam.

Doise, W and Mugny, G (1984) *The Social Development of the Intellect,* Pergamon Press, Oxford.

Donaldson, A J M and Topping, K J with Aithchison, R, Campbell, J, McKenzie, J and Wallis, D (1996) *Promoting Peer Assisted Learning among Students in Further and Higher Education* (SEDA Paper 96), Staff and Educational Development Association, Birmingham.

Donaldson, A J M and Topping, K J (1996) *A Student Self-Help Guide to Peer Assisted Learning,* Centre for Paired Learning, University of Dundee, Dundee.

Entwistle, N (1992) *The Impact of Teaching and Learning Outcomes in Higher Education: A Literature Review,* Universities and Colleges Staff Development Unit, CVCP, Sheffield.

Fantuzzo, J W, Dimeff, L A and Fox, S L (1989a) Reciprocal peer tutoring: a multimodal assessment of effectiveness with college students, *Teaching of Psychology,* 16(3), 133–5.

Fantuzzo, J W, Riggio, R W, Connelly, S and Dimeff, L (1989b) Effects of reciprocal peer tutoring on academic achievement and psychological adjustment: a component analysis, *Journal of Educational Psychology,* 81(2), 173–7.

Gartner, S, Kohler, M and Riessman, F (1971) *Children Teach Children : Learning by Teaching,* Harper & Row, New York.

Goldschmid, B and Goldschmid, M L (1976) Peer teaching in higher education: a review, *Higher Education,* 5, 9–33.

Greenwood, C R, Carta, J J and Kamps, D (1990) 'Teacher-mediated versus peer-mediated instruction: a review of educational advantages and disadvantages' in

Children Helping Children, H C Foot, M J Morgan and R H Shute (eds), John Wiley, London & New York.

Lawson, D (1989) Peer helping programs in the colleges and universities of Quebec and Ontario, *Canadian Journal of Counselling*, 23(1), 41–56.

Lee, R E (1988) Assessing retention program holding power effectiveness across smaller community colleges, *Journal of College Student Development*, 29(3), 255–62.

Maxwell, M (1990) Does tutoring help? A look at the literature, *Review of Research in Developmental Education*, 7(4), 3–7.

Moore-West, M *et al*. (1990) The presence of student-based peer advising, peer tutoring and performance evaluation programs among US medical schools, *Academic Medicine*, 65(10), 660–61.

Rogoff, B (1990) *Apprenticeship in Thinking: Cognitive development in social context*. Oxford and New York: Oxford University Press

Scoble, J, Topping, K J and Wigglesworth, C (1988) Training family and friends as adult literacy tutors, *Journal of Reading*, 31(5), 410–17.

Schunk, D H (1987) 'Self-efficacy and motivated learning' in *New Directions in Educational Psychology: Behaviour and Motivation in the Classroom*, N Hastings and J Schwieso (eds), Falmer Press, London and New York.

Schunk, D H and Zimmermann, B J (eds.) (1994) *Self-Regulation of Learning and Performance*, Lawrence Erlbaum, New York.

Topping, K J (1988) *The Peer Tutoring Handbook*, Croom Helm, Beckenham and Brookline, Cambridge, Massachusetts.

Topping, K J (1992) Co-operative learning and peer tutoring: an overview, *The Psychologist*, 5, 151–61.

Topping, K J (1995) *Paired Reading, Writing and Spelling: The Handbook*, Cassell, London and New York.

Topping, K J (1996) The effectiveness of peer tutoring in higher and further education: a typology and review of the literature, *Higher Education*, 32(3).

Topping, K J, Watson, G A, Jarvis, R J and Hill, S (1996a) Same-year paired peer tutoring in undergraduate mathematics, *Teaching in Higher Education*, 1(3), 341–56.

Topping, K J, Simpson, G, Thompson, L and Hill, S (1996b) Faculty-wide accredited cross-year student supported learning, *Higher Education Review*.

Topping, K J, Hill, S, McKaig, A, Rogers, C, Rushi, N and Young, D (1997) Paired reciprocal peer tutoring in undergraduate economics, *Education and Training International*, 39(2).

Vygotsky, L S (1978) *Mind in Society: The Development of Higher Psychological Processes*, M Cole, V John-Steiner, S Scribner and E Souberman (eds), MIT Press, Cambridge, Massachusetts.

Whitman, N A (1988) *Peer Teaching: To Teach is to Learn Twice*, ASHE-ERIC Higher Education Report, ERIC Clearing House on Higher Education Resources, Washington DC.

Details of relevant practical resources to assist the development of various kinds of peer tutoring are available from:
- Centre for Paired Learning, Psychology, University of Dundee, Dundee DD1 4HN
- cpl@dundee.ac.uk
- http://www.dundee.ac.uk/psychology/c_p_lear.html

Resources include: *The Peer Tutoring Video Training Pack; The Organising Peer Tutoring Audio Pack; The Effective Peer Tutoring Staff Development Pack; The Effective Student Tutoring Staff Development Pack; The Same-Year Paired Peer Tutoring Video; The Student Self-Help Guide to Peer Assisted Learning.*

Acknowledgement

The support of the Scottish Higher Education Funding Council, British Telecom and CSV 'Learning Together' is gratefully acknowledged.

THE CONTEXT
OF EDUCATION

CHAPTER 10

Adult Learning in a Workplace Context

Hitendra Pillay

Performance without knowledge is perilous

In light of the changing nature of contemporary workplaces, this chapter attempts to identify employer expectations and the associated skills required of workers to function effectively in such workplaces. Workers are required to participate in informed discussion about their specific jobs and to contribute to the overall development of organisations. This requires deep understanding of domain-specific knowledge, which at times can be very complex. Workers are also required to take responsibility for their actions and are expected to be flexible so that they can be deployed to other related jobs depending on demand. Finally, workers are expected to be pro-active, be able to anticipate situations and continuously update their knowledge to address new situations. This chapter discusses the nature of knowledge and skills that will facilitate the above qualities.

Changing employer expectation

The competitive nature of modern industry and the need to cope with the changing technology compel employers to move employees between jobs, thus creating the need for 'cross skilling'. Cross skilling is providing workers with more diverse skills by breaking down the traditional barriers between jobs. Workers are expected to have knowledge in a number of related domains. Thus, for example, in the catering industry, restaurant workers in large hotels are deployed during off-peak hours to other areas such as the banquet rooms and coffee shops. To facilitate cross skilling, training programmes on generic skills within each type of industry have been developed. It is argued that programmes in generic knowledge provide workers with the necessary base knowledge to develop skills in other related jobs. Through such a programme an electrician may have some generic knowledge and skill of electrical requirements in buildings, auto-electrical trade and domestic electrical appliances. However, the level of expertise that can be acquired through such cross-skilling efforts needs to be researched further. Available literature on this issue suggests that cross skilling through teaching generic skills may be appropriate for lower-level knowledge and skills only because more complex knowledge is often domain specific. For acquiring higher-level knowledge and expertise, domain-specific approaches may be more appropriate. Although in a domain-specific approach the initial knowledge acquisition may be limited to the domain, as we acquire a deep understanding and scaffold knowledge to an abstract level this is not constrained by contextual boundaries. Such knowledge can therefore facilitate cross skilling to other related jobs (Stevenson, 1991).

Support for the need for cross-skilled workers can be seen in the growing tendency among Australian and American companies to engage 'disposable workers': temporary, part-time and contract workers. In the USA these types of jobs accounted for almost half the new jobs in 1992 (Kilborn, 1993). To stay employed, disposable workers need to have a repertoire of skills and knowledge because full-time employment in a single domain may not be available. With workers often having so little tenure in the workplace and the employing organisations reluctant to invest in training it is essential that such workplace training as exists operates optimally. The ability to extend previous knowledge to new situations should be facilitated.

Furthermore, the change from mass production to flexible manufacturing, the introduction of information technology to office practice and the devolution of power to the workplace all indicate a shift from traditional, manual skills and employer-controlled procedures to cognitive skills and employee participation in decision making. In traditional workplaces job specifications did not require workers to have an understanding of the tasks they performed. They were only required to have an ability to perform specific procedural operations, in accordance with Taylorist philosophy. However, the modern day workplace requires workers to have a deep understanding of the task as well as the ability to perform the required skills. Biggs (1987) argues that deep understanding is being able to make relational connections between elements of given information to develop meaning. This encourages insight and restructuring of given and existing knowledge. The development of deep understanding (from pre-operational to extended, abstract understanding level) and complex domain knowledge (from naïve to expert level) is progressive. One needs to acquire the lower levels of understanding and domain knowledge before seeking deep understanding and complex knowledge. This progressive development of understanding and acquisition of complex knowledge is called 'upskilling'.

Also, with the increasing number of workplaces driven by new technology,

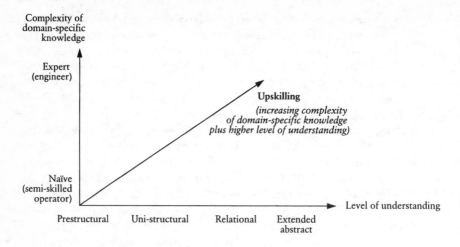

Figure 10.1   Upskilling (adapted from Biggs and Collis, 1982).

workers require more complex domain knowledge anchored in cognitive processes. For example, automotive technicians now have to deal with electronic fuel injection (EFI) systems instead of the old carburettors, which could be manually repaired. EFI systems require complex electronic knowledge regarding the systems as well as about the equipment that is used to work on them. While the need for complex knowledge may not be necessary in all workplaces a deep understanding may be required in most cases. This is illustrated in Suzaki's (1987, p.226) observation,

> 'in a contemporary Japanese radio manufacturing factory, a foreign visitor asked an operator, "Isn't it an engineer's job to make such an improvement [implying that it requires the complex knowledge that only engineers possess]...?" The operator's answer was, "I understand what you are saying. But I know this operation better than anyone else in the whole factory. I do this every day and I have developed an in-depth understanding of the operation. As such I realised the problem and made suggestions to fix it." '

Even though the operator did not have the complex domain knowledge of the engineer, his deep understanding of the job allowed him to participate in the improvement of the factory's operations. This exemplifies the need for deep understanding in making contemporary workplace systems such as total quality management (TQM) successful. Just assuming that workers will adopt TQM, just-in-time (JIT) principles and make positive contribution to improve work practices demonstrates a lack of appreciation of what makes such systems successful. Workers in the traditional systems were not expected to have a deep understanding of their jobs. They could only make suggestions based on their limited knowledge. Therefore it is imperative that contemporary workers have a deep understanding of their jobs irrespective of complexity of knowledge or job status if the new management and operational systems are to be successful.

The recognition that upskilling and cross skilling are essential for a productive workforce can be seen in the sentiment reflected in recent policy papers on vocational or workplace education from many countries. For example, the Australian Mayer report argues that 'competence is underpinned not only by performance but also by knowledge and understanding [upskilling], and that competence involves both the ability to perform in a given context and the capacity to transfer knowledge and skills to new tasks and situations [cross skilling]' (Mayer, 1992, p.4). To possess knowledge and skills that are not transferable is very limiting because it does not lend itself to a wide range of applications. Hence, such knowledge fails to facilitate cross skilling. Acquisition of deep understanding allows workers to organise their knowledge base in a well-connected, hierarchical structure. Clearly defined knowledge structure helps workers to recognise matching elements in different sets of information. Identifying matching elements in different sets of information is the first step in developing transfer knowledge and skills. Support for this contention can be found in Larkin's (1985) assertion that the ability to transfer knowledge and skills depends upon an individual's level of understanding of domain-specific knowledge, because transferable knowledge is intermingled with domain-specific knowledge. Low-level understanding implies that concepts may not be clearly defined, which means that knowledge about such concepts may overlap with other similar concepts. This type of understanding causes difficulties and sometimes makes it impossible for the worker to recognise matching elements in the given information. The use of transferable knowledge from domain-specific knowledge was noted by Pillay (paper in progress) in a study involving electronics students. He found that analog communication technicians with good understanding of domain-specific knowledge (at any level of complexity) had transferable knowledge such as technical terms and processes embedded in their domain knowledge. The technicians easily extended the transferable knowledge to digital communication problems. The transferred knowledge allowed the technician to gain a head start in acquiring expertise in digital communication. Therefore, possessing a good understanding of domain-specific knowledge and skills may increase transfer ability, which in turn may facilitate cross skilling.

Although there is a genuine need for upskilling and cross skilling, employers also seek higher-order thinking skills in their employees. Workers are required to have the capacity to analyse problems, become proactive and anticipate trends and take responsibility for work practices. Underbakke *et al.* (1993, p.138) describe higher-order thinking skill as the ability to 'combine information stored in memory with new information – that is interrelate or rearrange the information – to achieve a purpose such as to solve a problem, analyse an argument, negotiate issues or make a prediction'. Higher-order thinking skills involve critical reasoning, problem solving and creative thinking, which are cognitive processes that act upon domain-specific knowledge to help enhance deep understanding and consequently increase transferability of knowledge and skills. Trishman *et al.* (1993) analysed the above higher-order thinking skill and identified seven factors that contribute to higher-order thinking: being broad- and open-minded; having a sustained intellectual curiosity; seeking connections and explanations; making and executing plans and anticipating outcomes; being able to process information precisely; having the ability to weigh and assess reasons; and having the ability to monitor the flow of one's own thinking. As indicated above, these factors are not part of domain-specific knowledge, as they deal with thinking processes that assist individuals to dissect their domain-specific knowledge in meaningful chunks and explore the potential for creative applications. Individuals may have a deep understanding of domain-specific knowledge and yet be unable to engage in higher-order thinking skills. For example, medical students with deep understanding of domain-specific knowledge could not solve Dunker's radiation problems. In this study students were required to destroy a tumour by radiation without affecting any good tissue. Their inability to solve this problem was due to mental fixation about how radiation therapy is normally carried out. Their thinking was vertically aligned, which prevented them from considering other possibilities. De Bono (1971) noted this in his distinction between vertical and lateral thinking. He argued that vertical thinking developed meaningful understanding whereas lateral thinking used meaning to change settings and application. Individuals having good vertical thinking are not necessarily good in lateral thinking and vice versa.

The recognition of the need for higher-order thinking skill among contemporary workers can be seen in recent reports on training in workplace skills in both the USA (Perkins and Salomon, 1992) and Australia (Mayer, 1992). These reports suggest that workers need to develop higher-order thinking skills and be able to take control of their own learning and be responsible for their actions in work practice. Carnevale *et al.* (1990) argue that workers need to know how to learn because continuous changes in technology require employees to take initiatives to upgrade their knowledge and skills. If workers engage in the seven factors identified above by Trishman *et al.* (1993), it may facilitate continuous upgrading of their knowledge and skills. McKavanagh (1994) found that train drivers who could recognise non-routine problems, decompose them, set goals to solve the problem, engage in lateral thinking and be metacognitive about the overall process were able to continuously upgrade their knowledge and expertise. Similar evidence was noted by Pillay (in progress) in a study involving communication technicians, where higher-order thinking skills used in acquiring a deep understanding of domain-specific knowledge in analog communication informed technicians of the types of relationship to take note of, and the correct 'why' and 'how' questions to ask in order to develop a good understanding in digital communication. Furthermore, by engaging in higher-order thinking skills, technicians were able to identify congruity between related jobs and develop cross skilling.

Thus, to meet modern day employer expectations, workers need to be cross skilled, be high on upskilling and have the capacity to engage in high-order thinking. This cocktail of abilities is a prized commodity among contemporary workers and is referred to as 'multi-skilling'. It is not just acquiring complex knowledge in a single domain or just acquiring skills from a number of specific domains. Multi-skilling is acquiring thinking skills together with deep understanding of complex content knowledge, so increasing the versatility of one's knowledge and skill.

The nature of multi-skilling

The three dimensions, cross skilling, upskilling and higher-order thinking skills should not be seen as rivals. They are closely related and complement each other. As illustrated in Figure 10.2, individuals can be at varying levels of achievement on the three dimensions. To acquire a high level of multi-skilling ability one has to be high on upskilling and be able to engage in higher-order thinking in all cross-skill domains.

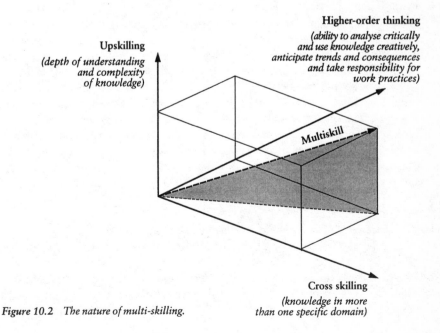

Figure 10.2 The nature of multi-skilling.

The growing need for multi-skilling ability involving skills such as reasoning and problem solving and acquiring a deep understanding of complex knowledge has been well described by Murnane *et al.* (1992). It is argued that lower-order understanding is reproductive and in learned behaviour achieved from contiguity experiences (in accordance with a behaviourist paradigm). This is typical of learning in many traditional trade subjects. There is no reflective or critical thinking involved, which is normally expected in adult learning programmes and other programmes aimed at developing meaningful understanding. For example, process workers may know which switch to press to get the task accomplished, but fail to have any understanding of what actually happens when the switch is pressed and how the raw material is changed into a required product. Should there be any irregularity in the product they will fail to take corrective action. Such workers have limited understanding of domain-specific knowledge and do not engage in higher-order thinking. Consequently, they are unable to participate in TQM issues beyond what they actually do. However, workers who engage in higher-order thinking are expected to draw on their deep understanding of different domain knowledge and apply it meaningfully to novel tasks. They engage in critical thinking and reasoning to make connections and apply processes to novel and non-routine situations, for example, in applying metal recrystallisation knowledge taught in metallurgy to automotive body repair. A deep understanding of the recrystallisation process will allow automotive body-repair apprentices to recognise that stress induced through repeated impact forces causing fatigue failure in metal is similar to what they do when working on metal panels. Having associated the above, they need to know how to neutralise the stress using heat-treatment procedures such as recrystallisation. By relieving stress the metal becomes more malleable and easier to work with. This requires the worker to engage in deep thinking regarding the recrystallisation process, heat treatment and stress induced in the panel, and to make a connection between the metallurgy knowledge and panel repair tasks. Such connections are difficult to make and should not be left to chance. It has to be explicitly taught and the barriers between domains have to be removed to encourage thinking across domains. Training programmes that go beyond delivering content and explicitly illustrate the connection of scientific principles and mathematical knowledge to work practice have far-reaching success in developing multi-skilling (Pillay, 1995).

Interaction between domain-specific knowledge and higher-order thinking skills in the acquisition of multi-skill

We know that acquisition of a deep understanding of domain-specific knowledge and higher-order thinking skills are closely related and are two main requirements for multi-skilling. These two attributes, as indicated by

Stevenson (1991), will enable the individual concerned to develop abstract knowledge beyond specific domains and facilitate high-level cross skilling.

There are two issues relating to these attributes. The first is whether we teach domain-specific knowledge or higher-order thinking skills first. The second is whether we teach higher-order thinking as generic skills applicable to a range of jobs or as specific to each job. Addressing the first issue, Sternberg and Lubart (1991) argue that in order to engage in higher-order thinking skills such as creative problem solving in any area, one must have an understanding of the knowledge in that domain. We cannot think in a vacuum. Without a sufficiently developed knowledge base it is difficult for individuals to assess the problem, which is the initial step in problem solving or critical thinking. Acquiring a rich, domain-specific knowledge allows one to make connections between new information and previous knowledge and between concepts within new or old knowledge. By understanding relationships between concepts we construct meaningful insights of given information, which should assist in critical thinking and problem solving and the ability to view information from multiple perspectives. However, it may also be argued that one first needs to have the skills to think creatively such as the lateral thinking skills of De Bono (1971) and the flexible thinking skills of Sternberg and Lubart (1991) in order to obtain multiple perspectives to a problem and consequently develop a deep understanding of domain-specific knowledge.

The second issue is summed up well by Perkins and Salomon (1989). They argue, in agreement with the growing evidence emerging from expert–novice studies, that since thinking is highly influenced by the structure of knowledge and the traditions of thought in different jobs, generic, higher-order thinking skills have limited utility. Furthermore, recent research in contextualised learning and authentic learning environments suggests that it would be most beneficial to the learner if higher-order thinking skills are embedded in the domain-specific knowledge (Resnick and Klopfer, 1989). However, when thinking skills are embedded in the content knowledge there may still be complex cognitive manoeuvres that remain inaccessible to learners (Prawat, 1991). In such cases the required higher-order thinking (cognitive manoeuvres) need to be explicitly taught. Although there is very strong theoretical support for embedding higher-order thinking skill in the domain knowledge there is still support for teaching generic, higher-order thinking skills as distinct from domain-specific knowledge (Edwards, 1991). Sometimes specific instruction in higher-order thinking is necessary: at other times an embedded approach ('immersion approach'; Prawat, 1991) may be suitable. In the immersion approach a way of thinking is learnt by osmosis, not by explicit instruction. A realistic resolution for each issue raised above may be to combine both dichotomous positions. A balance between explicit and implicit usage and domain-specific knowledge driving the thinking skill, and the higher-order thinking driving the understanding may be the best approach. The increased levels of upskilling thus achieved will also facilitate cross skilling.

The development of a deep understanding requires a generative or a productive approach to learning (Bain, 1994), rather than the reproductive approach commonly used in workplace education. A reproductive approach uses a limited set of ideas through an extensive set of examples, which have a limited set of solutions. This encourages repetitive learning on a limited set of tasks, thus limiting its applicability and potential for cross skilling. By contrast, the generative approach tends to use an extensive range of performances applied to a limited set of ideas that are transformed into a 'family of understanding' (Bain, 1994). The family of understanding concept suggests the development of multiple perspectives to a given set of ideas, which promotes deep understanding and cross skilling. The generative approach requires one to seek insight by engaging in higher-order thinking skills.

This allows the worker to recognise relationships between a number of performances and identify underlying principles that can be transferred to other related jobs, thereby facilitating multi-skilling. For example, in the drilling process, by working with different size drill bits and varying speeds, workers can develop a deep understanding reflected by an appreciation of the scientific principles underpinning the process. For example, the process induces torque and friction and there is a relationship between size, torque, friction, tool wear and quality of finish. Such knowledge can then be transferred to other similar processes such as milling. Workers need to recognise that there is certain congruity between the two operations despite their uniqueness. Critical thinking and reasoning, together with a deep understanding, should assist in recognising elements of congruity; in drilling and milling processes, both utilise a cutting tool mounted on a spindle, which rotates to cut metal. The difference between the two operations is that in the drilling process the cutting tool is moved to cut whereas in the milling process the work piece is moved while the cutter rotates in a stationary position. The drilling spindle is vertical and the milling one is horizontal. However, the cutting operations in both cases exert torque and friction, which are influenced by the size of the cutter and the speed. The selection of speed for cutting in both operations is therefore governed by common scientific principles. The cause of tool wear is also similar so workers learning to use the two machines should be explicitly taught these relationships. By doing this, workers acquire multi-skilling by developing a deep understanding, engaging in higher-order thinking and breaking the boundaries between the jobs (Pillay, 1995)

Cognitive capacity for developing multi-skilling

A concern for workplace educators and trainers is how to facilitate the acquisition of all three dimensions of multi-skilling in light of increasing domain knowledge and the decreasing training times. Like most learning tasks, for meaningful learning to occur, attention needs to be directed to all three dimensions of multi-skilling. The ability to attend to all aspects of the multi-skilling process depends on the availability of sufficient cognitive resources. We know that our memory resources are not infinite, so we need to plan for 'essentials' and 'desirables'. Often in training institutions and, in particular, workplaces, routine tasks of getting the work done or having the problems solved take priority over acquiring deep understanding, engaging in higher-order thinking skills and seeking cross-skilling relationships, all of which help develop powerful multi-skilling knowledge.

Furthermore, when confronted with multiple tasks we selectively prioritise them. When prioritising tasks in a learning context, often the strategies used for learning draw more attention. Consequently the insightful, domain-specific knowledge taught through the process is lost. For example, when using problem-based learning to teach both thinking skills and domain-specific knowledge, we have to be mindful that learners could easily lose sight of one if the other task imposes a large cognitive load (Baird and Mitchell, 1986). In such a case the knowledge generated may have information about the process but not about the domain-specific knowledge or links between the process and the domain knowledge. Similar implications of misdirected attention can be seen when learning domain-specific knowledge. If learners do not have the necessary understanding of lower-level domain knowledge to scaffold new knowledge then they resort to a search heuristic. This causes cognitive overload and in turn prevents learners from engaging in higher level thinking and acquiring deep understanding of complex information (Chandler and Sweller, 1991).

Research in cognitive science informs us that having appropriate schemata and categories allows us to process information with minimum effort (Chandler and Sweller, 1991). It further suggests that repetitive application of such schemata make them automated, which is an attribute of experts. Knowledge and skills that are automated are not consciously addressed, thereby imposing a reduced cognitive demand. The advantage of achieving automisation is that attention is freed from the primary task and can be focused on other aspects such as higher-order thinking skills and understanding cross-skill relationships across domains. As we progress from naïve to expert domain knowledge or from limited to deep understanding we must develop automation of the lower levels, thus freeing cognitive resources to attend to deeper-level understanding of complex information. Knowing one's prior domain knowledge and level of understanding can assist in structuring new knowledge so as to avoid unnecessary search processes. We also need to explicitly teach connection within and between new and old knowledge to make it meaningful rather then depending on an 'osmosis process'.

Evans (1994) investigated the development of expertise in trade skills such as welding and found that novices, because they had limited understanding of welding skills, had to devote most of their attention to the primary task. As a result, they could not attend to any other higher-order thinking skills, such as critical analysis of feedback information, while they were engaged in welding. By contrast, experts could operate quite effectively on a secondary task when engaged in welding because they had a deep and automated knowledge of welding. The secondary task was a critical analysis of the feedback with a view to improving the weld or searching for parallels between the various types of welding to develop cross-skilling knowledge. The monitoring of feedback is not normally discussed in welding instruction, but Evans (1994) found that such tacit knowledge is essential for expert performance. It is plausible to suggest that in developing multi-skilling we may need to automate aspects of the understanding, domain-specific knowledge and higher-order thinking dimensions, thereby freeing cognitive resources to deal with more complex domain knowledge, higher-order thinking and cross skilling or restructuring our understanding.

To sum up, workers are expected to function as multi-skilled workers yet they receive little encouragement in their training to develop all three dimensions of multi-skilling. The 'isolation by diversification' syndrome is a common problem. In an attempt to diversify, more specialised groups are constructed, which create more boundaries. With the increasing content knowledge in each domain and the decreasing time affordable by employers for training, a sound understanding of domain knowledge and higher-order thinking skills can assist in learning on the job. Most workers have a wealth of prior experience and knowledge which can be utilised in the learning process if new knowledge is structured in a manner that takes advantage of it (selecting and sequencing appropriate material in a manner that explicitly shows links and reduces cognitive load). Individuals can then optimise their limited cognitive resources in developing deep understanding of complex knowledge. Also, since the three dimensions of multi-skilling knowledge complement each other, instruction may be designed to eliminate redundancy. For example, embedding higher-order thinking skills within the domain-specific knowledge but explicitly pointing out the two aspects to learners may be a useful instructional strategy. The workplace training curriculum needs to reflect this by integrating instruction so that multi-skill schemata can be developed. An integrated approach involving innovative strategies, such as teaching about expert models explicitly, and using problem-based learning may help develop multi-skilling. No matter which strategy one adopts it will require planning and time.

The current trend of training for routine tasks through short-term workshops will only achieve an awareness of multi-skilling, which is not sufficient to be effective multi-skill practicians. Developing multi-skilling is neither easy nor fast, but if employers and governments want to become competitive internationally then they need to accept the fact that multi-skilled workers are necessary to achieve that goal and that appropriate time needs to be allocated to developing multi-skill.

References

Bain, J (1994) *Understanding by Learning or Learning by Understanding*, inaugural lecture, Griffith University, Brisbane, Australia.

Baird, J R and Mitchell, I J (1986) *Improving the Quality of Teaching and Learning: an Australian Case Study*, Monash University Press, Melbourne.

Biggs, J (1987) *Students' Approaches to Learning and Studying*, Australian Council for Educational Research, Hawthorn, Victoria.

De Bono, E (1971) *Lateral thinking for Management*, Penguin Books, Harmondsworth.

Chandler, P and Sweller, J (1991) Cognitive load theory and the format of instruction, *Cognition and Instruction*, 8(4), 293–332.

Carnevale, A P, Gainer, L J and Meltzer, A S (1990) *Workplace Basics*, Jossey-Bass, San Francisco, California.

Edwards, J (1991) 'The direct teaching of thinking skills' in *Learning and Teaching Cognitive Skills*, G Evans (ed.), 87–106, Australian Council for Educational Research, Hawthorn, Victoria.

Evans, G (1994) 'Learning in apprenticeship courses' in *Cognition at Work*, J Stevenson (ed.), 76–102, NCVER, Adelaide, SA.

Kilborn, P (1993) New job lacks the security in time of 'disposable workers', *The New York Times*, A1 and A6, 15 March.

Larkin, J (1985) 'Understanding, problem representations and skill in physics' in *Thinking and Learning Skills, Research and Open Questions*, vol.2, S F Chipman, J W Segal and R Glaser (eds), Lawrence Erlbaum, New Jersey.

McKavanagh, C (1994) 'Train simulators and the development of expertise' in *Cognition at Work*, J Stevenson (ed.), 103–37, NCVER, Adelaide, SA.

Mayer, E (1992) *Employment Related Key Competencies: a Proposal for Consultation*, The Mayer Committee, Ministry Of Education and Training, Melbourne.

Murnane, R J, Willet, J B and Levy, F (1992) *The Growing Importance of Cognitive Skills in Wage Determination*, Harvard Graduate School of Education, Cambridge, Massachusetts.

Perkins, D N and Salomon, G (1989) Are cognitive skills context bound? *Educational Researcher*, 18(1), 16–23.

Pillay, H (1995) Translating competency statements into desired outcomes: a representational model for conceptualisng the competency acquisition process, *Australian Journal of Adult and Community Education*, 35(1), 50–61.

Pillay, H (in progress) *Conceptions of learning and approaches to learning in electronics*, Center for Cognitive Processes and Learning, Queensland University of Technology.

Prawat, R S (1991). The value of ideas: the immersion approach to the development of thinking. *Educational Researcher*, 20(2), 3–10.

Resnick, L B and Klopfer, L E (eds) (1989) *Toward the Thinking Curriculum: Current Cognitive Research*, Association for Supervision and Curriculum Development, Alexandria, Vancouver.

Sternberg, R J and Lubart, T I (1991) An investment theory of creativity and its development, *Human Development*, 34, 1–31.

Stevenson, J (1991) 'The teaching of adaptability in vocational education' in *Learning and Teaching Cognitive Skills*, G Evans (ed.), 124–43, Australian Council for Educational Research, Hawthorn, Victoria.

Suzaki, K (1987) *The New Manufacturing Challenge: Techniques for Continuous Improvement*, Collier-Macmillan, New York.

Trishman, S, Jay, E and Perkins, D N (1993) Teaching thinking disposition: from transmission to enculturation, *Theory into Practice*, 32, Summer, 147–53.

Underbakke, M, Borg, J M and Peterson, D (1993) Researching and developing the knowledge base for teaching higher order thinking, *Theory into Practice*, 32(3), 138–49.

CHAPTER 11

Education, Work and Adult Life:

How Adults Relate their Learning to their Work, Family and Social Lives

*Loraine Blaxter, Christina Hughes
and Malcolm Tight*

Introduction

We live in an age in which adults, particularly those in or seeking employment, are expected to engage in education, training or learning throughout their lives. Such learning is believed to make individuals more productive, more adaptable and better citizens, and thus promote both the national economy and social well-being (Hughes and Tight, 1995). At the same time, the responsibility for organising and funding this learning is being shifted from the state to the employer and the individual.

These trends pose key questions for our understanding of the role of education in relation to both employment and the other domains of adult life. For example, how do individual adults use their learning within their work, whether paid or unpaid, and in their family and social lives? Is learning something that is linked to, or separated from, these other identities? How do these multiple identities contribute to learning? How do adults organise their lives to make space for learning? How important is education, training and learning within their lives? Does learning offer adults a means for making sense of their lives?

These and related questions have been a key focus for our research during the 1990s. This chapter will both draw upon, and attempt to synthesise, some of the results of this research so far. During this period we have collected a considerable amount of data from individuals and organisations, which is still being analysed. In order to present selected results from such 'work in progress', we have developed the technique of 'analytical vignettes'. These may be seen as analogous to critical incidents, with each vignette offering a particular reading of the data, and using particular concepts, theories or perspectives to illuminate our understanding. In this chapter we will proceed a stage further, and begin to weave some of these vignettes together.

The chapter is organised in four sections. The findings of relevant research carried out by others will be considered first. The methods we have used in our own research will then be summarised. The main body of the chapter will then use the data collected to explore the issues we have identified, offering alternative, but connected, interpretations. The final section will outline some of the main conclusions and indicate areas for future work.

Existing research

There is, of course, a vast array of literature drawn from a wide range of social science disciplines that is of relevance to the topic of this chapter. In another paper, this literature was categorised and reviewed in terms of possible combinations of the three topics suggested in the title: 'education'; 'work'; and 'adult life' (Tight, 1995). The findings of that analysis will be outlined here.

Research into *education and work* has included studies of the educational expectations of new employees, the work options available to them, and employers' training provision and practice. These suggest, among other things, that the relationship between education and work at the end of initial education has become increasingly complicated; that there is a continuing mismatch between the expectations of those entering work and the requirements of their employers; that the benefits of engaging in education prior to labour market re-entry in mid-career are questionable; and that, while there are examples of good practice, in-company provision for training and learning is very varied and in many cases inadequate.

Studies of *work and adult life* have examined the varied patterns that careers in and out of employment may take, and the place of the individual within organisations. Two particular focuses for research have been the changing nature of employment careers and the conflicting demands faced by women seeking to combine jobs with family responsibilities. Women in this position are steered towards part-time and short-term patterns of working, severely limiting their opportunities for advancement and training.

Research into *education and adult life* has involved surveying adult participation and non-participation in education and training, their motivations and progression and the factors affecting their success or failure. Surveys have confirmed the increasing extent of adult participation in education, training and learning activities, shown how this is related to previous individual participation and indicated the importance of social differentiation and gender in understanding the varied patterns revealed. A growing amount of more theoretical work has attempted to explain why adults participate and the effects it has upon them.

Studies that have attempted to examine the relations between all three of the areas identified, *education, work and adult life*, are more limited in number. Much of this work has focused on the idea of life cycles or courses, examining the changes or transitions that adults progress through during their lives, and their relation to family and employment circumstances.

A number of conclusions may be drawn from this range of studies. First, much of the existing research that has been carried out on education, work and adult life has been located within one disciplinary perspective – economics, psychology or sociology, for example – or within a particular branch of a discipline. There is a need for both broader and different forms of research to better explore and understand such an interdisciplinary field.

Second, the existing research seems over focused on formal educational provision, and on higher education in particular. There is a need for more research into, for example, further education, training, informal and self-directed study in their relation to work and other aspects of adults' lives.

Third, most of the research that has been undertaken is, or appears to be, informed by the assumption that more participation in (formal) education and training is necessarily a good thing for all concerned; individuals, employers and society. There is a need for more open and questioning research that seeks to identify when further participation might be disadvantageous, or that focuses on the kinds, levels and qualities of participation that are likely to be most beneficial.

Fourth, there is relatively little available research that attempts to link the domains we have identified and consider how adults understand and relate their learning to their work, family and other roles throughout their lives. Such research, and the theoretical development building upon it, is certainly needed if we are to not only understand, but also contribute to, policy and practice on education, work and adult life. It is in this area that our own research is attempting to make a contribution.

Methods

The research that we have been undertaking on education, work and adult life has taken the form of two major projects. The first of these focused on students on two part-time degree programmes (Blaxter and Tight, 1995). The second has moved away from focusing on formal education, and has been examining the experiences of adults working with six organisations (Blaxter *et al.*, 1996).

The part-time degree study involved extensive questionnaire and interview surveys of students on two substantial local part-time degree programmes. One of these programmes, offering general degrees in historical, literary and cultural, and social studies, was based at our own institution, Warwick University. The other, a degree in business administration, was offered by Coventry University. In all, 308 students completed a survey questionnaire, which included questions on their studies, their educational and work experience and their personal, social and family situation. Thirty-six selected respondents were then interviewed in more detail about their study experience and its relation to other aspects of their lives.

The second project has been based within six medium-to-large organisations – two from each of the private, public and voluntary sectors – in the West Midlands region. Each was chosen for study because it exhibited 'good' practice in terms of providing for the education and training of its workforce. The project has been examining both organisational and individual perspectives on the learning experience. For the latter purpose, twenty workers were chosen within each organisation for in-depth interview. Each interview focused on the interviewee's lifetime experience of education, training and learning, and how they related these to their work and the rest of their lives.

There are, of course, so many ways in which such data can be analysed and presented. In the case of the second project described, much analysis also remains to be done. Given these constraints and the space available, we have chosen to use the method of analytical vignettes. These allow for the selective presentation and discussion of research findings, without suggesting that a definitive analysis has been carried out.

The following two sections present some of our research findings in terms of two main themes, each of which has two sub-themes:

1. The changing role of education throughout adults' lives:
   - the way in which education may appear as a separate activity during the early adult career; and
   - how education can come to be placed in an integral position later on.
2. The relation between education and other life domains:
   - adults' use of time for different life roles; and
   - whether and how they perceive their educational participation in relation to other life roles.

The first set of themes offer a longitudinal understanding of adult educational career paths. This owes a lot to the life-cycle literature. It presents the analysis as a chronological account, one that was indeed encouraged by the way in which questions were posed during the interviews. It also bears an obvious relation to both policy developments and the ways in which educational provision is institutionally structured. However, it is only one way of interpreting the data and of perceiving adult lives.

The second set of themes presents a more cross-sectional understanding of the relations between the different domains of adult life. It relates to individual adults' considered perceptions of their use of education, and its meaning and place in their lives. This is based on their own personal experiences, and will, of course, develop over their lifespan. It will also depend on the individual's other commitments, and the nature and scope of the educational participation they engage in.

There are, of course, close interconnections between these two ways of examining the issues considered in this chapter, and we will return to these in the concluding section.

The changing role of education throughout adults' lives

It is still, of course, commonplace to think of education in terms of school and/or college. Education may then be perceived as something undertaken as a child, adolescent or early adult, which is put aside in, but serves to support, adult life. While this may continue to resonate for many adults today, we are also aware of the growing pressures to engage in further education and training throughout life.

How, then, does the role of education change during the life course? The two vignettes presented in this section adopt a chronological account. They suggest that two contrasted views of the role of education may commonly be taken in early and mid adulthood. The first of these supports the 'front end' view of education, while the second places it in a more central role, integrated with other aspects of life. These two vignettes should not, however, be seen as oppositional, as the latter develops from the former. Both vignettes demonstrate the ways in which social divisions such as class and gender have impact, in affecting life chances and 'choices', throughout the life course.

Separate early careers

We prefer to take a broad view of the term 'career', seeing it not as confined to paid work, but encompassing unpaid forms of work as well as overall life choices and circumstances (Goldschmidt, 1990). Seen in these terms, each adult's career can be seen to involve a number of possible roles – employee, partner, parent, voluntary worker, learner, and so on – at different times and in varying combinations. Our research suggests that it is normal for adults to regard these roles as essentially separate during the early part of their lives. Indeed, the way in which the state orders our lives during childhood, adolescence and early adulthood encourages such a view.

Thus, after the early years of childhood, we spend ten or more years in compulsory, full-time education. Increasingly, we are expected to engage in further periods of full-time initial education. Then, in our late teens or early twenties, we aim to enter full-time employment, typically involving a period of initial training. This, of course, is a summary of what might be called the 'classic' career model. To say that it has never applied to all adults, and that it is of little relevance to those becoming adults today, is not to deny its relevance in influencing prospective adults' views of their own careers.

This is indicated by an analysis of the career expectations and choices at the time of completing full-time initial education of 40 people, 37 of whom were women, in two of the organisations we have studied: a local authority social services department and a voluntary organisation delivering a counselling service (Blaxter *et al.*, 1995). They were aged between 30 and 67 at the time of interview. Most were either qualified counsellors or social workers, or working towards this status, though a few were working in managerial or secretarial capacities.

Our analysis identified six contrasting themes, of which five will be illustrated here: individuals' acceptance of the work career options seen as open to them; their rejection of other options; their perceived lack of choice or advice in deciding upon their options; their perceptions of themselves as either channelled or drifting into particular options; and, for the women interviewed, their views on motherhood as a career option. These themes have, of course, been reflected in many other studies (eg Sharpe, 1994).

The majority of those interviewed could readily recall their initial interest in a particular range of work career options. These were usually drawn from a very narrow range – nursing, teaching or office work – reflecting the class and gender composition of the sample. For some, their initial work career was a positive 'choice':

'Well the only thing I ever really wanted to do was to be a nurse... I just couldn't have thought of being in an office environment.' (woman, 50s)

For others, the rejection of options was at least equally important:

'I wasn't going to work in a factory like my parents. My one thought was to get some money, I didn't want to go to college.' (woman, 30s)

Most of those interviewed, in looking back, saw themselves as having had few choices about their careers at the time when they left school:

'at sixth form level I remember my headmistress saying "you won't make university, so what do you want to do other than that?"... we didn't have any careers advice, so it was go to university, teaching, nursing.' (woman, 50s)

They tended to perceive themselves as having either been 'channelled' into a particular narrow range of options, or as 'drifting', without effective guidance, and lacking an understanding of what they might best do:

'I ended up doing a YTS scheme in the local hospital, just sort of clerical work really, but then got offered a placement at the local school with people with learning difficulties, and that is how I ended up doing what I do really.' (woman, 30s)

Some of the respondents, however, presented themselves as more purposive actors. For example, one of the men interviewed stated:

'I had always wanted to be a statistician for reasons that I couldn't possibly explain... So I applied to universities with the objective of doing a degree in statistics.' (man, 50s)

Channelling was also apparent in the accounts given by women regarding their future roles as wives and mothers. This was most clearly expressed by the older women, who typically saw these roles as following on from a brief period of employment:

'I think the future in those days was that you took a small job, and then you got married and had a family.' (woman, 50s)

This analysis confirms the view of separate early careers, with employment and motherhood following on from, and supplanting, education. Education may be seen here as having a key role, together with gender and class, in channelling young people into their future career paths. At this stage, few perceived their options to combine two or more roles; and fewer still saw a continuing, and central, role for learning beyond initial education. As indicated in the next section, however, experience of adult life soon changes these perceptions.

Education in a central role later on

A considerable amount of recent research suggests that there is a problem of individual commitment and motivation to train (Crowder and Pupynin, 1993). This is too frequently read as a problem of attitudes, values or culture, but has at least as much to do with issues of social division, such as class and gender. These issues will be explored through the following vignette of seven working-class, white women, who left school with low levels of qualifications. Our analysis indicates that these women may be representative of a workforce that is already learning and exhibits a considerable commitment to learning throughout their lives (Blaxter et al., 1996).

The public-sector employer for which these women work aims to be a total quality organisation, and successfully completed the Investors in People process in 1993. A system of appraisal that encouraged the development of skills by manual staff was in place. The seven women concerned were employed as waitresses and chambermaids at a training centre. Their experiences as workers, wives and mothers exhibited common features of women's careers: initial full-time participation in the labour market, leaving at the birth of their first child and subsequently returning to a lower-status or lower-paid occupation (Arber and Gilbert, 1992).

These women all left school at the earliest possible point, all but one with no qualifications. Their initial career paths took them into jobs as office juniors, typists or factory workers. Their initial participation in full-time work, prior to the birth of children, varied in length from two years to twelve years. On returning to work, they had all found jobs in cleaning or catering, mostly beginning part time and gradually increasing their hours as their domestic work load declined:

> 'I went to work evenings at my first employment, waitressing in the same place. I keep going back there... She [her second child] was six weeks but we were so hard up. I worked Saturday night and Sunday lunch... I used to go and do a few evenings in the week.' (woman, 40s)

Education, in its broadest sense, manifested itself in their lives in many ways, through voluntary work, courses and self-directed learning:

> 'Learning how to make the money stretch... Oh gosh it was hard... how to make the cheapest meals... I remember buying a book... recipes for £1 and under.' (woman, 40s)

For most of them, educational participation came to be a recurrent or continuous activity:

> 'I started at night re-doing typing and I went up to RSA II and I passed all those and got a distinction and I thought, hey I like this, this is brilliant. So I went on to the computers. Didn't know a thing about computers and I did the whole lot of Word Perfect 5.1 and sat all the exams and got a distinction and I thought hey up, I quite like this you know.' (woman, 40s)

This attitude was encouraged and further developed by the organisation they now work for, though this is not to say that the training arrangements were perfect:

> 'they sent a tutor from the college into work, but it had to be done, it was such a rush thing, between 9 and 11 in the morning. You knew that when you got out of there at 11 the people came in for lunch at 12, and you had to get all the work you should have done between 9 and 11 done between 11 and 12... But we all did it, we all passed it.' (woman, 40s)

In short, this group of women, despite leaving school early, entering low-skilled employment and having a break from full-time employment to bring up their children, had become committed, lifelong learners:

> 'My outlook is different. I want more... I like change and I like to learn new things, so I am quite happy to do that, or if they want me to go somewhere else and they are quite happy to teach me, I would go.' (woman, 40s)

Their experience, in coming to see learning as having a central role in their lives, is not, we would suggest, unusual for women. While we have yet to analyse fully the data we have on men's experiences in this respect, their changing experience of learning would appear to be broadly similar.

The relation between education and other life domains

The second theme to be discussed here also involves two analytical vignettes. Unlike the first theme, which took individuals' life stories as the narrative, and used these to explore their involvement in learning at different times in their lives, here the respondents' accounts are more reflective. Thus, the first vignette focuses on adults' views of their usage of time for different activities. The second vignette then considers the general issue posed in the subtitle of this paper: how adults relate their learning to their work, family and social lives. Both use data collected from the part-time degree students we studied.

Use of time

For a minority of adults, the availability of time to engage in learning is not problematic. Thus, as young adults, they may be supported by the state, their family and/or their prospective employers to devote themselves to full-time study. Or, as older adults, they may, when retired, have sufficient time and resources to satisfy their desires for further study. In between these ages, however, it is much less likely that adults will be free from other major demands on their time, most notably those associated with their roles as employees and family carers.

This has two main implications for most adults' use of time in relation to education. First, adults are unlikely to voluntarily engage in learning unless it has considerable meaning or significance for them. Second, most such engagements, whether voluntary or compulsory, are likely to exert substantial pressure on their other major roles, and require the development of time management strategies (Blaxter and Tight, 1994b). The strategies that they adopt are many and varied, but three basic responses may be recognised:

giving up other activities in order to engage in education; giving up education; or somehow managing to combine education with other life roles and coping with the resultant pressures.

Thus, on the part-time degree programmes we studied, most students reported cutting back on activities, most notably watching television. In some cases, major life roles, such as employment and voluntary work, would also be given up:

> 'I was in a sort of conflict all the time... I suppose I like to give a lot of my time to the things I'm doing.' (woman, 20s, who resigned from her job in order to do justice to her studies)

The tendency for overburdened students to withdraw from courses, and the supportive or remedial responses that are open to institutions, have been extensively studied by researchers (eg Tinto, 1987). Most adult students are likely to have seriously considered the option of withdrawal if they are engaging in education over a lengthy period of time. However, many people, particularly women with family responsibilities, clearly feel compelled to somehow manage the 'triple shift' of family, work *and* education. Their time-management strategy is commonly described as 'juggling' (Blaxter and Tight, 1994a):

> 'I always seem to be juggling with half a dozen balls in the air... Coursework, work, family I suppose. I don't see enjoyment as a separate thing, though I skim enjoyment off the top of those things... the house' (woman, 30s)

The pressures faced by such jugglers have a habit of getting more extreme at times, and affect men as well as women:

> 'I used to manage very well until the beginning [of the year] when the employer began shedding staff... My time has been eaten up at work, but I'm still on track... I used to be able to plan the [course] work in spare time at lunch, and stop off at the library on the way home. But now...' (man, 40s)

In such circumstances, study gets compressed into whatever time is left over, often encroaching on sleep, and not uncommonly placing pressure on relationships.

Educational participation in relation to other life roles

We have argued that education and other roles tend to be viewed as separate early on in the adult's career, but that education later often comes to assume an important, central and linking role. This is, obviously, not the case for all adults, as many do not participate to any significant extent in learning activities, whether formal or informal. It is also very much a matter of circumstances and perception, with some individuals perhaps choosing to stress or reject linkages. This is indicated by another analysis of the interviews we carried out with part-time degree students, which showed a nearly even split between those who linked their educational involvement to life transitions, and those who did not (Blaxter and Tight, 1995).

This analysis identified six kinds of responses: three groups where clear or possible links could be identified between transitional events and educational participation, and three groups where no evidence of linkage was presented or identifiable. The former related to changing family patterns, retirement and employment prospects. For example:

'When the youngest started school I went to [a further education college]... and did two A levels with the eventual aim of doing something with them.' (woman, 30s)

The cases where the interviewee made no clear linkage between transitional events and educational participation, and where no linkage was apparent in the analysis of the interview records, include examples where participation was related to boredom at work, was described as a continuing activity, or was related to chance or opportunity. For example:

'I don't really enjoy the work that I do so I look forward to college... It gives me a bit of energy and... takes the drudgery out of... I don't know what I'd do if I didn't do it.' (man, 20s)

Clearly, an involvement in education or learning in adult life will be easier to sustain where it is complementary to other activities, or where it does not demand constant juggling of available time. The voluntariness of the activity may be as important as its relevance. However, where education has come to assume a major, and perhaps fulfilling, role in an individual's life, it may be given priority over other activities. An understanding of the different ways in which educational participation may be linked to other aspects of life, and of the need to make space for such activity, is of major importance to policy makers and educators, given the emphasis now placed on lifelong learning and the learning society.

Conclusions

Before coming to any conclusions, it is best to enter some caveats. While we have been researching the question of how adults relate their learning to their work, family and social lives for a number of years, this is clearly an enormous topic, and much more work remains to be done. We would be the first to admit that there is much more data to be collected, as we cannot imagine that the adults we have studied so far are wholly representative. In particular, there is more work to be done among groups of adults who are not directly involved in either employment or education.

These caveats aside, however, we would wish to argue that the analytical vignettes we have presented are suggestive, and make a significant contribution to our developing understanding of this area. From the work presented in this chapter, we draw three broad conclusions.

First, the relations that adults make between their educational involvement and their other life roles develop throughout their lives. We all enter adult life having spent a great deal of time in education, not all of it fruitfully, and for many of us our immediate subsequent response is one of rejection: education is not allowed a further role. For many, possibly most of us, it later comes to assume, at least from time to time, an important role. Indeed, this role may be central; the one that helps to make sense of the whole of our lives.

Second, the ways in which adults use education, and relate it to other aspects of their lives, are manifold, varied and multifaceted. They may link it to their work, to their family life, to their leisure interests or to a number of these, or they may see no need to relate it to anything else at all. The ways in which they see these linkages will change over time and as their engagement in learning changes. Others, such as their employers and their partners, will have an influence over these linkages, but the real meaning is made by the individual adults themselves.

Third, as the discussion so far should have demonstrated, a key to understanding how adults use and locate education is the recognition that this is, at root, perceptual. As outsiders, and as researchers, we may see linkages between individuals' life roles, but if they are not perceived as such by the individuals themselves, how much meaning do they have? Thus, when an organisation sets out to create a culture of learning among its members, its success might be judged by how far the meaning of education has changed for them. That is not, of course, to deny the importance of developing appropriate, institutional structures for supporting learning.

This linkage between changing individual perceptions and developing support structures parallels the interconnection between our two themes: the changing role of education throughout life, and the relationships between education and other activities. These cross-sectional and longitudinal perspectives are intimately related, as each adult's account of their educational and life history is necessarily placed within the succession of contexts they have experienced. Moreover, our actions today, as policy makers, students, researchers or whatever, will change these contexts for future learners.

For the policy maker, the concern is primarily about how developing improved structures to support learning, and attempting to change individuals' perceptions, may strengthen both the role of education and its linkage to other domains in adult life. For the student, the responses are likely to be more practical and personal. Do you, for example, as the reader of this chapter, find elements that ring true or relate to your own experiences? For the researcher, while there is an interest in both policy and practice, the primary focus remains the continuing endeavour to better understand how adults relate their education to their work, family and social lives.

References

Arber, S and Gilbert, N (1992) 'Re-assessing women's working lives' in *Women and Working Lives: Divisions and Change*, S Arber and N Gilbert (eds), 1–13, Macmillan, Basingstoke.

Blaxter, L, Hughes, C and Tight, M (1995) *Nursing, Teaching or Office Work? Revisiting Women's Initial Career Expectations and Choices*, (unpublished), Department of Continuing Education, University of Warwick, Coventry.

Blaxter, L, Hughes, C and Tight, M (1996) Living lifelong education: the experiences of some working class women, *Adults Learning*, 7(7), 169–71.

Blaxter, L and Tight, M (1994a) Juggling with time: how adults manage their time for lifelong education, *Studies in the Education of Adults*, 26(2), 162–79.

Blaxter, L and Tight, M (1994b) Time management and part-time study, *Adults Learning*, 5(5), 126–7.

Blaxter, L and Tight, M (1995) Life transitions and educational participation by adults, *International Journal of Lifelong Education*, 14(3), 231–46.

Crowder, M and Pupynin, K (1993) *The Motivation to Train*, Department of Employment, Sheffield.

Goldschmidt, W (1990) *The Human Career: the Self in the Symbolic World*, Blackwell, Oxford.

Hughes, C and Tight, M (1995) The myth of the learning society, *British Journal of Educational Studies*, 43(3), 290–304.

Sharpe, S (1994) *Just Like a Girl: How Girls Learn to be Women. From the Seventies to the Nineties*, Penguin, Harmondsworth.

Tight, M (1995) Education, Work and Adult Life: a Literature Review, *Research Papers in Education*, 10(3), 383–400.

Tinto, V (1987) *Leaving College: Rethinking the Causes and Cures of Student Attrition*, University of Chicago Press, Chicago.

THE PARTICULAR CONTEXT OF THE MATURE STUDENT IN HIGHER EDUCATION

CHAPTER 12

The Personal Experience of Learning in Higher Education:
Changing Views and Enduring Perspectives

Elizabeth Beaty, Gloria Dall'Alba
and Ference Marton

Differing views of learning

As should be evident from the various contributions to this book, there are many ways in which adult learners can be characterised. One of the options is to describe what they are like (in terms of background, characteristics, personality traits and other attributes). Another option is to describe what they do (in terms of the characteristic ways of studying engaged in or the characteristic ways of learning).

An alternative, or rather a complementary option, is to reveal how learning and the learning situation appear to the learner. One might argue, for instance, that we get a better understanding of the learners' acts if we manage to find out what the situation in relation to which they act looks like from their perspective. Säljö (1982) has pointed out that once the learner defines the situation as a 'learning situation' their perception of it is contingent on what learning (in general) means to them. Accordingly, Säljö (1979) distinguished five different ways in which adults see learning. His findings have been given support by other researchers (for instance, Van Rossum and Schenk, 1984). In an earlier study of students at the Open University in the UK (Marton *et al.*, 1993), we have found similar variation to that described by Säljö but were able to elaborate it further and found six (instead of five) ways in which learning was viewed by the students, as follows.

A *Increasing one's knowledge*
  There is a strong quantitative and taken-for-granted flavour to this way of experiencing learning. Its indicators are the collection, consumption and storage of ready-made pieces of knowledge (information), together with a quantitative, discrete character of knowledge (information).

B *Memorising and reproducing*
  Learning is typically seen in quantitative terms, as a (rote) reproduction

of something memorised and the orientation to a test or performance. The distinction between this way of experiencing learning and the previous one primarily relates to the formal educational situations to which it refers, where a requirement to reproduce something memorised is anticipated.

C *Application*
The emphasis is on the ability to apply some knowledge or procedure when the need arises. What is to be applied is taken in and stored for later use, as required. While there are similarities with A and B above, this view of learning can be distinguished from A through the emphasis on application. It differs from B in the sense that the knowledge or procedure is to be used, not merely reproduced, and it is not confined to tests or performance in formal educational situations.

D *Understanding*
In A–C above, what is acquired through learning is seen as ready made or given, to be taken in and stored. The views of learning described in D–F can be distinguished from those described above in the sense that what is learned is no longer taken for granted or given. Rather, the learner has a critical role in the making of meaning. In D the emphasis is on grasping the meaning of learning material in the study situation. Visual metaphors, such as looking into or having a view of the learning material, are common.

E *Seeing something in a different way*
As for D above, this view of learning involves coming to grasp or see something in a certain way. In E, however, the emphasis is on change to a new way of seeing. Furthermore, situations for learning are no longer limited to study settings and course material. Instead, the student typically comes to see something in the world outside the university in a new way, often from material learned within the university context.

F *Changing as a person*
In this case learning is afforded a more personal character than for those described above. Seeing something in the world in a new way enables change as a person. Learning is an integral and ongoing part of the life of the person concerned.

Longitudinal studies of learning and related phenomena

Unlike Säljö's investigation, the Open University study was longitudinal, following a group of students over their six years of undergraduate study. This allows us to examine what changes and what remains unchanged during the course of studies. This is the focus of the present chapter.

While our specific focus here is closely related to how learning is viewed,

Beaty and Morgan (1992), making use of other parts of the same data set, concentrated on the development of the student's skill in learning.

The analysis revealed a consistent link between three aspects of development from the student's point of view. The first development was in confidence. Over the six years of the study the students referred frequently to their feeling of growth in confidence and illustrated this in what they felt able to do. The second area of development was that of competence in studying; the development of their own approach to study tasks. Again this was illustrated by their description of the ways in which they approached studying particular courses. The third area of development was shown in the control the students had over their own study patterns. In the beginning of their studies they described studying in terms of attempting to do what the course expected them to do. In subsequent years they described taking more decisions about what and how and how much they studied different parts of the courses. The authors described this as a development in autonomy in relation to their own work on the course.

Two frequently quoted longitudinal studies are relevant here: that of William Perry who followed students at Harvard (all male) throughout their college years, and Mary Field Belenky and her colleagues who studied women students and recent alumni of formal educational institutions and women consulting maternal and child health clinics.

Perry characterised intellectual and ethical development in terms of a scheme with nine positions, as follows.

1. Right answers for everything exist in the absolute, known to authority, whose role is to mediate (teach) them.
2. The student perceives diversity of opinion and uncertainty, accounting for them as unwarranted confusion in poorly qualified authorities or as learning exercises set by authority.
3. The student accepts diversity and uncertainty as legitimate but still temporary in areas where authority 'hasn't found the answer yet'.
4. (a) The student raises legitimate uncertainty to the status of an unstructured epistemological realm of its own in which 'anyone has a right to his own opinion'.
   (b) The student discovers qualitative, contextual, relativistic reasoning as a special case of 'what they want' within authority's realm.
5. The student perceives all knowledge and values (including authority's) as contextual and relativistic and subordinates dualistic right–wrong functions to the status of a special case, in context.
6. The student apprehends the necessity of orienting himself in a relativistic world through some form of personal commitment.
7. The student makes an initial commitment in some area.
8. The student experiences the implications of commitment, and explores the subjective and stylistic issues of responsibility.
9. The student experiences the affirmation of identity among multiple

representations and realises commitment as an ongoing, unfolding activity through which he expresses his lifestyle (derived from Perry, 1970, pp.9–10).

Belenky *et al.* (1986, p.156) described 'frameworks of meaning making' that evolve. In response to Perry's focus on men, Belenky *et al.* focused on the experience of women. The ways of knowing described by the women in the study by Belenky *et al.* are,

- 'silence, a position in which women experience themselves as mindless and voiceless and subject to the whims of external authority;
- received knowledge, a perspective from which women conceive of themselves as capable of receiving, even reproducing, knowledge from the all-knowing external authorities but not capable of creating knowledge on their own;
- subjective knowledge, a perspective from which truth and knowledge are conceived of as personal, private, and subjectively known or intuited;
- procedural knowledge, a position in which women are invested in learning and applying objective procedures for obtaining and communicating knowledge; and
- constructed knowledge, a position in which women view all knowledge as contextual, experience themselves as creators of knowledge, and value both subjective and objective strategies for knowing.' (p.15)

In general, the pattern of development from reliance on authorities for truth and knowledge to construction of one's own knowledge and commitments, with recognition of the contingent nature of knowledge and truth, are similar for both the studies by Perry and Belenky *et al.* However, one of the features of the results from the study by Belenky *et al.* which differs from Perry's results is the prevalence of the metaphor of voice and the integration of a sense of voice, self and mind during intellectual and ethical development:

> The tendency for women to ground their epistemological premises in metaphors suggesting speaking and listening is at odds with the visual metaphors (such as equating knowledge with illumination, knowing with seeing, and truth with light) that scientists and philosophers most often use to express their sense of mind.... Unlike seeing, speaking and listening suggest dialogue and interaction (Belenky *et al.*, 1986, p.18).

Development is a strong emphasis in these longitudinal studies and it was also the initial interest in our study of the Open University students. In analysing the data, however, we were struck by the fact that there are threads running through individual cases.

Individually characteristic themes in changing views of learning

The Open University context

The Open University has an open admissions policy whereby any adult who is able to study may gain entry. The degree courses are primarily designed for students to study part time through distance learning. To gain an ordinary degree, students must pass six credits (normally students take one credit per year although they may take up to two credits). All students are required to begin with a foundation course.

The students

The 29 students in the study (18 women and 11 men) all began with a social science foundation course in 1980; thereafter their course choice diverged widely. Therefore, in this study we follow students on very different degree courses over six years. The students were randomly sampled from among those living within a 100-mile radius of the Open University central offices. None of the students in the sample had any qualification beyond A level. For each year of the study all students in the sample who registered for a course were interviewed about their experiences of studying. One of the issues raised in each interview concerned how the students viewed learning. This part of the interview was the focus of a previous paper (Marton *et al.*, 1993). Here we also take the remainder of the interview into consideration.

The interviews occurred at the beginning and end of the first year and, subsequently, towards the end of each year in which they took a course. The sample was depleted over the six years through drop-out and students moving away from the area. After ten years, only eight of the original group of students had gained their degrees. This pattern is consistent with Open University statistics which reveal a very high drop-out rate in the early stages of the degree. During the six years of the study, there were six students who were interviewed on five or six occasions. As it happened, all of these students were women. The case studies that follow therefore describe women studying at a distance.

Changing conceptions of learning

The conceptions of learning for the six students for whom we have data across five or six occasions are shown in Table 12.1. The intra-individual differences are striking in two cases (Downs and South), in two cases (Baker and Field) less so and in the remaining two (Larkin and Williams) we cannot claim a develop-

Table 12.1 Ways of experiencing learning at university over five to six years.

Interview	1980 1a	1980 1b	1981 2	1982 3	1983 4	1984 5	1985 6
Baker	D	C	D	D			E
Downs	B	B	D	E	F	F	
Field	E	D	D	D	E		F
Larkin	D	D	E	D		D	
South	A	E	E	E	F		F
Williams	E	D	E		E	E	E

ment or progression. There are, however, no conceptions of learning lower than D after year one. In four of these cases (described below), the different conceptions of learning were expressed in individually characteristic ways.

Four Open University students

Eleanor Baker

Baker had been interested in doing a degree for a number of years and had waited until her children were at school before enrolling. She joined the Open University with a clear wish to become better educated. She described this as a need to understand everything, to see what lay behind things, and considered that this would help her to find out what she might go on to do. She also hoped that her studies would enable her to cope with an indistinct future. She described the path towards this as being through an understanding of course material.

During her time on the course Baker was the student who studied in the way intended by the course team: not slavishly following procedures but trying hard to give the course her full attention. She tended not to cut corners and was one of the few students who read recommended texts that were not part of the core course material. In the last interview she described doing some participant observation out of interest in a local political debate. She was fascinated by the way the courses allowed her to understand these local events in quite a different way, but she looked rather than acted.

There is a developmental pattern in Baker's conception of learning that is not immediately evident in the pattern of conceptions expressed from one interview to the next (Table 12.1). In the first interview (1a), she was searching for a conception of learning that involves more than 'to reproduce what you have learned'. What is learned must mean 'something more than just in the way in which you've learnt it'. Learning is a matter of application, which means 'looking at it from the point of view of different discipline explanations'. What is being looked at seems to mean the content of the learning material (conception D).

In interview 1b, she expressed the idea that learning is more than reproducing. You have to apply it; 'you turn it round and make use of it in other
ways' (C). In interview 2, she said that learning is 'understanding, relating
new things to what you already know' (D). In interview 3, she talked about
understanding as 'coming across something fresh and sort of tossing it around
a bit and become sufficiently familiar with it... to have some views, some sort
of informed views about it'. She was not referring to 'just remembering
things'(D). In interview 3 we can see the continuity and the difference (development) between conception C (in interview 1b) and conception D (in interview 3). The expression 'turn it round and make use of it' was found in the
former case and the expression 'tossing it around... to have some views' was
found in the latter case. The spatial metaphor (with a revolving movement) is
common in both cases. However, in conception C, as mentioned above, you
do something with the tool, with that retrieved knowledge, while in conception D you see the phenomenon in a different way.

Interview 6 was conducted three years later. The familiar, everyday world
was no longer seen as separate from what is learned from courses. The difficulty of relating the two was resolved. Their integration evolved from the
framework provided by disciplinary knowledge. This framework equipped
Baker with particular ways of thinking (such as 'seeing things as systems' and
not 'just as isolated facts'). The disciplinary knowledge enabled her 'to look at
the world with those eyes' and discover the structures and patterns located in
the world (the skill aspect of conception E).

We can see that there is a common theme or thread running through the
different interviews; the emphasis on disciplinary knowledge. There is development, however, in the sense that disciplinary knowledge becomes integrated with everyday reality. The development takes place in accordance with
the theme, the everyday world is seen from the point of view of disciplinary
knowledge.

Abigail Downs

Downs had a clear orientation; she wanted to broaden her horizons. She had
a very successful husband, whom she described as a tycoon. She wanted to be
more interesting to him as well as to have something that was beyond looking
after the two small children. (She had the second child halfway through her
first year of study.)

In her second year of study a relative committed suicide and this was a
devastating event in her life. She struggled to keep up with the coursework
and yet she said that the Open University became more important during that
time, as it represented a safe normality that the rest of her life lacked. The
experience in this year appears to have made her stand back from her life and
ask the question, 'What is important to me?'

Over a number of years she completely changed her style of dress, her house and her politics and became a radical feminist. She commented that if it had not been for the Open Univeristy her marriage would not have survived. The Open University became her own project that allowed her to keep up with her husband. One thing that showed her enormous growth in confidence was that she successfully challenged the Open University rules on the need to take a second foundation course. Over the six years she gradually took more control over her studying so that, finally, she felt she did not need to study with the Open University but could go out and study what she wanted on her own.

In interview 1a Downs clearly expressed a conceptualisation of learning as memorising (conception B).

> 'If I read something I'm so bothered about taking in what it says that I read it and I think, what have I just read? I don't even know who wrote it or what it was about and I think at the moment I feel worried about not taking in what I am doing or what I am learning.'

In interview 1b she said that learning is 'the learning of facts – more like school work' (conception B) and she argued that the course was about 'seeing things in a different light' which was definitely not learning. In interview 2 she claimed that learning is something that 'gives me a new awareness… I am aware now of things that I possibly wasn't aware of before… I just look further into things and maybe think a bit more, and think of the other person's point of view'. Her awareness is related to the study situation and the learning material (conception D), but in interview 3 she spoke about an awareness of her relation to the world around her.

> 'I'm very aware of everything affecting me… this has sort of grown with being with the Open University… just knowing that I know why or that I can see a let-out or I can see that I can affect me in what happens to me more than I thought I could.'

She recognised that she had developed ways of seeing that made her more capable; she had a feeling of being more in charge of her own life. This means that a conceptualisation of learning that is framed in terms of the skill aspect of conception E (being more capable of seeing the world in certain ways) enabled a change in her perception of herself and of the relation between herself and the world. Downs affords the clearest expression of an element that is implicit both in conceptions E (especially in its skill aspect) and F; the most important outcome of education is developing ways of seeing or ways of experiencing certain phenomena in, or aspects of, reality.

In interview 4 the distinction between learning and changing your view of reality, that was introduced in interview 1b, arose again. She seemed to regard

157

it as a paradox that the study of books might change her view of the world beyond the study situation. The paradox was, however, resolved by focusing on the continuity of the person.

> 'The unit is probably only a hundredth of the learning and the rest goes on once you put it down. And the next time you read your newspaper it might look different... or you might think about different things.... I can close the book now. It doesn't stop there, that's just where it starts.'

This means that learning is,

> 'something personal and it's also something that's continuous, once it starts it carries on and it might lead to other things. It might be like a root that has other branches coming off it... it is for the person before and for the person afterwards sort of thing.'

The paradox is resolved by seeing formal learning as a small, but critical and indistinguishable, part in the continuous change of the person. Formal learning contributes significantly to the change and, thus, to the person's changed view of the world (conception F; the person changes). The same conception is expressed in interview 5, albeit in somewhat different words.

> 'Learning is self-realisation... when I've been made aware of something... the effect of learning how I feel... I've got more positive views and more positive ideas and I know which side of the fence I am on.'

Again, learning is seen as a change of the person (conception F).

Downs shows the clearest developmental pattern of the six cases (BBDEFF). Yet, there is something stable. There is an overarching theme; her focus is herself. Although she conceptualised learning in widely varying ways, it was always seen from the point of view of her own person and it culminated in some straightforward statements about the organic character of learning and human cognition in general. The experiences you have continue to grow, to lead further on, and they become interwoven with other experiences in the present and the future. There is an interesting similarity with the view of a young female student participating in an earlier study on student learning.

> 'When you read something, then just afterwards you're not really quite sure about it. But after perhaps a day or an hour or so, as a result of experiences or events which jog your mind, it sort of works its way into a more solid perception in some way, which you stick to.... And other people's comments provide an impetus to get your think-

ing along different lines. And they help, even if they don't give you the idea directly.' (Marton and Säljö, 1984, p.45).

Mary Field

Field felt that she had wasted her time earlier in life. She had been clever at school but had not wanted to carry on studying after school. She felt unable to express all her views at home and, at first, tended to keep quiet in tutorials. As she moved into the later years of study, she described feeling more able to participate in discussions over dinner and to have informed conversations with friends. In describing her study and interest in the Open University courses she frequently spoke about her past life, which was northern working-class and very different from her current southern, affluent, middle-class environment. She described her views as emanating from her background.

Married with two children at school, but not employed outside the home, Field wanted to use the Open University to do something interesting and worthwhile. She envisaged going back to work when the children were older and thought that Open University study would help in a general way to get a job. Towards the end of the course she began work in the Citizens Advice Bureau. She said that she now felt she could surprise people with her knowledge when she wished to. In interview 1a she expressed a conceptualisation of learning as seeing things in a different way. Learning 'changes the perspective on things and makes me look at things in ways that I haven't thought of before'. One example of the 'things' she saw differently is immigration (one of the three examples used in the first unit of the course), clearly a phenomenon in the 'real world' (conception E). Her conceptualisation has a skill aspect that is evident when she said, 'I hope that learning will make me see things a lot clearer... look at life differently'.

In interview 1b she clearly expressed a view of learning as understanding. Learning is 'to understand on my own terms... what the person who's writing it means'. She was referring to the learning situation (conception D). In interview 2 the study situation was still in focus, although the skill aspect of learning as understanding was emphasised.

> 'have a process of thought that sort of "sets in motion" when you look at something... looking at something new in a far more logical way, and seeing the steps and the moves towards arriving at some sort of conclusion... learning is thinking clearer.'

She was talking about applying what she has learned earlier, but 'applying' in this case refers to the act of understanding. She said, 'Whatever I am thinking about, whatever I have done before becomes relevant to a new problem, or a new area of study'. Learning was seen by Field in terms of the skill aspect of learning as understanding; 'Perhaps it is just the skill you have learned of thinking more coherently' (conception D).

In interview 3 she said that learning is 'personal development'. In the absence of further explanation we make the interpretation that personal development means for her what it did in the previous interview, namely, thinking more clearly and more coherently (conception D, skill aspect). In interview 4 she conceptualised learning in terms of 'understanding how things work... and why things are like they are... You see things in different ways so your perceptions are different'. The 'things' to which she referred are things in the world beyond the study situation. Learning is 'understanding how things work in the world and how you fit into the world, particularly your experience'. Furthermore, the skill aspect is present: 'widening your horizons and opening up your mind a bit more' (conception E).

In interview 6 Field said that learning is,

'expanding yourself. It is being more alive, more aware, feeling more in control. You tend to think that life just took hold of you and did what it wanted with you and I think that you come to realise that now you should take hold of life and make it go your way because you know that it is possible.'

This feeling of 'being in charge' is similar to the feeling described by Abigail Downs in interview 5 and, as was the case there, learning is understood as a change of the person (conception F).

Throughout the interviews Field seemed to focus on the ways of seeing, the ways of thinking, and emphasised the capability of doing so (that is, the skill aspect of learning). On two occasions she also gave an explanation of how those ways of seeing or thinking develop: 'all that you have learned earlier affects how you learn the new' (interview 5); and 'you try to fit your previous experiences into the world: whatever I am thinking about, whatever I have actually done before becomes relevant to a new problem, or a new area of study' (interview 2). This is a distinct and interesting idea, namely, that all previous experiences are present and mould new experiences. A similar idea was expressed by the 1982 Nobel Laureate in Chemistry, Aaron Klug, in a television discussion entitled 'Science and Man', which was broadcast in Sweden shortly after the Nobel Prize ceremony. 'One doesn't see with one's eyes, one sees with the whole fruit of one's previous experience' (Marton *et al.*, 1994, p.467).

Emily South

South initially displayed a lack of confidence in her own ability. She said in the first interview that she didn't know how she had the courage to participate in the interview as she had almost not had the courage to enrol in the Open University. Among all of the students, she was the least confident in the beginning. She had married an older man and since marriage had worked in support of his business. She felt this had weakened her general knowledge about the world and she looked to the course to improve this. She wanted to be more informed in a general way. South showed a great deal of change in her approach to studying after entering the Open University.

In interview 1a South conceptualised learning as an increase in one's knowledge, 'gaining new knowledge of different subjects you know' (conception A). In interview 1b, however, she expressed the E conception (seeing things in new ways). She said, 'You might have seen it in one way before and you sort of see it in a different way now'.

In interview 2 she went further in the sense that she explained what the change of view meant; instead of only seeing things from one's own perspective (how it affects me), things can be seen from different perspectives. Furthermore, there is a skill aspect; learning is 'knowing how to approach things so that you can understand them' (conception E). This skill aspect is emphasised in interview 3 when she said that learning equips us 'with tools to analyse things' (in the real world) and these tools are 'different ideas, complex ones' (the skill aspect of conception E). In interview 4 she picked up the themes from interview 2 (replacing the egocentric perspective) and interview 3 (the skill aspect). She said that to learn is 'to understand why things are the way they are, instead of seeing things from one's own point of view'. This knowledge about why things happen seemed to give her a feeling of being in charge (conception F), similar to that in Abigail Downs's (interview 5) and Mary Field's (interview 6) cases.

> 'Before I was studying at all I thought, "Just lead your own life and things happen or they don't happen". But not now; just knowing more about how things work doesn't give you more of a say but at least it makes you realise sometimes why things are the way they are, that some things that you might not like are perhaps unavoidable.'

In interview 6, she emphasised the awareness of differing points of view and the insight into why people have those points of view and, again, she talked about herself as being a more competent and confident person (conception F).

The overarching theme is how one progresses from having only one's own point of view to becoming able to see things from different points of view and thus arriving at a better grasp of why things (including the various points of view) are the way they are. This widening of horizons has important implications for seeing oneself as a participant (rather than only a spectator) in what is happening. This is a clear example of re-centering with a somewhat paradoxical result: by transcending your own point of view, by distancing yourself

161

from it, you consider yourself as a much more capable person. Through being able to adopt multiple perspectives you become more confident.

Learning as lived

The structure of variation

As was pointed out above, in this chapter we are dealing with an idea that originates from an earlier study (Marton *et al.*, 1993). There we made use of a phenomenographic approach (Marton, 1994), aimed at revealing qualitative differences in views of learning expressed by Open University students. In the section above we showed how these views varied over six years of studying (see Table 12.1). We have argued, however, that regardless of the extent of variation there are individually characteristic themes underlying this variation. Eleanor Baker focuses mainly on disciplinary knowledge. Abigail Downs's focus is herself, as a person. Mary Field focuses on the act of learning; on capability, on the skills that originate from learning. Emily South can also be said to have herself as a focus but in a different way to that of Abigail Downs.

At the same time, there is commonality among the four cases; one main motive for enrolling in the Open University is to become more capable, to become more confident. As was pointed out above, Beaty and Morgan (1992) showed that a growth of confidence is a central feature of development at the Open University. So studying there is deeply personal both as far as motive and actual development are concerned. But within this commonality there are thus individually characteristic themes. By studying something, disciplinary knowledge (the object), you become capable of acting in a more competent way (the act) and thereby you see yourself in a different way (the subject). As Marton *et al.* (in press) have pointed out, subject, act and object are fundamental components of the variation in how learning is experienced. We can thus conclude that although these different components are intrinsically related to each other there are differences in centring (from the point of view of which component the other components are seen). These differences in centring are visible in our case-study data and constitute individually characteristic dimensions against which variation is evident, representing different but related aspects of the ways in which learning is experienced.

Orientations to studying and individually characteristic themes

Within one interview it might be expected that a theme would emerge, being the focus of attention at the time, but it is certainly more significant when these themes are demonstrated over interviews a year apart over six years.

How can we make sense of these consistencies? A clue lies in the first interviews where the students were asked about their intentions when enrolling with the Open University and the place of studying in their lives. For all these students, taking an Open University degree was a project, something they took on to fulfil a particular purpose in their lives and they were all able to describe their aims, hopes and fears. Eleanor Baker, for example, talked about wanting a better understanding of things; to feel that she really understood, and was looking forward to having time to read. Abigail Downs wanted to broaden her horizons, to become a more interesting person. She was looking forward to the pleasure of studying. Mary Field wanted to widen her view of life and to increase her ability to join the job market and Emily South wanted to gain confidence, to prove to herself that she could study at a higher level and to become 'more than a mother and a wife'.

These projects relate to their orientation in studying (Taylor, 1983; Gibbs *et al.*, 1984). Orientation describes students' personal reasons for studying, what they want to gain. It can be seen that all the four case studies show students with personal orientations, either seeing study as a way of developing themselves or proving that they are capable of university study. Their particular orientations appear to act as a filter through which they experience learning over the six years. In the original research on orientation, personal orientation was demonstrated mostly with older undergraduates. Vocational, academic and social orientations were more common among the younger students. Since all Open Univeristy students are mature (in the cases above aged between 30 and 42 at first interview), it is not surprising to find this emphasis on aspects of personal orientation in our case studies.

Research looking at students' experience of reading texts has also found a relationship between the different experiences and the reasons for studying (Mann, 1987). In this study, students both defined the task of reading differently and approached the task differently from each other. The activity of reading itself means something different for each student. The meaning reading had for each student is related to the meaning of being a student. Although Mann's analysis is not in terms of orientation and is looking at a more micro setting of reading a text, her conclusions are very similar to our own in linking themes within views of learning to the life project or what it means to be a student.

Gender and the experience of learning

As we noted earlier in the chapter, those students for whom we have interview data across five or six occasions were all women. The question arises, then, to what extent similarities emerge between the women in our study and those in the study by Belenky *et al.* described above. As in Belenky *et al.*, and also in Perry's studies, there is evidence in our data of a development from reliance on authorities for truth and knowledge to construction of one's own knowledge and commitments, with recognition of the contingency of knowledge and truth. As for Belenky *et al.*, the women in our study tended not to align themselves with authority.

Belenky *et al.* report the prevalence among the women of an emphasis on development of self, voice and mind. For the women in our study, such development was closely related to their motives for studying and the focus of their development. They described broadening their outlook and becoming more informed as being related to their reasons for studying and the gains they make. They emphasised understanding other perspectives and points of view, as for the study by Belenky *et al.*, but in contrast to the emphasis placed on judging among Perry's men. One of the conceptions identified in our earlier study, learning as changing as a person, explicitly expresses a focus on development of self. Three of the four women for whom change occurs from the first to the final interview reach a position of conceiving learning in terms of changing as a person.

Conclusion

Beyond the differences over time and the differences between individuals there are fundamental commonalities in the experience of learning. Although we expect the architecture of the variations and commonalities in the experience of learning to be generalisable, the individually characteristic themes may be gendered. In the four cases above, the students experience their studies as personally transformative. They want to become more capable and be seen as such. They want to become more confident, and this actually happens. These commonalities of experience reasonably have to do with similarities in their conditions of life; they are all women, for instance, at a particular stage of life. Learning in these cases is thus something that concerns the person, that concerns one's life. What we have been dealing with here is the existential aspect of learning or, in other words, learning as lived.

References

Beaty, E and Morgan, A (1992) Developing skill in learning, *Open Learning*, 7, 3–11.
Belenky, M F, Clinchy, B M, Goldberger, N R and Tarule, J M (1986) *Women's Ways of Knowing: The Development of Self, Voice, and Mind*, Basic Books, New York.
Gibbs, G, Morgan, A R and Taylor, E (1984) 'The world of the learner' in *The Experience of Learning*, F Marton, D Hounsell and N J Entwistle (eds), 165–88, Scottish Academic Press, Edinburgh.
Mann, S J (1987) *Revealing and Understanding Reading: an Investigation with Eighteen Readers*, PhD thesis, Department of Educational Research, University of Lancaster.
Marton, F (1994) 'Phenomenography' in *The International Encyclopedia of Educa-*

tion, 2nd edn, T Husén and T N Postlethwaite (eds), Pergamon Press, Oxford.

Marton, F, Dall'Alba, G, and Beaty, E(1993) Conceptions of learning, *International Journal of Educational Research*, 19, 277–300.

Marton, F, Fensham, P and Chaiklin, S (1994) A Nobel's eye view of scientific intuition: discussion with the Nobel prize winners in physics, chemistry and medicine (1970–1986), *International Journal of Science Education*, 16, 457–73.

Marton, F and Säljö, R (1984) 'Approaches to learning' in *The Experience of Learning*, F Marton, D Hounsell and N J Entwistle (eds), 36–55, Scottish Academic Press, Edinburgh.

Marton, F, Tang, C and Watkins, D (in press) Continuities and discontinuities in the experience of learning: An interview study of high-school students in Hong Kong, *Learning and Instruction*.

Perry, W G (1970) *Forms of Intellectual and Ethical Development in the College Years: a Scheme*, Holt, Rinehart and Winston, New York.

Säljö, R (1979) *Learning in the Learner's Perspective I. Some Common-sense Conceptions*, no. 76, Reports from the Department of Education, University of Göteborg, Sweden.

Säljö, R (1982) *Learning and Understanding: a Study of Differences in Constructing Meaning From a Text*, Acta Universitatis Gothoburgensis, Göteborg, Sweden.

Taylor, E (1983) *Orientations to Study: a Longitudinal Interview Investigation of Students of Two Human Studies Degree Courses*, PhD thesis, University of Surrey, Guildford.

Van Rossum, E J and Schenk, S M (1984) The relationship between learning conception, study strategy and learning outcome, *British Journal of Educational Psychology*, 54, 73–83.

CHAPTER 13

Dispelling some Myths about Mature Students in Higher Education:

Study Skills, Approaches to Studying, and Intellectual Ability

John T E Richardson

Introduction

In most countries institutions of higher education have traditionally endeavoured to recruit from among the more highly qualified young people leaving secondary schools. As a consequence, older students have been few in number and have had a relatively marginal role. However, the situation in the UK has changed over the last ten years. National policy and funding arrangements have been revised to stimulate considerable expansion of provision of higher education, and yet there has not been a concomitant increase during this period in the number of qualified students supplied by secondary schools. A largely unintended aspect of these national developments has therefore been a proportionately larger increase in the number of 'mature' students, officially defined as those aged 21 or over who are admitted to undergraduate courses or those aged 25 or over who are admitted to postgraduate courses.

The UK is by no means unique in this regard. Indeed, the numbers of older students have been increasing since the mid-1970s in both Australia, where those students aged 25 or over on admission are described as 'mature-age' students, and the USA, where those students aged 22 or over on admission are described as 'adult' students. In both cases, the increases in question have been the result not of initiatives from the national government, but of demands for greater access to higher education for older students in the light of demographic, economic and technological developments. Of course, similar demands were expressed in the UK with regard to mature students and other groups who had traditionally been under-represented in higher education.

Nevertheless, discussions about the role of mature students in higher education tend to emphasise their supposed needs rather than the potential benefits that they can bring. Indeed, many accounts characterise the situation of mature students as one that is inherently problematic. For example, a recent volume published by the American Psychological Association referred to mature students solely in terms of their special needs and problems (Ware et al., 1993, pp.53, 62–3). Similarly, a British volume considered mature students solely in terms of the problems and issues that they might present (Wheeler and Birtle, 1993, Chap.6). The authors proposed that these could be understood in terms of the life cycle and the concept of the 'mid-life crisis'. Their account culminated in the warning, 'If a crisis has not yet occurred then watch out for it' (p.88).

Haselgrove (1994) suggested that institutions of higher education have been led to construe the experience of mature students as problematic because it stemmed from roles other than that of learners. In other words, mature students tend to be regarded as having 'difficulties' studying in higher education because the rest of their lives (financial, emotional and personal) impinge on the only role in which institutions are prepared to recognise them. As Haselgrove shrewdly commented, 'The unacknowledged reality is, of course, that these roles have always impinged on students' experience of higher education but the prevailing culture did not permit its articulation' (p.6). Nowadays, indeed, 'non-academic' factors affect the lives and experiences of increasing numbers of younger students, too.

Mature students are however consistently stigmatised by even the most well-intentioned authors with respect to their capacity to benefit from higher education. Moreover, these pejorative stereotypes are often shared by mature students themselves. This does not of course validate those stereotypes, although the resulting levels of anxiety among mature students might well constitute a means by which they could be led to behave in ways that confirmed those stereotypes as a 'self-fulfilling prophecy'. The arguments that tend to be given in justification of those stereotypes usually concern the study skills, approaches to studying and intellectual capacities of mature students.

Study skills in mature students

Many mature students seeking entrance to higher education undertake a period of study in further education by way of preparation. In the UK, this might include studying for one or more qualifications at A level or undertaking an 'Access' course. However, other older applicants lack recent experience of formal education, and many commentators therefore suggest that they may be out of practice in learning. As a result, such students might be expected to encounter problems in effective studying and time management.

The notion that studying in higher education relies upon a variety of basic skills is a fairly plausible one, but the far stronger position that one particular set of skills constitutes effective studying and guarantees good academic attainment has been discredited. Although it is possible to identify a 'study skills' factor in self-reports of studying behaviour, this does not show any consistent relationship with academic performance. Moreover, although manuals and guides intended to promote study skills have a long history, it is also a fairly chequered one. The available evidence suggests that any skills involved in being an effective learner need to be acquired in the context of everyday academic activities.

One domain in which mature students are sometimes said to encounter problems is that of time management (eg Wheeler and Birtle, 1993, p.85), despite the fact that many mature students have been successfully juggling a variety of domestic and occupational responsibilities for several years. Trueman and Hartley (1996) built upon previous research carried out in the USA to try to develop a self-report scale on time management for use with British students. Although there were statistically significant correlations between scores on long-term planning and subsequent academic performance, these relationships were fairly trivial in their magnitude. Moreover, Trueman and Hartley found that mature students who were aged 25 or over on their admission to higher education reported making more use of time-management strategies than either younger mature students who were aged between 21 and 24 on admission or traditional-age students. Clearly, this pattern of results does not support the stereotype of mature students being deficient in terms of the skills needed for effective studying.

Approaches to studying in mature students

The notion that mature students are in some sense inferior to younger students in how they go about the business of learning can be addressed in a different way by comparing their approaches or orientations to studying. There is a general consensus within the research literature that students in higher education manifest a number of different approaches to learning. For example, students may adopt a 'deep' approach that is directed towards comprehending the meaning of the materials to be learned; or they may adopt a 'surface' approach that is directed towards just being able to reproduce those materials for the purposes of academic assessment (see Chapter 12). These different approaches were originally identified in structured interviews carried out with students in connection with particular learning tasks. However, a number of standardised questionnaires have been developed to try to operationalise students' dispositions to adopt specific approaches to learning within their normal academic studies (see Richardson, 1995b).

It is typically assumed that students display particular approaches to learning in response to the perceived context, content and demands of their learning tasks. On the one hand, students are considered to exhibit a deep approach (or a 'meaning orientation') in so far as they acknowledge the more abstract forms of learning that are demanded in higher education and are motivated by the relevance of the syllabus to their own personal needs and interests. On the other hand, they are thought to exhibit a surface approach (or a 'reproducing orientation') in so far as they encounter an overloaded curriculum and methods of assessment that stress the superficial properties of the material that is to be learned.

Different subject areas are associated with different approaches to studying, so that students taking arts courses are more likely than those taking science courses to manifest a deep approach and other aspects of meaning orientation, whereas the reverse is the case for certain aspects of reproducing orientation (see Entwistle and Ramsden, 1983, pp.181–4). Students' approaches to studying are also related to their perceptions of the institutional context, so that a reproducing orientation is associated with perceptions of a heavy workload and a lack of freedom in learning, whereas a meaning orientation is associated with perceptions of freedom in learning and good teaching (Eley, 1992).

Further, there is evidence that individual students adopt different approaches to studying in different contexts in response to the perceived demands of the immediate learning situation. Much of this evidence comes from the use of structured interviews (for example, Gibbs, 1992, pp.8–9). However, Eley (1992) administered questionnaires concerning concurrent pairs of courses that seemed to encourage different approaches to studying. For some students, but not all, 'the course unit perceived as having a significantly greater metacognitive focus, higher emphasis on independent learning, and better support for higher education study, was the unit for which higher rates of deep approaches and lower rates of surface approaches were reported' (p.247).

Moss (1982) administered a questionnaire on learning processes to students who had been referred for remedial tuition in the light of weak academic performance, and she found that they showed a greater dependence upon repetitive methods of studying at the expense of any deep approach. However, two subsequent studies have found that academically unsuccessful students produced incoherent or 'unorchestrated' patterns of responses to formal questionnaires (Entwistle *et al.*, 1991). If mature students are genuinely deficient in their study skills, it would follow that they too should be more likely to adopt a surface approach or a reproducing orientation or perhaps might fail to show any coherent pattern in their orientations to academic learning at all.

In fact, the available evidence on this matter obtained from the use of several different questionnaires is remarkably consistent in confirming neither of these predictions. Adult students are more likely than younger students to exhibit a deep approach or a meaning orientation towards their academic studies; whereas, conversely, they are less likely than younger students to adopt a surface approach or a reproducing orientation towards their academic studies (see Richardson, 1994b, 1995a). Harper and Kember (1986) suggested three possible explanations for this: first, that mature students were motivated more by intrinsic goals than by vocational goals; second, that younger students acquired a surface approach to learning in their final years of secondary education; and, third, that the prior life experience of mature students promoted a deep approach to studying.

Intellectual ability in mature students

To justify the negative stereotyping of mature students as deficient in study skills, some commentators even appeal to the research literature on age-related deficits in cognitive performance. Thus, Woodley (1984) proposed that the capacity for learning may have decreased among older students, 'both in terms of memory and in terms of the mental flexibility required to adapt to new perspectives' (p.47). Similarly, Wheeler and Birtle (1993) suggested that mature students might be 'at a disadvantage compared to younger students with respect to their adaptability, the speed with which they are able to work, and their retentive capacities' (p.92). In a recent article (Richardson, 1994a), I have extensively criticised the notion that mature students are impaired by deficits in intellectual ability, but two points are particularly worth mentioning here.

The first point is that age-related changes in intellectual capacity often amount to a reduction in 'fluid intelligence' or what psychologists nowadays characterise as the available central capacity for information processing. Conversely, there may be little decline with advancing age, and even continuing growth, in 'crystallised intelligence', and especially in tasks that have to do with expertise and the development of systems of knowledge (see Baltes *et al.*, 1984) or what in everyday parlance would be referred to as 'wisdom'. Indeed, Hoyer and Rybash (1994) argued that cognitive expertise (or crystallised intelligence), wisdom and other adaptive competencies might well ensure that the period of adulthood offered the greatest potential and opportunity for utilising the rest of one's capabilities. Moreover, the analysis of 'wisdom' that was proposed by Dittmann-Kohli and Baltes (1990) implies that older people would be more capable of exhibiting the interpretive, contextualised and relativistic conceptions of learning that other commentators have claimed constitute genuine intellectual development amongst university students.

The second point is that age-related cognitive deficits can usually be demonstrated only in people drawn from the general population who are over the ages of 50 or 60 (Baltes *et al.*, 1984). Very few institutions of higher education contain significant numbers of students who fall in this age range. In fact, most mature students in full-time higher education both in the UK and in the USA are aged between 25 and 34, and the evidence suggests that their intellectual abilities are broadly the same as those of younger students. Moreover, cognitive performance in this age range exhibits great inter- and intra-individual variability, which implies that biological and maturational factors are less important than idiosyncratic and contextual influences (Hoyer and Rybash, 1994).

Conclusions

In this chapter, I have tried to rebut the prevalent stereotype that the situation and the experience of mature students in higher education is inherently problematic. I have reviewed three different types of argument and evidence that individually call this stereotype into question and that collectively render it quite untenable. The findings are as follows.

1. The idea that mature students are deficient in their study skills is meaningless, because there is simply no one specific set of skills that constitutes effective studying in higher education.
2. Mature students exhibit approaches to studying that are more desirable than those of younger students, in the sense that they are more compatible with the avowed aims and objectives of higher education.
3. There is essentially no evidence that mature students are subject to age-related deficits in the intellectual capacities needed for studying in higher education.

To these findings, one might add those discussed in Chapter 14, showing that mature students tend to perform as well as younger students on courses in higher education.

One qualification that needs to be added regarding these conclusions is that they are based solely upon research carried out with undergraduate students. Very little has been written concerning the experiences and the capability of mature students who are working for postgraduate degrees by research. The most obvious exception to this is an in-depth study of ten students carried out by Salmon (1992). Very little has been written, too, concerning the increasing numbers of mature students who undertake taught Master's courses. The *Handbook for Personal Tutors* has a chapter entitled 'Mature and postgraduate students' (Wheeler and Birtle, 1993, Chap. 6), which refers only to undergraduate and research students, apart from a brief discussion of a retired army officer who was undertaking a higher degree in engineering as a change of career. This is not a very typical example, since many mature students undertake postgraduate courses to develop their careers rather than to change them.

Gibbs (1992, pp.100 ff.) reported an evaluation of an oceanography module involving independent group field-work which was taken by students on a conventional undergraduate programme and by mature students working for a postgraduate diploma. When requested to complete a questionnaire on their approaches to studying, both groups of students achieved high scores on meaning orientation, but the postgraduate students produced much higher scores on reproducing orientation than the undergraduate students. It is interesting that in discussing the latter finding Gibbs attributed it to a heavier curriculum and the pressure of examinations on the diploma course, and he concluded that the mature students' orientations to studying were deter-mined more by the nature of their experience of higher education than by their age or by the extent of that experience (p.163).

Nevertheless, at least with regard to undergraduate programmes, one can be fairly definite about endorsing the conclusion of Woodley (1984) that 'universities should have few qualms about increasing their mature student intake' (p.189). Elsewhere, I have gone further and argued that the quality of university courses is enriched by the admission of mature students, because it provides school-leavers with opportunities to learn by example from their superior approaches to studying (Richardson, 1994b). In fact, the pejorative stereotypes with which this chapter is concerned do not appear to be shared by those academic staff who have had experience of teaching mature stu-dents. According to a survey that was carried out in Australia by Boon (1980), these academic staff believe that 'mature age students perform better overall than normal age students, that they have a positive influence on the course, and that their tutorial contribution is considerably better than that of normal age students' (p.130).

References

Baltes, P B, Dittmann-Kohli, F and Dixon, R A (1984) 'New perspectives on the devel-opment of intelligence in adulthood: Toward a dual-process conception and a model of selective optimization with compensation' in *Life-span Development and Behavior*, vol 6, P B Baltes and O G Brim, Jr (eds), 33–76), Academic Press, Orlando, Florida.

Boon, P K (1980) 'Attitudes of staff towards mature students' in *Mature Age Students in Australian Higher Education*, T Hore and L H T West (eds), 122–39, Higher Edu-cation Advisory and Research Unit, Monash University, Clayton, Australia.

Dittmann-Kohli, F and Baltes, P B (1990) 'Toward a neofunctionalist conception of adult intellectual development: Wisdom as a prototypical case of intellectual growth' in *Higher Stages of Human Development: Perspectives on Adult Growth*, C N Alexander and E J Langer (eds), 54–78, Oxford University Press, New York.

Eley, M G (1992) Differential adoption of study approaches within individual stu-dents, *Higher Education*, 23, 231–54.

Entwistle, N, Meyer, J H F and Tait, H (1991) Student failure: integrated perceptions of studying and the learning environment, *Higher Education*, 21, 249–61.

Entwistle, N J and Ramsden, P (1983) *Understanding Student Learning*, Croom Helm, London.

Gibbs, G (1992) *Improving the Quality of Student Learning*, Technical and Educa-tional Services, Bristol.

Harper, G and Kember, D (1986) Approaches to study of distance education students, *British Journal of Educational Technology*, 17, 212–22.

Haselgrove, S (1994) 'Why the student experience matters' in *The Student Experience*, S Haselgrove (ed.), 3–8, Society for Research into Higher Education and Open University Press, Buckingham.

Hoyer, W J and Rybash, J M (1994) Characterizing adult cognitive development, *Journal of Adult Development*, 1, 7–12.

Moss, C J (1982) Academic achievement and individual differences in the learning processes of basic skills students in the university, *Applied Psychological Measurement*, 6, 291–6.

Richardson, J T E (1994a) Mature students in higher education: Academic performance and intellectual ability, *Higher Education*, 28, 373–86.

Richardson, J T E (1994b) Mature students in higher education: I. A literature survey on approaches to studying, *Studies in Higher Education*, 19, 309–25.

Richardson, J T E (1995a) Mature students in higher education: II. An investigation of approaches to studying and academic performance, *Studies in Higher Education*, 20, 5–17.

Richardson, J T E (1995b) 'Using questionnaires to evaluate student learning' in *Improving Student Learning Through Assessment and Evaluation,* G Gibbs (ed.), 499–524, Oxford Centre for Staff Development, Oxford.

Salmon, P (1992) *Achieving a PhD: Ten Students' Experiences*, Trentham Books, Stoke-on-Trent.

Trueman, M and Hartley, J (1996) A comparison between the time-management skills and academic performance of mature and traditional-entry university students, *Higher Education*, 32, 199–215.

Ware, M E, Busch-Rossnagel, N A, Crider, A B, Gray-Shellberg, L, Hale, K, Lloyd, M A, Rivera-Medina, E and Sgro, J A (1993) 'Developing and improving advising: challenges to prepare students for life' in *Handbook for Enhancing Undergraduate Education in Psychology,* T V McGovern (ed.), 47–70, American Psychological Association, Washington, DC.

Wheeler, S and Birtle, J (1993) *A Handbook for Personal Tutors*, Society for Research into Higher Education and Open University Press, Buckingham.

Woodley, A (1984) The older the better? A study of mature student performance in British universities, *Research in Education*, 32, 35–50.

CHAPTER 14

What's the Bottom Line?
How Well do Mature Students
do at University?

James Hartley and Mark Trueman

Introduction

Recent changes in educational policy in the UK have led to an increasing number of mature students entering higher and further education. According to the Department for Education (1994), the number of mature students (defined as being 21 years old or older) entering higher education in Britain more than doubled between 1982 and 1992 (from 139,800 to 319,400), and these figures did not include Open University students. The Department for Education also indicated that in 1992 there were more mature students entering higher education (319,400) than there were young students (281,600). Questions arise, therefore, concerning the opportunities and difficulties for such students, and for their teachers, and how well such students might be expected to perform under traditional (but perhaps now changing) teaching methods.

Table 14.1 summarises the results obtained from a series of studies carried out since the 1970s that have compared the academic performance of mature students in higher education with that of younger traditional-entry ones in different institutions. It can be seen that:

- the older students usually perform as well as, or sometimes better than, younger ones;
- the results are sometimes affected by the nature of the discipline with most students – mature or otherwise – doing better in the arts and the social sciences than in the sciences;
- there are sometimes gender differences in the results, but these are not wholly consistent; often mature women seem to do better than mature men but this is not always the case; and
- there is some suggestion that older mature students do not do as well academically as younger mature ones, but the evidence for this is weak.

It is difficult, of course, to draw such clear conclusions from such a diversity of studies. Two significant points to bear in mind are (1) that some studies use polytechnic students (eg Brennan, 1986; Hoskins *et al.*, 1996) whereas others use 'older' universities (eg Woodley, 1984), and (2) that mature students do not comprise an equal proportion of the total number of students in every discipline: a much larger number of mature students study arts and social science subjects than science ones (Brennan provides some useful figures here).

For these, and for other reasons – such as the fact that there are variations in the number of good and poor degrees awarded within different disciplines in different institutions – the most reliable data may come from studies of students taking particular courses in particular institutions. It is these kinds of studies that we have attempted to carry out at Keele (see Hartley *et al.*, 1993).

All but two of the studies summarised in Table 14.1 have provided data concerning the final degree performance of mature and traditional-entry students. In these studies these final degrees were usually awarded in the final (third or fourth) year of study when the students had completed numerous 'final' examination papers in different subject matters. 'Coursework' marks and 'part-one' marks from earlier years were also included in some courses when arriving at these overall assessments. However, in 1993 or thereabouts, most universities in the UK abandoned the notion of assessing accumulated knowledge in 'finals' and instituted a modularised system. Students now study several modules independently to obtain their final degree, and each module is assessed upon its completion.

The University of Keele introduced both a semester and a module system in 1993. In each year a Keele student now completes eight modules, independently of each other, four per semester, and twenty-four overall. Normally half of these modules are taken from one discipline, and half from another, thus maintaining the joint-honours system. We thought it of interest, because of these changes, to examine the performance of mature and traditional-entry students on these smaller, individual modules, and especially the first-year ones, as it is the first year that is crucial for many students (Rickinson and Rutherford, 1995).

Method

The module marks obtained by 30 mature and 30 traditional-entry students, matched on gender and subjects studied, were collated for each of four introductory psychology modules studied in the session 1993–94 and again for 26 mature and 26 traditional-entry students on the same four modules for the session 1994–95. Overseas students were not included in these analyses. Drop-out rates were compared, and these were equally small in the different groups.

Table 14.1 An overview summary of comparison studies of the academic performance of mature and traditional-entry students.

Author	Place	N (mature)	N (traditional entry)	Results
Hopper and Osborn, 1975	Birkbeck	240	5,106	35% of mature students got good degrees. 38% of traditional-entry students got good degrees.
	LSE	73	413	Mature students did as well as traditional-entry ones.
	Reading	31	32	Mature students did rather better than traditional-entry ones.
Walker, 1975	Warwick	231	3,314	Mature students in the arts and social sciences did better than traditional-entry ones but slightly worse in the sciences.
Sear, 1983	Degree results of graduates in 1979	?	?	The percentage of traditional-entry students gaining first and upper-second class degrees was slightly, but not significantly, higher (42%) than that of mature students (40%).
Woodley, 1984	All universities (1972–74)	18,343	165,400	Mature students were just as likely to get a good degree as traditional-entry ones. Mature students in arts and social sciences did better than traditional-entry ones, but the reverse was true for science subjects. Mature women did better than traditional-entry women. Mature men did slightly worse than traditional-entry men.
Lucas and Ward, 1985	Lancaster (3-year period)	263	3,498	Mature students were twice as likely as traditional-entry ones to gain firsts or upper seconds. Mature men students gained more first class degrees than did the mature women. Mature women students gained more upper and lower second class degrees than mature men.
Brennan, 1986	Courses in polytechnics and colleges validated by Council for National Academic Awards (CNAA)	452	2,190	39% of the mature students achieved first or upper-second class degrees, whereas only 30% of the younger students did so. Mature students were more likely than younger students to obtain good degrees in 21 out of 31 subject areas.

Author	Place	N (mature)	N (traditional entry)	Results
Smithers and Griffin, 1986	5 universities (1975–80)	600	16,300	Mature students did as well as traditional-entry ones.
Marshall and Nicholson, 1991	A London polytechnic	33	47	There was no significant difference between the performance of mature and traditional-entry students who were all studying psychology.
Hartley and Lapping, 1992	Keele University	51	51	There was no significant difference between the performance of matched mature and traditional-entry students who were all students of psychology between 1978 and 1990.
Hartley et al., 1993	Keele University	324	324	There was no significant difference between the performance of mature and traditional-entry students who were matched in terms of gender and subjects studied.
Richardson, 1995	Brunel University	32	44	There was no significant difference between the performance of mature and traditional-entry students who were all studying psychology, sociology and social anthropology.
Hoskins et al., 1996	Plymouth University	3213	3653	Mature students were divided into two groups: those aged 21–5 (N = 1894); and those aged over 25 at entry (N = 1319). The results showed a systematic improvement with age and there was a trend for females to perform better than males.

The four modules were of two different kinds. Modules 1 and 2 comprised lectures and tutorials, and were assessed by an essay and an examination. The weighting of the essay mark in arriving at the overall module mark was 40 per cent, and that of the examination mark was 60 per cent. Module 1 was taught in the first semester, and module 2 in the second. Modules 3 and 4 comprised laboratory and statistical classes, and were assessed by two laboratory reports, each with a weighting of 50 per cent. Module 3 was taught in the first semester, and module 4 in the second.

In order to avoid distorting the overall mean scores, students who missed one piece of work, or failed components within the modules, were given a mark of 40 for these elements in the present calculations. There were a total of 27 such adjustments for the mature students, and 20 for the traditional ones. In modules 1 and 2 nearly all of these adjustments were made to examination marks, rather than to essay ones.

Results

The overall results obtained are shown in Table 14.2. Initial analyses of the results showed that there were no significant differences between the results of the men and the women students. Thus the data shown in Table 14.2 were analysed for each module separately using a three-way analysis of variance (with one repeated measure). The variables under consideration were age (mature vs. traditional-entry students), year group (1993–4 vs. 1994–5) and method of assessment (eg exam and essay).

Table 14.2 The mean percentage marks of the mature and traditional-entry students for the different components of the four modules.

| | | 1993–94 | | 1994–95 | |
		Traditional-entry $N = 30$	Mature $N = 30$	Traditional-entry $N = 26$	Mature $N = 26$
Module 1	Essay	59.8	58.9	59.1	58.8
		5.5	5.2	5.3	8.3
	Exam	55.1	56.6	57.1	51.7
		8.8	7.6	6.3	9.5
Module 2	Essay	59.3	57.7	59.0	59.5
		8.4	8.4	5.8	6.2
	Exam	54.0	52.7	56.3	51.7
		7.8	7.8	7.1	8.0
Module 3	Report 1	57.8	54.2	62.9	57.3
		8.3	7.6	8.9	11.7
	Report 2	56.9	55.5	62.2	58.1
		9.8	9.0	7.9	9.8
Module 4	Report 1	57.8	54.8	63.8	63.2
		9.4	10.8	12.9	12.3
	Report 2	59.8	57.1	59.2	60.8
		10.1	9.5	10.5	8.8

Modules 1 and 2

For modules 1 and 2 the analyses of variance showed that there were no significant differences between the performances of the mature and the traditional-entry students ($F = 1.26$ and 2.02, respectively). Nor was there any significant effect for the different year groups ($F = 0.73$ and 0.11). There was, however, a significant difference between the marks obtained on the essays and the marks obtained in the examinations ($F = 13.46$ and 20.39, $p < 0.001$ respectively). As Table 14.2 shows, the mean percentage marks obtained for the essays were higher than those obtained for the examinations.

Modules 3 and 4

For modules 3 and 4 the results were somewhat different. There was a significant difference between the performance of the mature and the traditional-entry students in module 3 ($F = 6.12$) that was not apparent in module 4 ($F = 0.33$). In module 3 the traditional-entry students outperformed the mature students in writing laboratory reports, but this difference had disappeared by the time these students had completed module 4. Also in both modules 3 and 4 there were significant year effects ($F = 7.49$ and 5.85). In each case the marks obtained in 1994–95 were significantly higher than those obtained in 1993–94.

Discussion

The results described above are in line with those reported previously, in that there were no significant differences between the overall performance of the mature and the traditional-entry students for modules 1, 2 and 4. The results of module 3 were of interest, however, for here the mature students did do significantly worse than the traditional-entry ones. None the less, it appeared that these students had learned the necessary skills of report writing, at least to the same extent, as the traditional-entry students by the time they had completed module 4. Perhaps it should be noted here that, although it appears that all the students did better in modules 3 and 4 in 1994–95 than they did in 1993–94, this finding was probably a consequence of using a new method of marking laboratory reports that was introduced in 1994–95.

Another interesting finding was the fact that the marks obtained in modules 1 and 2 were higher for the essay components than were the marks obtained for the examination components. Such a finding is not new, of course, but the particular point of interest here is that the mature students did not do better than the traditional-entry ones on the essay component and worse than them on the exam component, as might have been predicted from other work (eg Clennell, 1984).

Finally, we should note that the results obtained in most of the studies reported in this chapter, although encouraging from the point of view of mature students, and a sharp corrective to ageist stereotypes, do not do much to help teachers and administrators learn from and understand the qualitative differences between mature and young students. Individual students may arrive at the same degree class by a variety of different routes, and our procedure of examining students' end of year marks or degree classes does not enable us to differentiate between students with vastly different background experiences. An unmarried mature student aged 21 years living in a hall of residence is probably closer to a traditional-entry student than is one aged 30 years, married and living at home with young children. Several researchers have documented clearly these different ranges of experience, and their importance (eg Britton and Baxter, 1994).

So perhaps what is needed now are prospective rather than retrospective studies: ones that identify rather different groupings within the category of mature student and follow them through to graduation and beyond. In such studies it might be possible to identify the particular needs of various groups (based on the descriptions given by the authors cited above) and to follow up their progress. It might be possible, for example, to follow cohorts of students in different age bands (eg 26–30 and 41–50), with different aims (eg instrumental vs. personal) and in different social situations (eg maintaining a family at home vs. living alone in hall of residence).

Some work on identifying such different groupings in mature students has already begun (see Chapter 13), and there is beginning to be a greater interest in studies of the life events of mature students, particularly those of women (eg Cox and Pascall, 1994). In addition there is interesting new work on the learning styles of mature students (see Chapters 11 and 12). Now we have the baseline data, these new developments are to be encouraged.

References

Brennan, J (1986) Student learning and the 'capacity to benefit': The performance of non-traditional students in public sector higher education, *Journal of Access Studies*, 1, 23–32.

Britton, C and Baxter, A (1994) Mature students' routes into higher education, *Journal of Access Studies*, 9, 215–28.

Clennell, S (ed.) (1984) *Older students in the Open University*, report from the Older Students Research Group, Open University, Milton Keynes.

Cox, R and Pascall, G (1994) *Women Returning to Higher Education*, SRHE and Open University Press, Milton Keynes.

Department of Education (1994) *Statistical Bulletin*, issue no. 16/94, September, Department of Education, London.

Hartley, J and Lapping, C (1992) Do mature students of psychology perform as well as traditional entry ones? An analysis of archival data, *Psychology Teaching Review*, 1, 76–81.

Hartley, J, Trueman, M and Lapping C (1993) *The Academic Performance of Mature and Traditional Entry Students: a Review and a Case-study*. Paper to the London Conference of the British Psychological Society, December.

Hopper, E and Osborn, M (1975) *Adult Students: Education, Selection and Social Control*, Frances Pinter, London.

Hoskins, S, Newstead, S and Dennis, I (1996). *Degree performance as a function of age, sex, prior qualifications and discipline studied*, unpublished paper, Department of Psychology, University of Plymouth.

Lucas, J and Ward, P (1985) Mature students at Lancaster University, *Adult Education*, 58, 151–7.

Marshall, H and Nicholson, P (1991) 'Why choose psychology? Mature and other students' accounts at graduation', in *The Choice of Psychology*, J Radford (ed.), The British Psychological Society, Leicester.

Richardson, J T E (1995) Mature students in higher education: II. An investigation of approaches to studying and academic performance, *Studies in Higher Education*, 20, 5–17.

Rickinson, R and Rutherford, D (1995) Increasing undergraduate student retention rates, *British Journal of Guidance and Counselling*, 23, 161–72.

Sear, K (1983) The correlation between A level grades and degree results in England and Wales, *Higher Education*, 12, 609–19.

Smithers, A and Griffin, A (1986) *The Progress of Mature Students*, Joint Matriculation Board, Manchester.

Walker, P (1975) The university performances of mature students, *Research in Education*, 14, 1–13.

Woodley, A (1984) The older the better? A study of mature student performances in British Universities, *Research in Education*, 32, 35–50.

CHAPTER 15

Older but Wiser?
The Motivation of Mature
Students in Higher Education

Stephen E Newstead, Sherria Hoskins, Arlene Franklyn-Stokes and Ian Dennis

The recent massive increase in student numbers in higher education in the UK has been achieved in no small measure through an increase in the number of mature students. According to data released by the Higher Education Statistics Agency (HESA, 1995), one-third of the new entrants to undergraduate degrees in UK universities in 1994 were over 21 years of age, and half of these were over 25 years of age. In total, there may be close to half a million mature students studying for first degrees.

It is difficult to assess the impact that this recent growth in the number of mature students has had on higher education in general. In fact, we know very little about these mature students: what motivates them; what backgrounds they come from; what skills they bring with them; and what problems they encounter as undergraduate students. There is a very simple reason for this lack of knowledge. Most of the research that has been conducted on students' personality, aptitude, ability, motivation, learning style and so on was carried out before the recent expansion and hence used predominantly traditional-age students, since these formed the great majority of the population (see, for example, Entwistle and Ramsden, 1983).

Despite the paucity of objective information, a number of assumptions are often made: that mature students have a greater tendency to drop out of higher education; that they need special treatment due to the lack of study skills resulting from their absence from the education scene; that they have extra needs for pastoral care; and that they will tend to perform worse at degree level than their younger counterparts. Underlying all these there seems to be an implicit assumption that mature students are motivated in different ways to traditional-age students.

Only recently has there been any systematic attempt to obtain hard information about the characteristics and performance of mature students. In this chapter we try to bring together some of this research, with a specific focus on some of our own research in this area, and with special emphasis on what this research tells us about the motives of mature students.

There are four main themes underlying the research to be discussed in this chapter.

- The attainment of mature students in their final degree classification, in particular whether they perform better or worse than traditional-age students.
- The drop-out rates among mature students and how these compare to those of other student groups.
- The incidence of academic dishonesty (cheating) and whether this occurs more frequently in mature than in younger students.
- The motives, aims and objectives of mature students who are studying for a degree and what this tells us about their performance at degree level.

How well do mature students perform at degree level?

The studies that have investigated the relative performance of mature and younger students have produced conflicting results, but the consensus to emerge from most recent British studies is that: 'older students usually perform as well as, or sometimes better than, younger ones' (Chapter 14).

We have recently analysed the computerised statistical records of our own institution in an attempt to throw further light on the performance of mature students (Hoskins *et al.*, in submission). We found that mature students performed better than younger students in terms of the number of good degrees obtained. Sixty per cent of students aged over 25 obtained good degrees, compared with only 47 per cent of those aged 18–20 years and a similar number (47 per cent) of those aged 21–24 years (see the overall means in Table 15.1). Our results confirm previous findings that mature students perform at least as well as younger ones, but are slightly unusual in that relatively few studies have reported an actual superiority of mature students.

Table 15.1 Percentage of good degrees as a function of age at entry and qualification (per cent).

	Age at entry (years)		
	Under 21	21–25	Over 25
A levels	48	58	58
Non-traditional qualifications	41	44	63
Mean	47	47	60

It may be of relevance that our university is a former polytechnic. An earlier study that found evidence for the superiority of mature students was that of Bourner and Hamed (1987), which also used data from the former polytechnics. It would be interesting to know if this superiority is also found in more traditional universities, or whether it is restricted to the newer ones. Many of the latter have large numbers of mature students, and they may also tend to use different assessment systems, with more emphasis on coursework and continuous assessment than in the old universities. They may also tend to attract the more able mature students because of the reputation that they have for supporting such students.

Mature students typically enter university with a wider range of qualifications than do younger students. Previous studies have shown that A levels are not as good a predictor of degree performance in mature students as they are with younger students (Sear, 1983), although in neither case was the correlation a very high one. In our study, we were able to investigate the effects of type of qualification on degree performance. There was little difference between the overall performance of students with A levels and those with other qualifications, but there was an interesting interaction between this variable and age (see Table 15.1). In both of the younger age groups, degree performance was better among students with traditional A level qualifications on entry, but the reverse pattern was obtained with those students aged over 25 years.

We can only speculate as to the source of this interaction. Younger students who have non-traditional qualifications may be ones who have struggled within the school system and have looked for alternative modes of training. They may thus be less suited to an academic career than those who take A levels. Mature students who take non-traditional qualifications may do so for less negative reasons; often because of the vocational relevance or general interest of the course. Mature students bring many qualities to university education, and traditional A levels may not be the most appropriate way of assessing these abilities. Certainly, a lack of conventional academic qualifications should not in itself deter universities from recruiting mature students.

The general picture to emerge from these studies is that mature students perform well at university. The myth that they are somehow at a disadvantage in higher education appears to be just that, a myth. Much of the evidence suggests that they actually perform better than younger students, although this is, clearly, not an entirely consistent finding. Their motives may be different to those of other students, but seemingly not in ways that lead to inferior performance.

Drop-out rates in mature students

Drop-out rates among students have become increasingly important in higher education, since institutions are funded according to the number of students they recruit and retain. Hence it is surprising how little research has been conducted into drop-out rates in general and into drop-out rates in mature students in particular. The only large-scale study that has looked at the latter is that of Woodley (1984), who found that 13 per cent of traditional-age students failed to complete their courses, compared with 17 per cent of mature students. However, other, smaller-scale studies have tended to find little, if any, difference (see Richardson, 1995, and Chapter 13 for a review).

The database relating to our own institution had data on drop-out rates, which we decided to examine. The findings are presented in Table 15.2, and provide a clear and consistent picture. Firstly, there was no discernible difference in drop-out rates between students in the two youngest age groups. However, there *was* a difference between these two groups and those students aged over 25, with the older students showing considerably higher drop-out rates. This difference occurred both in the first year of study (where most drop outs occur) and in subsequent years.

Table 15.2 Drop-out rates as a function of age (per cent).

Age (years)	Year 1	Post year 1	Overall
18–20	6.7	1.8	3.2
21–25	6.7	1.9	3.6
25+	9.1	3.8	5.3

Unfortunately, the database contained no information on the reasons for dropping out of university, so we cannot tell whether students left for academic or other reasons. Richardson (1995) has claimed that mature students are no more likely to drop out for academic reasons but may be more likely to leave for personal reasons. We suspect he may well be correct but have no data to report in this connection. This, then, is an instance where there may be substance to the academic folklore that claims that mature students are more likely to drop out of university. However, we need to know much more about the sources and the generality of these differences before jumping to any conclusions.

Do mature students cheat?

It may seem strange to look for age effects in academic dishonesty (student cheating); and, indeed, when we first embarked on this research it was not one of the main factors that excited our interest. We were more motivated by wanting to know whether the high incidence of cheating reported in American studies (eg Davis *et al.*, 1992) would also be found in the UK. Nevertheless, the studies we have conducted have produced interesting and revealing differences between age groups.

One of the first studies we carried out examined respondents' perceptions of the seriousness of a number of different behaviours that would be regarded by most people as constituting cheating, for example taking crib notes into an exam or copying work from another student (Franklyn-Stokes and Newstead, 1995). Seriousness was rated on a six-point scale, where 1 indicated 'not at all serious' and 6 indicated 'very serious'. Respondents were first-year undergraduates and academic staff. The older students gave significantly higher average seriousness ratings than the younger ones: for students aged 25 years and over, the mean was 4.8; for students aged 21–24 years it was 4.0; and for students aged 18–20 years it was 4.1. The mean ratings given by the oldest age group were actually nearer to the ratings given by university lecturers (4.7) than they were to the ratings given by the younger students. This suggests that mature students have a different concept as to what is acceptable behaviour than do younger ones.

In a number of subsequent studies we have investigated the frequency with which various types of cheating occur. In doing this we have used a self-report method with guarantees of absolute confidentiality and anonymity to respondents. The findings were in many ways surprising, as they suggested that cheating is much more common in university students than most lecturers would have believed. From the present perspective, however, the main findings of interest concern age differences in the reported incidence of cheating. We calculated a 'cheating index', which was essentially an indication of the percentage of the cheating behaviours a student or group of students admitted engaging in. Thus a cheating index of 33 per cent would mean that a student admitted cheating in one-third of the more than 20 behaviours on the questionnaire. There were very large differences between age groups, with those aged 18–20 years producing a cheating index of 27 per cent, those aged 21–24 years an index of 25 per cent, and those aged 25 years and over an index of 13 per cent (Newstead et al., 1996).

We were intrigued by these age differences, as they were largely unexpected. The voluminous American research on academic dishonesty has not systematically investigated the effects of age, though there are some suggestive findings in that literature. For example, Davis et al. (1992) found that cheating was more commonly reported by high-school students than by those in colleges and universities. However, it is by no means clear that this difference is attributable to age, since the two types of students are working in very different environments and cultures. The only study that seems to have looked directly at the effects of age is that by Haines et al. (1986). These authors found that there was a strong, negative correlation (–0.4) with reported incidence of cheating. Indeed, of the demographic variables they investigated, age was the best predictor of cheating. Our studies seem to be the only other research that has included age as a variable.

What, then, are the reasons for these age-related differences? One plausible possibility is that moral development is something that continues into adulthood, and that the older students have better developed moral consciences than younger students. We cannot rule out this possibility but incidental findings in our research suggest it is, at best, only part of the cause. In one of our studies (Newstead *et al.*, 1996, study 1) students were asked to give their reasons for cheating and for not cheating. One of the possible reasons for not cheating was that it would be immoral/dishonest. It would be expected that this reason would be given much more frequently by the mature students if they have a better developed sense of morality. However, this was not the case. A more attractive explanation is in terms of student motivation, which will be considered in some detail in the following section.

Motivation and reasons for studying in mature students

In our research on student cheating, a number of our studies enquired as to the reasons why the respondent was studying for a degree. This was a completely open-ended question and we were not sure how informative it would be. In the event, it proved to be of considerable use and provided real insights both into why there are age-related differences in cheating and also into the motivations of mature and traditional students. The responses to the question were classified into three main categories, which we labelled 'stop gap', 'means to an end' and 'personal development'. Table 15.3 gives an indication of the kinds of responses that were placed into the different categories.

Table 15.3   Reasons for studying.

Stop gap	avoiding work
	laziness
	allowing time out to decide on career
	social life
	fun and enjoyment
Means to an end	improving standard of living
	improving chance of getting a job
	developing career
	getting a good qualification
	getting worthwhile job
Personal development	improving life skills
	reaching personal potential
	gaining knowledge for its own sake
	furthering academic interest
	gaining control of own life

There were large differences in the cheating index associated with each of these categories. Those students studying for stop gap reasons produced an index of 32 per cent, those studying as a means to an end one of 23 per cent, and those studying for personal development one of 17 per cent. Such differences seem perfectly understandable. For example, there seems little sense in students who are studying for personal development reasons engaging in cheating. If they are studying mainly to prove to themselves that they are capable of obtaining a degree, then they would really only be cheating themselves if they indulged in academic dishonesty.

Interestingly, the occurrence of these reasons for studying varied substantially as a function of age (see Table 15.4). With respect to means to an end, there was little difference between the various age groups, but there were large differences for the other two categories. In general terms, mature students (those aged over 25) were much less likely to be studying as a stop gap than were younger students, and much more likely to be studying for personal development reasons. It is likely that these differences in reasons for studying are fundamental to the age-related differences in cheating. Mature students are studying for different reasons to younger ones and, given their motivations for studying, cheating makes little sense to them.

Table 15.4 Occurrence of reasons for studying as a function of age (per cent).

Age (years)	Stop gap	Means to an end	Personal development
18–20	14	65	21
21–24	11	71	18
25+	4	62	34

In our research we have also asked students to indicate their reasons for cheating (if they admitted to carrying out a specific cheating behaviour) or for not cheating (if they said they had not indulged in a specific behaviour). The relative frequencies of the different types of reasons among the different age groups again provided insights into students' motivations. The main age-related difference in the reasons for cheating occurred with 'to increase the mark', which constituted 24 per cent of all reasons given by the youngest age group but only 13 per cent of those given by the oldest students. With respect to reasons for not cheating, the major differences appeared with 'it would devalue my achievement', which was given much more frequently with the older students; and 'fear of detection/punishment', which occurred more commonly with the younger students. The picture that emerges from this is that the mature students are more intrinsically motivated than their younger counterparts. The mature students are motivated more by the concern that cheating would undermine their own achievement than they are by fears of punishment or by the desire to increase their grade by fraudulent means.

This picture is confirmed by other data, as yet unpublished, on the relative scores of mature and nonmature students on a battery of questionnaires measuring motivation, anxiety and approaches to learning in first-year students (Dennis *et al.*, in preparation). Our results on approaches to studying are broadly similar to those that have been obtained elsewhere and summarised by

Richardson (1994; see also Chapter 13). The mature psychology students we studied produced consistently higher scores on measures of meaning orientation than did younger students (in this analysis, we regarded mature students as those aged over 21 on entry). The picture with reproducing orientation was a little less clear cut. Richardson's research suggested that mature students were less likely to use this orientation, but we found no consistent differences between the age groups.

Of more interest in the present context are the more purely motivational measures used in this research. The picture is a fairly consistent one across the various measures that were used, with mature students emerging as more intrinsically motivated than younger ones. Mature students scored more highly on the 'intrinsic motivation to know' and the 'intrinsic motivation to experience stimulation' scales of the academic motivation scale (Vallerand *et al.*, 1992). Students who score highly on the first of these scales indicate that they are studying for the pleasure and satisfaction of learning new things and in order to gain more knowledge about subjects that interest them. Students scoring highly on the second scale indicate that they are studying for the pleasure of reading about interesting topics and communicating ideas to others.

Mature students also scored more highly than younger ones on the 'intrinsic goal orientation' measure on the motivated strategies for learning questionnaire (Pintrich *et al.*, 1991). Items loading on this measure are ones in which students indicate that they like challenging material so that they can learn new things, and choose assignments that will enable them to learn new things even if this might lead to a lower grade. In our studies we also asked students what classification of degree they expected to obtain and what degree they would be satisfied with. There was no difference on the first measure, but mature students indicated that it would require a higher class of degree to satisfy them than it would younger students. Interestingly, however, there was a suggestion that, after their first semester at university, the mature students would be satisfied with a lower class of degree than they would when they first started out.

There was an indication in our results that mature students scored less highly on measures of extrinsic motivation, though this did not achieve significance on all of the measures used. Mature students gave significantly lower scores on the 'external regulation' scale of the academic motivation scale. Items included in this measure include ones where students indicate that they are taking a degree to get a better paid or more prestigious job, and to be able to lead a more comfortable life later on.

The parallels between these findings and those arising from the studies of student cheating reported earlier are clear. The questionnaire measures confirm that mature students are more likely to be motivated by personal development and interest in the subject. This lends support to our claim that individual differences in motivation hold the key to explaining many of the obtained differences between mature and nonmature students.

In conclusion, the evidence we have presented suggests that mature students are likely to enrich and to make major contributions to university life. The picture that emerges from the research is that mature students are a highly motivated group, who wish their degree to be the result of their own work and effort, and who tend to achieve good degrees. They may be more likely to drop out of university but this seems to be a small price to pay in the light of all the benefits they can bring.

References

Bourner, T and Hamed, M (1987) *Entry qualifications and degree performance*, Council for National Academic Awards, London.

Davis, S F, Grover, C A, Becker, A H and McGregor, L N (1992) Academic dishonesty: prevalence, determinants, techniques, and punishments, *Teaching of Psychology*, 19, 16–20.

Dennis, I, Jones, S M, and Newstead, S E (in preparation), *Predictors of Success in Higher Education*, Department of Psychology, University of Plymouth.

Entwistle, N J and Ramsden, P (1983) *Understanding Student Learning*, Croom Helm, London.

Franklyn-Stokes, B A and Newstead, S E (1995) Undergraduate cheating: Who does what and why? *Studies in Higher Education*, 20, 159–72.

Haines, V J, Diekhoff, G M, LaBeff, E E and Clarke, R E (1986) College cheating: immaturity, lack of commitment, and the neutralizing attitude, *Research In Higher Education*, 25, 342–54.

HESA (1995), *Students in higher education institutions*, Higher Education Statistics Agency, Cheltenham.

Hoskins, S, Newstead, S E and Dennis, I (1997) Factors affecting degree outcomes: sex; type of entry qualification; age and course, *Assessment and Evaluation in Higher Education*, 22(3).

Newstead, S E, Franklyn-Stokes, B A and Armstead, P (1996) Individual differences in student cheating, *Journal of Educational Psychology*, 88, 229–41.

Pintrich, P R, Smith, D A F, Garcia, T and McKeachie, W J (1991) *A manual for the use of the Motivated Strategies for Learning Questionnaire*, Technical Report no. 91-B-004, University of Michigan.

Richardson, J T E (1994) Mature students in higher education: I. A literature survey on approaches to studying, *Studies in Higher Education*, 19, 309–25.

Richardson, J T E (1995) Mature students in higher education: II. An investigation of approaches to studying and academic performance, *Studies in Higher Education*, 20, 5–17.

Sear, K (1983) The correlation between 'A' level grades and degree results in England and Wales, *Higher Education*, 12, 609–19.

Vallerand, R J, Pelletier, L G, Blais, M R, Briere, N M, Senecal, C and Vallieres, E F (1992) The academic motivation scale: a measure of intrinsic, extrinsic and amotivation in education, *Educational and Psychological Measurement*, 52, 1003–17.

Woodley, A (1984) The older the better? a study of mature student performance in British universities. *Research in Education*, 32, 35–50.

IMPLICATIONS FOR TEACHING

The Implications of Research on Approaches to Learning for the Teaching of Adults

Peter Sutherland

In the first five sections of this book, 15 sets of authors present evidence and/or ideas on the learning of adults. Some point explicitly to the implications of their work for teachers (eg Chapters 3 and 4). Most, however, do not. The aim of this chapter is hence to tease out the impact of the other chapters for the teacher of adults. Generally this will assume a formal setting, a university or a further education college, for example, but informal, distance learning or self-directed settings are not completely ignored.

In this chapter we shall use Malcolm Knowles's (1978) dichotomous model for the teacher of adults: both the traditional pedagogue who imparts knowledge and the andragogue who enables students to develop their own potential for learning by setting suitable challenges.

Mezirow (Chapter 1) has developed Habermas's (1978) three different types of learning: technical learning, 'practical' learning and emancipatory learning. Each requires a different method of teaching. For example, in order to achieve emancipatory learning in their students, teachers need to encourage perspective transformation. In mature adults this may well fit in with the changes that are taking place in their lives anyway; for example, promotion, midlife crisis or retirement. In young adults the massive transition out of adolescence itself requires a major perspective transformation.

Boulton-Lewis (Chapter 2) is interested in memory and the concepts of stages of development in adult learning. With respect to memory, she presents evidence that there is no serious decline in memory until people are well into their 60s. Therefore adults of up to that age are quite as well equipped as younger adults to cope with such learning situations as their teachers provide for them. In fact she presents evidence that the mechanisms whereby memory operates for adults tend to be knowledge based and therefore top-down, rather than operating from experience (bottom-up), as the information processing model would have predicted. Unlike the ideas of most authors in this book (other than Owens, Chapter 6), Boulton-Lewis's ideas point to adults being able to operate successfully with a traditional teacher-centred pedagogic model of teaching, rather than a student-centred andragogic one.

Her review of some of the literature on the postformal thinker (in Piagetian terms) points to adult students who absorb knowledge rapidly within their best domains; yet are very flexible between domains. A picture of a top-level post graduate research student is built up, but it may have little relevance to a first-year student aged 18 years with very little metacognitive awareness of learning strategies.

Dart (Chapter 3) points to the relative failure of teachers of adults to encourage metacognitive strategies (which to him largely means constructivist strategies). This is surely a matter that adult educators should give priority to, particularly as part of study skills schemes. He argues that, if students do offer such constructivist strategies for learning, this implies that teachers must be facilitators and not mere purveyors of knowledge. (Like Mezirow he favours an andragogic rather than a pedagogic model of teaching.) He argues that teachers should try to improve their students' knowledge about the learning process: particularly in the direction of learning for understanding. Such a deep approach is essential for true metacognition to take place.

This may be expedited by the students keeping learning diaries. Additionally students should be encouraged to form collaborative learning groups and to negotiate learning contracts with their teachers. In particular, students should be helped to attain what he calls an elaborative strategy. In other words students should personalise new ideas by relating these ideas to their own prior learning. At the same time the teacher should create small group interaction situations, following this up with whole class discussion. Assessment should be carried out by the student himself and by a peer, as well as by the teacher. According to Dart, men are on the whole less cognitively aware than women. This may create a problem for teachers to try redress this.

Section II, *Learning and education*, has, by definition, implications for teaching. Hettich (Chapter 4) reviews four epistemological theories of intellectual growth in young adults. He points out that the authors of the theories themselves saw plenty of implications for teaching. For example, King and Kitchener see the aim of teaching advanced students as promoting reflective thinking. For a start teachers need to show respect for their students as people. This establishes a climate in which teachers can create opportunities for students to examine problems from different perspectives. Once this has been established, teachers should create opportunities for students to make judgements.

King and Kitchener (1994) recognise a range of individual differences across the student population, particularly in the assumptions they make about knowledge (epistemic assumptions). In order to be realistic about the bases on which their students are learning, teachers should, according to King and Kitchener, informally assess these assumptions, although this may be challenging for hard-worked teachers (as opposed to researchers) to do in practice.

At the same time teachers need to recognise the emotional dimension of learning and provide both challenge and/or support when either is needed. This involves teachers of adults accepting that they have a counselling/guidance role similar to that of teachers of children and adolescents. Perhaps realistically, in view of current trends towards higher teacher–student ratios and shorter modular courses, King and Kitchener's ideas are more appropriate to roles such as that of supervisor of a research student, that is 1:1 situations.

Baxter Magolda (1996) argues that teachers of advanced students should require the students to analyse and evaluate knowledge acquired on lower-level courses and to develop belief systems that encompass these. To promote independent knowing, teachers should design a learning environment that provides students with independence, direct experience in decision making, accountability for their actions and interaction with other students to explore and evaluate options; that is, many of the aspects of self-directed learning. Teachers should encourage students to connect points learnt academically with real life. One technique that Hettich (like Dart) recommends is for students to keep study journals in which they relate concepts encountered on the course with their real-life experiences. Simultaneously, teachers should encourage their students to think critically and to collaborate with their peers. Teachers should develop genuine relationships with their students and treat them with respect as equals (as King and Kitchener also advised). It is difficult to argue with the desirability of these teaching strategies for advanced students (or, for that matter, for undergraduate students).

Schmeck (Chapter 5) narrows the learning focus to tactics rather than strategies. He then argues that a person's personality largely decides the tactics he will choose. However, if one accepts that adult learners' personalities are largely decided by the time they reach adulthood, teachers of adults can have relatively little influence on the personalities of their students. Nevertheless, Schmeck finds that the learning of traditional-age adults is determined by basic personality to a much greater extent than is the learning of mature adults.

In few institutions is personality moulding considered part of the adult educator's job. On the other hand, teachers should try to provide teaching that is compatible with the personalities of their students. In order to do this, Schmeck's personality scale is one that can be used to diagnose the basic broad characteristics of a student, such as whether he is positively oriented towards work (which Schmeck calls agentic) or not. Teachers need to think through what can be done to cope with those students whose personality is not positively oriented towards work.

Schmeck implies that *literal memorisation* and *conventional* students require teachers who basically provide the facts; pedagogues. On the other hand *reflective* and *self-actualising* students require teachers who help them to reflect and thereby fulfil their potential; andragogues. Both *deep semantic* and *elaborative self-actualising* students would also seem to need andragogues. Schmeck implies that no one teacher can fulfil both demands simultaneously, but perhaps teachers of subjects such as education and psychology should try to do so.

A number of Schmeck's broad personality categories seem suitable for distance learning, such as the *agentic serial, elaborative, self-actualiser* and *methodological study* categories (although a *methodological study* student could also thrive under an andragogue when they meet in regular face-to-face sessions).

It would seem that those who are *self-assertive* would thrive on group work, such as seminars, as discussed in Section III, *Adults interacting in groups*. It is interesting to note that Schmeck found that female teachers are generally better in the role of eliciting discussion from groups.

The implications of Owens's (Chapter 6) behaviourist approach for teaching adults would seem to point to two areas in particular: those who have problems with motor skills and those who have acute general learning difficulties. The motor skills could be shaped by the teacher until they were of a standard considered to be satisfactory. Adults with acute general learning difficulties could be helped by providing them with behaviourist programmes on computers, where they can obtain unlimited practice. The computer can also provide unlimited reward (or reinforcement) in the form of feedback on the progress made.

Sutherland (Chapter 7) argues that the concepts of experiential learning and constructivism are strongly related and that a merger of the two traditions would be beneficial to adult learning and teaching, particularly where the teacher is seen as an andragogue facilitating the learning of the students. If this argument is accepted, there are enormous implications for the teaching of adults. This would involve a shift of emphasis away from a teacher or an examination board designing courses, towards students negotiating courses based on their prior experiential learning, and utilising the constructs that have already been established in their cognitive repertoires. There are many opportunities for teachers to use the informal learning of students (using this term as an umbrella for both experiential and/or constructivist learning). The list includes the students choosing essay, project or dissertation topics for themselves.

In addition experiential and constructivist concepts of learning can underlie the process of a course, as well as its content. Students can be encouraged to go out and seek informal learning experiences. Alternatively teachers can build in experiential learning as part of the course; for example, first-year student nurses visiting crèches or student teachers taking part in teaching-practice lessons. Teachers using distance learning have perhaps the greatest scope for implementing these ideas. In the UK the Open University has been a pioneer for over 25 years.

Despite the financial pressures to lecture to big numbers, most British teachers of adults believe that seminar work is of great value in the teaching of adults, whether they are traditional age or mature. Hence the importance of Section III, *Adults interacting in groups*, which focuses on the group situation.

Mowatt and Siann (Chapter 8) draw attention to the benefits of learning in small groups (this may include using brainstorming). However an implication of their findings is that teachers need to become more sensitive to the non-verbal cues within the groups they are teaching if they are to manage the interaction effectively. Nominal groups (where students contribute in writing as well as orally) have the advantage of helping the more retiring adult to enter into the group activity, while simultaneously reducing the over-contribution of the dominant members.

Mowatt and Siann argue that assessment remains an abiding problem of group work. How to assess an individual's contribution to group efforts remains a problem for teachers and adult educators generally. Maybe we should agree with Callaghan *et al.* (1994) that it is better not to assess group work. They also argue that how the teacher approaches the task depends on the aptitude differences and gender composition of the group.

Their idea of using peer evaluation links up with Topping's (Chapter 9) Vygotskyan notions of teaching and learning. The idea of peer tutoring, which Vygotsky pioneered, is applied by Topping to a model that assumes a single learner; one-to-one, dyadic tutoring. If small-group work is to be pre-served, peer tutoring is one of the strategies that universities need to consider in order to solve the problem of increasing teacher–student ratios. So the vari-ous possibilities that Topping considers all need to be taken seriously by the managements of universities and colleges.

He particularly recommends peer tutoring in pairs, both where the more able student is the tutor throughout, and where roles reciprocate over time according to the specialist competencies of the partners. According to the evidence that Topping reviews, peer tutors gain in metacognitive awareness and transfer this skill to new situations. From his own studies Topping claims that the tutor develops more awareness of his or her own learning style and that of other students.

The implications of peer tutoring for the teaching of adults with learning difficulties are particularly interesting and promising. For instance, an adult with moderate learning difficulties could tutor one with greater difficulties. Likewise a spouse or friend could act as the tutor in home-based learning or a workmate in work-based learning.

In Section IV, *The context of education*, authors focus on how learning is experienced in various settings. In industry, Pillay (Chapter 10) argues, it is often difficult to teach both domain-specific and generic knowledge at the same time. This finding may well apply to colleges as well. If it does, what does the teacher do: first lay foundations of principles, then build domain-specific knowledge on these foundations (using a measure of deduction) or first facilitate the acquisition of domain-specific knowledge, then induce general principles?

Blaxter *et al.* (Chapter 11) point to the links that mature adults make between the various aspects of their lives: education, work, family and leisure. They argue that the relationships between these aspects change as people go through adult life. It is how an adult perceives the links that is crucially important. For instance study might be seen as so important to a woman (possibly because she came from a background where one automatically left school aged 16 years and went out to work) that she was prepared to give up her job in order to improve her performance in studying. Since Blaxter *et al.*'s study is conceived sociologically, there are not so many direct implications for teaching as with the psychologically oriented authors. Nevertheless it does point to a clear need to provide a maximal support service within the institution to help the adult; for example a crèche, a library service that allows longer loans for part-time students and study cubicles for those who don't have them at home.

Section V, *The particular context of the mature student in higher education*, focuses on mature adults and the circumstances under which they do learn successfully and those that inhibit learning. Beaty *et al.* (Chapter 12), like Blaxter *et al.*, focus specifically on the mature female learner. Teachers should also be aware of background factors that affect women far more than men. These include the effect on the employment position of the husband; for example, if she needs him to look after the children at times when classes clash with his work. If a child is sick, it is usually expected that the mother will stay at home. However, if the husband is not working, this handicap may not arise. For reasons of child care, travelling any distance to class may also be a problem and many women prefer the option of distance learning. On an emotional level the husband may feel threatened intellectually by the wife's academic advance, as in the well known play, *Educating Rita*. However, many women have a support network of female friends, which men largely lack.

Empirical findings remain limited on the cognitive capabilities of 'middle-aged' adults. However, Richardson (Chapter 13) presents a considerable amount of evidence that, at least up to the age of 50 years, mature students perform, if anything, better than those aged 18–22 years, and are more likely to operate at a deep level than their younger counterparts. According to his evidence mature students are not generally lacking in adequate study-skill strategies, as the prevailing stereotype indicates. If Richardson's case is accepted by higher education institutions, they have no need to provide study skill courses for many mature students. Furthermore teachers can expect a deep approach and intrinsic motivation from their mature students. Courses should therefore be planned and assessment demands made on these assumptions. According to Richardson, the problem lies more with the traditional-age students: whether they will be able to cope with expectations of a deep approach; or whether they will need to be catered for by means of a surface approach and extrinsic motivation.

Richardson's evidence of a more efficient time-management strategy among mature students is something that teachers and counsellors can pass on to their traditional-age students.

However Hartley and Trueman (Chapter 14) found that there were no significant differences between 18–22-year-olds and older Keele University students in their performance on modules. So, according to them, teachers do *not* have to modify their teaching significantly if they have mature as well as traditional-age students in their class.

Newstead *et al.* (Chapter 15) compare mature with traditional-age students in motivation. The overall picture they paint is one of a far higher degree of intrinsic motivation in the mature than in the traditional-age students. Mature students are therefore more likely to study for personal development rather than for vocational need. Teachers should cater for this form of motivation by offering plenty of opportunities for mature students to work on topics that they find inherently interesting.

Because they are so interested in the subject, mature students are less likely to cheat. So teachers don't have to be so vigilant in this task as they need to be with traditional-age students; although it is not a problem that can be totally ignored.

The implications for teaching of all the contributions have now been worked through. It is now time to synthesise some of the diverse ideas presented and to draw conclusions. Some of the ideas now put forward are largely speculative, but hopefully constructively so. This exercise should not be seen in isolation, but as forming part of a larger (hopefully international) picture of fundamental research on adult learning (both traditional age and mature), which should lead to curriculum development and more appropriate teaching.

What, then, is the ideal teaching structure for the learning of mature adults? We shall limit our discussion to mature adults at this point, since most authors focused on this category. The dilemma being posed here is a rerun of an old debate in memory psychology: part or whole learning?

The part method might involve a series of lectures once a week lasting for the semester. Each lecture is then followed up by a seminar. At the end of this students have seven days in which to mull over the ideas and (hopefully) integrate them with their existing conceptual frameworks. By the end of the unit, they should be in a position to write essays in which they show a deep approach to the topic.

Inglis (1994) advocates a drip-feed approach: regular doses of input from staff so that adult learners have an opportunity to integrate new learning with their experiential learning and existing concept hierarchies.

Another option is distance learning, so successfully used by the Open University for over 25 years. This is not conceptually different from the drip-feed approach, except that the input comes not directly from a teacher, but from television and radio programmes and printed material. There is often a brilliantly successful summary of the essentials of a topic, communicated in clear, simple language with a minimum of jargon.

A third option is self-directed learning (or Boud's autonomous learning; 1998). This has many elements in common with distance learning and can be virtually synonymous if the teachers using distance learning assume that the learning of their students is self-directed.

Learning in wholes would be represented by a large block of time devoted to a thorough immersion in the material of the course. Models for this are the Open University summer school or study week-ends for Doctorate in Education students. This approach would seem particularly suitable for foreign language courses where the student would have time to be able to think in the foreign language. However, it might be less successful at a lower level of competence where the students are still struggling to make connections between different concepts and facts and to immerse themselves in an appropriate theoretical framework. Here the fatigue factor might outweigh the benefits of concentrated exposure.

Of course another vital question is, what is the best way of assessing mature adults? Formal examinations mean that mature students are given only the same time as those aged 18–22 years in which to recall the salient points on a topic, as well as to use them in a constructive logical way in a response. There would seem to be a great deal of evidence, even if retrospective, that such exams are not a suitable or fair means of measuring the performance of mature adults, particularly if study notes are not permitted in the exam. The work of Richardson (Chapter 13) and Hartley and Trueman (Chapter 14) confirms this.

An obvious alternative is the essay or some other form of continuous assessment. Another is the grading of the seminar presentations of mature students and also of their contributions to seminar discussions. In both of these formats mature students can bring all their experiential learning to bear. Admittedly there are considerable problems of obtaining objective and reliable assessment, but these problems are essentially the same as exist for essay assessment. Whether multiple-choice testing is suitable for the mature learner is also questionable. Providing them with the correct answer as one of the alternatives relieves mature learners of the burden of having to recall the correct answer. However, if they are in direct competition with young adults, the time pressure is still a handicap for mature learners. In principle, however, there is no necessity for multiple choice tests to have a fixed time. They could be adapted to fit the needs of the person being tested, as are the comparable IQ tests, which can be either time-limited or not.

We shall now leave this speculation. The authors of this book have made various contributions to the fields; mainly on the nature of the process of adult learning and on the capabilities of the mature learner. For their teachers a challenging picture has built up, both from the research and teaching points of view. As Hartley and Trueman (Chapter 14) pointed out, there is a need for more longitudinal research on mature students and how they fare at university or college. The evidence of Dart and Hettich points to a need to establish more study skills programmes. The evidence of Chapters 12–15 is that the needs and capabilities of mature students are so different from those of their traditional-age classmates. This has led to this speculation on various problems to be solved. Hopefully, the readers of this book will provide the solutions to some, if not all, of the problems.

References

Baxter Magolda, M B (1996) Epistemological development in graduate and professional education. *Review of Higher Education*, 19(3), 283–304 (in press).

Boud, D (ed.) (1988) *Developing Student Autonomy in Learning*, 2nd edn, Kogan Page, London.

Callaghan, M, Knox, A, Mowatt, I and Siann, G (1994) Empirical projects in small group learning, in *Group and Interactive Learning*, H C Foot, C J Howe, A Anderson, A K Tomlin and D A Warden (eds), Computational Mechanics Publications, Southampton.

Habermas, J (1978) *Knowledge and Human Interest*, Heinemann, London.

Inglis, W (1994) (oral communication).

King, P M and Kitchener, K S (1994) *Developing Reflective Judgment: Understanding and Promoting Intellectual Growth and Critical Thinking in Adolescents and Adults*. Jossey-Bass, San Francisco, California.

Knowles, M (1978) *The Adult Learner: A Neglected Species*, 2nd edn, Gulf Publishing Co., Houston.

Author Index

Subject Index